D0983037

A Century of
HIGHER EDUCATION

A Century of
HIGHER
EDUCATION:

CLASSICAL CITADEL
TO COLLEGIATE COLOSSUS

WILLIAM W. BRICKMAN

**PROFESSOR OF EDUCATIONAL HISTORY, GRADUATE SCHOOL OF EDUCATION,
UNIVERSITY OF PENNSYLVANIA; EDITOR, SCHOOL AND SOCIETY**

and

STANLEY LEHRER

**VICE-PRESIDENT AND MANAGING EDITOR,
SCHOOL AND SOCIETY**

Society for the Advancement of Education
NEW YORK, 1962

First Edition

Printed in the United States of America

To

MURRAY BRICKMAN *and* ZELLA B. PINE

and to

DORA SCHWARTZ *and* PAULINE GOODMAN

for kindness and affection

most priceless through the years

Preface

*M*ANY CONCEPTS have gone into developing the kind of higher education we find today in the U. S. One of the most significant—land for the lamp of learning—was embodied in the Morrill Act, which created our land-grant colleges and which this book commemorates on the 100th Anniversary of the Act's passage.

The Morrill Act takes us back to the day of 1859, when Congress first approved it. President James Buchanan refused to sign the bill, how ever, because, among other reasons, he opposed any Federal participation in state-controlled education. Under the Presidency of Lincoln in 1862, the Act finally became law, helping to stimulate agricultural education.

During the 1860's, it was necessary to encourage college teaching of agriculture because of inadequate attention to agrarian demands of the country. Perhaps the 1960's will reveal the need for other Morrill-type legislation to infuse vitality into areas of sluggish enrollments, such as science and engineering, because of the nation's interests in the fiercely competitive space age.

In 100 years, higher education has shifted its national emphasis from the soil to the stars in accordance with the needs and circumstances of the times. The purpose of this book is to examine the forces of change, the needs and demands, that have influenced the growth of higher education inside—and also outside—America and made it one of the most important keys to a better life—and even survival on this planet and beyond.

Here, in effect, is the story of the dynamic transformation of higher education from a citadel of limited curricular offerings to a colossus of learning with expanding courses, expanding enrollments, and expanding research facilities and new buildings. Indeed, nostalgia is mixed with progress as the ivy-covered façades fade into the shadows of tomorrow's sprawling, sparkling structures.

The editors are deeply grateful to the following contributors for making it possible to recreate 100 years of higher education: Willis Rudy, professor of history, Massachusetts State College, Worcester; M. M. Chambers, executive director, Michigan Council of State College Presidents, Lansing; George P. Schmidt, professor emeritus of history, Rutgers University, New Brunswick, N. J.; John S. Brubacher, professor of higher education, University of Michigan, Ann Arbor; Earle D. Ross, university historian, Iowa State University of Science and Technology, Ames; Tyrus Hillway, professor of education, Colorado State College, Greeley; Allan O. Pfnister, associate professor of higher education, University of Michigan, Ann Arbor; Everett Walters, dean, Graduate School, Ohio State University, Columbus; Lloyd E. Blauch, former director, Division of Higher Education, and assistant commissioner, U. S. Office of Education, and now assistant director, Retired Professors Registry, Washington, D. C.; Paul Woodring, editor, *Saturday Review Education Supplement;* Saul Sack, associate professor of education, University of Pennsylvania, Philadelphia; Horace Mann Bond, dean, School of Education, Atlanta (Ga.) University; and Robert M. Hutchins, president, Center for the Study of Democratic Institutions, The Fund for the Republic, Santa Barbara, Calif. To chronicle all the major events and to analyze significant developments in higher education would not have been easy tasks without the help of these eminent educators and administrators. The comprehensive coverage of the book attests to the exceptional scholarship of every contributor.

Laurel F. Lehrer, this writer's wife, deserves special thanks for her helpful suggestions concerning certain phraseological trouble spots in some of the chapters, but particularly for her understanding and co-operation when work on the book occasionally upset some of the normalcy in household routine and schedules.

STANLEY LEHRER

New Hyde Park, N. Y.
July, 1962

Introduction

THE CENTENNIAL ANNIVERSARY of the Morrill Land-Grant College Act is a good time to take another look at the situation of American higher education. This has been a century of growth and development, expansion, and even explosion in the number of higher educational institutions, the size and variety of the student body, and the concept of the curriculum. From a time when the classics and other traditional subjects prevailed, we have reached a period where these have been subordinated to more functional fields of study.

The financial aid by the Federal government to 68 land-grant colleges and universities during the century gave a mighty forward push to the modern subjects. It made possible the higher instruction of the children of workers and farmers and thus enabled social mobility and the equality of educational opportunity to become realities in a political democracy. It helped the realization of the broader nature and purposes of the modern university—the addition of services to the state, the nation, and the international community. Perhaps no land-grant institution, or, indeed, any university, has propelled itself within a short time into a position where it now is a world university as has Michigan State University.

Scholarship and pure research appear no longer to be the major functions—if they ever were—of the American college and university. Practical research projects for the state and nation, adult courses for the people, and educational assistance to developing nations are absorbing the attention and energies of administrators, faculties, and trustees. The new image of the university is, in a large measure, a product of the development of the land-grant institutions.

A lesson that can be learned from a centenary of the land-grant college and university is that it is possible for the Federal and the state governments to co-operate in educational work without the imposition of any unwarranted control from Washington. The state universities not only have served their own states, but also other states and the nation at large. Accordingly, it is logical and fair for the national governmental authority to furnish aid minus control for the further development of the higher educational institutions. As President John F. Kennedy stated, the land-grant colleges and universities constitute "one of the finest examples of our Federal system, the fruitful cooperation between national and state governments in the pursuit of a decent education for all of our citizens."

The American Association of State Universities and Land-Grant Colleges, the prime promoter of the 1962 centennial celebration, points out some statistical facts of significance. The 68 land-grant institutions make up less than four per cent of all colleges and universities in the country, but their combined enrollment represents 20% of all the undergraduates. Perhaps even more impressively quantitatively is the fact that they grant close to 40% of all the doctorates in every branch of study. Surely, the facts and figures prove the lasting impact by the land-grant institutions upon higher education in the U. S.

But the status of colleges and universities cannot be viewed with pleasure and placidity at the present time. There are too many problems of personnel, administration, enrollment, curriculum, and finance which confront the higher institutions. It is too easy, in appreciating the growth and development of higher education in America, to become overly complacent. Both the state and the private institutions must consider some fundamental issues. One of these is the question of the basic purposes of higher education. Are the colleges and universities contributing substantially to the raising of the intellectual level of the nation? Might there not be too much flexibility and informality with respect to standards of scholarship? Has the university gone too far in trying to be all things to all men and all nations? Is the university losing its peculiar position in society as the possessor and propagator of the intellectual heritage of man?

One might learn also from a review of a century of the American college and university that the provision of plentiful funds might be a contributory cause to a change in values. The Federal and state governments gave aid to the universities for such a practical purpose as the teaching of agricultural and engineering subjects. It was but a matter of time when these fields and others, which were generously endowed by private individuals and foundations, began to outshine in importance the traditional areas of learning. The National Defense Education Act of 1958, it is true, did help considerably the teaching of modern foreign languages, science, and mathematics. However, let it be noted that the objective of this law was once more a practical one. It is proper to ask if the overstressing of the functional and the practical in colleges and universities is not contributing materially to the establishment of a curricular imbalance where, to use Newman's phrase, there is "so little for the mind."

The past century has witnessed the transformation of colleges and universities from institutions of spiritual emphasis and moderate scholarship to those of stress on secularism, scientism, and societism. They seem to be overreaching themselves in all directions at the same time. The moment has arrived when the objectives and content of higher education must be reappraised. The essentials must be emphasized and the trivial and the ephemeral must be relegated to the periphery or to a far distance. The university should not try to teach or do everything for its clientele. Students should be expected to do something for themselves and, as they mature, to embark upon a self-educational process. Universities must insist upon the highest possible standards of scholarship and integrity on the part of administration, faculty, and students. To do less is to debase and demean the only institution in society which has the responsibility and the potential of pointing out the path of intellectual progress.

The next century of the American college and university, it is hoped, will be marked by a closer approach to the essential nature of higher education.

WILLIAM W. BRICKMAN

Contents

A Century of
HIGHER EDUCATION

1

Higher Education in the United States, 1862-1962

WILLIS RUDY

OR MORE THAN 300 YEARS the development of civilization in that part of the western hemisphere which is now the U. S. has been intertwined closely with the evolution of higher education. Each type-form of academic institution which has arisen—the New England hilltop college, the state university, the technological institute, the urban university, the community college—reflects a stage in the growth of the American society.

In the midst of the mass of facts with which we have to deal in order to describe this complex phenomenon, is there some central organizing principle which we can find to help bring order out of chaos? Perhaps there is such a keynote, and it may be just this: the history of American higher education, particularly during the last 100 years, is, in essence, the record of a long-continued interaction between transplanted European concepts and institutions of higher learning and New World conditions. As part of this process, some elements were accepted readily and even copied more or less literally; some were rejected on the ground that they were unsuited to American conditions; and still others were transformed so as to fit a new pattern. While hardly novel, this generalization goes to the heart of the American experience in the realm of higher education.

If we begin with this premise, what meaningful examples can we cite, from the 1862-1962 period, of transplantation and adaptation in American higher education? At least six main areas come to mind where processes of this kind may be seen at work. Let us briefly consider each in turn.

1. European Models and American Adaptations. Just as in colonial days, when North American higher learning was influenced decisively by the English college ideal, so in the years from 1862 to World War I, the U. S. was deeply impressed by the example of the German university.[1] Thousands of American students went to Germany during these years to pursue higher studies of one sort or another. Many of these young people returned to their native land with the conviction that American university procedures must be transformed to conform to German standards. The seminar method of investigation, the laboratory system of scientific teaching, the lecture method, the Ph.D. degree—all these were brought across the seas at this time. What was even more important, the German university spirit of search for knowledge and its

---

[1] For the early English influence, see Samuel E. Morison, "The Founding of Harvard College" (Cambridge: Harvard University Press, 1935).

concomitant emphasis on productive research were transplanted in large measure to America. We have it on authority of the eminent German philosopher, Friedrich Paulsen, that by 1900, American institutions of higher learning had been more thoroughly "Germanized" than any other universities outside of Germany itself.[2]

Even before the 1917-18 war put a temporary stigma on German ideas, a reaction had set in which involved a renewed interest in various aspects of the English college structure. For example, the system of university extension which had been developed by Cambridge University was copied widely in America. In addition, experiments began to be launched about the turn of the century which aimed to realize some of the values which were said to be inherent in the English residential college pattern. William Rainey Harper's dormitory and house plan at the University of Chicago was clearly influenced by considerations of this type, as were Woodrow Wilson's preceptorial plan at Princeton and the Harvard and Yale house or "college" experiments.

In certain cases, however, European-derived university concepts had to be modified and readjusted to new roles before they were finally accepted in the New World. Thus, it soon became apparent that it would be impossible to establish independent graduate-level universities in America which strictly would follow the German model. The broader preparatory base on which the German university rested—namely, the *gymnasium*—was lacking in the U.S. It was also a serious question whether the American people felt it was justifiable or expedient to support a

---

[2] Friedrich Paulsen, "German Universities" (New York, 1895), p. 15.

group of advanced schools which would devote *all* of their energies to postgraduate teaching and research. Nevertheless, the Ph.D. degree took root in American academic culture, especially after the founding of Johns Hopkins University in 1876. The result was that a German-inspired graduate school granting the Ph.D. degree came to be superimposed in American universities upon a four-year, English-derived undergraduate college granting the baccalaureate, which in origin was a general education degree. Indeed, in many institutions, the graduate faculties remained closely associated with the undergraduate college faculties. On many American campuses, the same teachers frequently served both types of schools. It is due to this situation more than any other, some observers feel, that those perennial American academic problems—general education *versus* special education and teaching *versus* research—have arisen.

2. A Dual System of Colleges and Universities. In one respect, the American structure of higher education has diverged sharply from continental European precedents, though not quite as sharply from those of Great Britain. This divergence is apparent in the dual system of financing and administering institutions of higher learning which has emerged in the U. S. American historical development has produced two great academic systems—the private and the state-supported—and these have grown up contemporaneously and in some cases literally side by side. The Dartmouth College decision of the U. S. Supreme Court gave, as early as 1819, strong legal sanction for this dualistic system.[3] Subse-

---

[3] Richard G. Axt, "The Federal Government and Financing Higher Education" (New York: Columbia University Press, 1952).

quent grants by state and Federal governments and donations by private individuals and organizations have served only to confirm the trend.

In this particular area, the most important tendency which has developed since 1862 was for Federal financial support for *both* the private and the public sectors to become increasingly vital and perhaps even determinative. Federal grants for higher education went back to 1787 and the Confederation land grants to the Ohio and Scioto companies. A series of similar grants was made to other new western states as they entered the Union. This precedent was followed in 1862 by the first Morrill Act, which provided Federal land donations for colleges of agriculture and mechanic arts. A second Morrill Act in 1890 renewed and expanded these grants. In this picture we should not overlook the importance of the Hatch experiment station act of 1887, which provided state universities and agricultural colleges with additional special Federal subsidies. Also, it should be noted that, in 1914 and 1917, new Federal legislation was put on the statute books authorizing grants to state colleges for agricultural extension programs and vocational education work.

Thus far, this Federal support had been tendered exclusively by means of grants-in-aid to the states and was not given directly to the colleges themselves. In 1944, with the passage of the "G. I. Bill of Rights," the first departure from this pattern occurred. Federal grants now were made directly to institutions of higher education within the states as part of a system of veterans' benefits, and people began to become accustomed to the idea that Washington, in propriety, might financially assist young people to attend college. In addition, since the money technically was granted to the student who then attended the college of his choice, the Federal grants now came to include *private* as well as public institutions.

The pressing necessities of the stormy era of global war and Cold War produced still other departures from what had been, up to this time, the norm. Contracts now began to be negotiated directly between Washington and various universities, public and private, for the undertaking of research in fields vital to the national interest. This was quickly followed by a program of Federal loans for college and university housing and other physical facilities. Thus, over the last 100 years, American traditions hostile to centralization have been revised gradually to accommodate themselves to a larger measure of Federal financing, with possibly increasing Federal influence, in many vital areas of the nation's dualistic system of higher education.[4]

3. Democracy in Higher Education. In the years since 1862, perhaps the most significant instance of the influence exerted by the American cultural environment upon patterns of higher learning imported from Europe has been that deriving from the impact of democracy. American civilization generated an almost irresistible drive for the popularization of opportunities for learning, and one of the most notable aspects of this movement was a constant increase in the percentage of the population enjoying the benefits of a higher education. This phenomenon was accompanied by the emergence of institutional

---

[4] Willard L. Thorp, *et al.*, "Financing Higher Education, 1960-1970" (New York, 1959).

patterns peculiar to America, such as the state university, the land-grant college, the municipal university, and the junior or community college.[5] Federal land and money grants for college purposes, state and local appropriations, and private endowments all combined by 1962 to establish as almost a cardinal principle of national policy the ideal that at least the chance for some form of post-secondary education should be proffered to all interested American youth.

In the 20th century, various allied self-improvement agencies, including the summer school, the afternoon or evening session, and the university extension division, have extended further the opportunities for college-level study to Americans. At the same time, the sweeping movement for coeducation and women's colleges made giant strides toward eliminating ancient barriers due to sex. Finally, strenuous efforts have been made, most successfully in the years since 1933, to end restrictions on academic opportunity due to economic status, race, or ethnic origin. The upshot of all of this was that, by the mid-point of the 20th century, more equality of opportunity for post-secondary training existed in the United States of America than in any other part of the world.[6]

4. A Higher Learning, Broad in Scope. The traditional university on the European continent had four great faculties—law, medicine, theology, the liberal arts. While the English university diverged somewhat from this blueprint, the

---

[5] I. L. Kandel, "The Humanities in Search of Students," *American Scholar*, 14:323, 325, Summer, 1945; A. Monroe Stowe, "Modernizing the College" (New York, 1926), pp. 48-49.

[6] Merritt M. Chambers, "University Student Population in the World," *Bulletin*, Association of American Colleges, 34:265-266, October, 1948.

American system of higher education, particularly since 1862, has revised it even more fundamentally. Of course, it is only fair to state that many continental European institutions have considerably broadened and diversified their courses of study in modern times. It still remains a fact, however, that American universities have demonstrated an even greater readiness to admit, as integral members of the academic family, many new and different fields of study. Thus, schools of journalism, library service, nursing, business administration, architecture, and agriculture have been accepted readily as proper parts of a university organization on scores of American campuses.

Significant examples of this catholicity of the American university are the Wharton School of Finance and Economics (founded at the University of Pennsylvania as early as 1881), the Harvard Graduate School of Business (founded in 1908), and Teachers College, Columbia University (first established in 1894).[7] New branches of university work such as the ones served by these schools were pioneering the way for a more flexible approach to the higher learning and at the same time serving areas of human life which were of the greatest importance. Perhaps this effort to diversify opportunities on the university level for advanced training can best be understood if it is seen in the context of the pragmatic bent of the American people—their willingness to try new things if only to see if results of tangible value could be secured.

---

[7] On the foundation of Teachers College, Columbia, see Lawrence A. Cremin, David A. Shannon, and Mary E. Townsend, "History of Teachers College, Columbia University" (New York: Bureau of Publications, Teachers College, Columbia University, 1954), pp. 3-41.

5. Higher Education for Life. According to all indications, the system of higher education which evolved in the U. S. in the decades following the Civil War was genuinely popular with most Americans. Why was this so? For one thing, we already have noted that a greater proportion of people in the U. S. than in other countries were able to look forward to the possibility of enjoying the benefits of college training. This factor is important in explaining the generally favorable attitude toward the American college, but it is not the whole story. Probably just as important was the fact that Americans had come to see these institutions as actively seeking to serve the manifold interests of the evolving democratic community. This concept of service is the one aspect of higher education in America which, more than any other, has impressed a succession of visitors from Europe and other continents.[8]

The idea of service was expressed by 20th-century American universities in various ways. Pure research in sciences and the humanities has been pushed forward by scholars on university staffs. Investigations in the applied sciences, sponsored by university laboratories, experiment stations, and seminar groups, have produced discoveries as diverse as hybrid corn and anti-polio vaccine. Thousands of Americans have been furnished by colleges and universities with the specialized and professional training they re-

---

[8] As samples of this kind of literature, see Eugene Kuehnemann, "Charles W. Eliot" (Boston, 1909); Hugo Munsterberg, "The Americans" (New York, 1905); and Maurice Caullery, "Universities and Scientific Life in the United States" (Cambridge, Mass., 1922).

quired to play a useful role in the complex society of the modern era.[9]

All this Americans came to expect of their colleges and universities. From the "watchtower" philosophy as embodied in the "Wisconsin Idea" to the "community college" program of the University of Minnesota, the world of American higher learning eschewed academic isolation in favor of an active involvement in the concerns of the sustaining society. In so doing, colleges were in close relationship with the work of the entire structure of democratic education at every grade level. In so doing, too, they showed a greater interest than was true elsewhere for the student's personal and psychological well-being. Thus, American institutions of higher education upheld an ideal which has been termed "characteristically American"—the urge to put knowledge to work for the public weal.[10]

6. Harmonizing the Liberal and the Professional. Throughout the western world, scholars and educators for decades have been wrestling with the problem Herbert Spencer raised as being particularly important for the Age of Science—"What Knowledge Is of Most Worth?" The educational question involved struck pragmatic America with particular impact and the solutions worked out from 1862 to 1962 are important for the history of education.

The "old-time" American college, deviating very little from the European (and especially the English) model, served the needs of a limited clientele which was preparing for a small number of the traditional, so-called "literary," pro-

[9] Yandell Henderson, "Universities and Unpreparedness," *Science*, 43:242-243, Feb. 18, 1916.

[10] James B. Conant, "America Remakes the University," *Atlantic Monthly*, vol. 177, May, 1946.

fessions. The Civil War, acting as a kind of social catalyst, forced upon American college administrators recognition of the academic respectability of a number of new lines of specialized work. More money became available to sponsor these rapidly emerging fields—Morrill Act funds, for example, and also private donations by the great American industrialists. The development of new academic and social disciplines in sciences and social sciences led on the one hand to the proliferation of specialized subject-matter courses and on the other to a greater degree of departmental specialization within college faculties. At the same time, the nationwide influence of Charles W. Eliot's elective curriculum at Harvard and of the host of German-trained specialists who were being engaged as college teachers speeded even more the trend toward diversification and specialization. As a consequence, by the end of the 19th century, the traditional liberal arts college with its limited and strictly prescribed course of study had virtually disappeared in the U. S.[11]

During the first six decades of the 20th century, the movement described above went forward apace. Liberal arts colleges now involved themselves heavily in the business of offering a wide variety of specialized and pre-professional programs, as well as some courses that were purely professional. As time went on, the last two undergraduate years came very generally to be devoted to professional or specialized concerns, just as the first two years concentrated upon a more

---

[11] Clarence Shedd, "Higher Education in the United States," in W. M. Kotschnig, editor, "The University in a Changing World" (London, 1932), pp. 128-130.

general or liberal education.[12] During this same period, many colleges training for professional fields came in turn to seek to broaden their offerings to include more emphasis on general education. The net result was that something like a generalized pattern of American post-secondary education, on the collegiate level at least, began to emerge.[13] In this pattern, many hoped that a better balance would be attained than heretofore between general and specialized studies, *i.e.*, between the "liberal" and the "professional" in college curriculums of diverse types.[14] This, of course, is essentially what the Harvard Committee on General Education recommended when it drew up its influential report in 1945.

Conclusion. During the fateful span of years from 1862 to 1962, American higher education demonstrated a continuing vitality and driving force which in itself may be said to constitute a unifying pattern. It is true that standardization was not carried to the extreme, as in certain other countries, but this very situation made possible fruitful experimentation and healthy rivalry within the framework of a dualistic system of support and control. European methods and concepts continued to be enormously influential, as indeed they had been from the time of

---

[12] Richard M. Gummere, "The Bisected A.B.," *Bulletin,* Association of American Colleges, 28:567-571, October, 1942.

[13] On this trend, see John T. Rettaliata, "Synthesizing Science and Liberal Education," *School and Society,* 86: 51-53, Feb. 1, 1958; also Quentin Oliver McAllister, "Business Executives and the Humanities" (Chapel Hill, N. C.: University of North Carolina Press, 1951).

[14] I have discussed this problem at greater length in a monograph published by the Institute of Higher Education, Columbia University. See Willis Rudy, "The Evolving Liberal Arts Curriculum: A Historical Review of Basic Themes" (New York: Bureau of Publications, Teachers College, Columbia University, 1960).

the first colonial settlements. From across the Atlantic, academic procedures were freely borrowed, reappraised, and adapted to the needs of American civilization. Leaders of American higher education were quick in most instances to revise old ideas to meet new conditions, to broaden the scope of university organization, to expand and diversify college curriculums, and to strive to serve ever more directly the people of their nation and the fundamental needs of contemporary civilization. By 1962, a veritable revolution had occurred in American higher education. A dynamic system had emerged which radically transformed traditional concepts of the higher learning. To a greater extent than in other lands and times, its keynote was democracy.

2

Legal Developments in Higher Education, 1862-1962

M. M. CHAMBERS

*L*OOKING BACKWARD across a century in the American law of higher education brings into view a crowded panorama. This period encompasses the development of the great nationwide system of land-grant colleges. It sees the total number of students in the nation's colleges rise from fewer than 100,000 to 4,000,000. It sees higher education for women progress from an extreme rarity to a point where about 38% of all college students are female. It sees the American Negro rise from slavery, devoid of civil rights, to where his privilege of being admitted, when qualified, to a public college or university in his own state can generally be enforced in court.

In this period, the practice of regular appropriation of state tax funds in support of state universities and colleges moved from near nonexistence to its status today, when the appropriations by the 50 states for operating expenses alone substantially exceed $1,500,000,000 a year. Although these appropriations have doubled within the last decade, they amount to only about eight per cent of the total of state tax collections and are far from constituting a catastrophic dollar drain upon the states.

This past century has witnessed practically all of the development of graduate work in the arts and sciences and its associated advanced research work. The research and "extension teaching" of the land-grant colleges have revolutionized American agriculture and inundated the nation with surplus food and fiber, while half the world is underfed and ill-clad. Our scientists and technicians from the universities go at the invitation of underdeveloped nations in both hemispheres to teach their peoples literacy, sanitation, community co-operation, public administration, and how to make the best of their unused or wasted resources of soil, water, forest, and minerals. This is largely by virtue of Federal statutes and Federal appropriations enacted in pursuance of a national public policy suited to the circumstances of today's world.

Acts of Congress. Long prior to 1862, the government had granted public lands to individual states and territories for the endowment of higher education, and the practice was continued for many decades thereafter, often embodied in the Enabling Act for the admission of a new state. These grants are not to be confused with those made under the Morrill Act of 1862, which stimulated the creation of the great chain of 69 land-grant colleges over a period of 60 years — up to the opening of the University of Alaska in 1922.

It is notable that the number (69) came to

exceed the number of states and territories chiefly because 17 states of the southeast maintained racial segregation and each established two land-grant colleges — one for white students and one for Negroes. The number recently has dropped to 68 because West Virginia, after unequivocally opening West Virginia University at Morgantown to qualified applicants of all races, withdrew the designation of "Morrill Act land-grant college" from West Virginia State College at Charleston, which continues to flourish as a multi-purpose non-land-grant institution.

The Morrill Act was the beginning of a long series of Federal statutes, outstanding among which were the Hatch Act of 1887, inaugurating the habit of annual appropriations of money to the states for higher education (in this instance for agricultural research and experimentation); the Second Morrill Act of 1890; the Smith-Lever Act of 1914 (for the co-operative agricultural extension service); and the Smith-Hughes Act of 1917 (for the education of teachers of vocational agriculture and home economics).

This series is by no means ended, for the national interest in the land-grant colleges and universities continues to be augmented. The fact that the farm population has greatly declined and that we are currently beset by surplus agricultural products must not divert attention from the advancement of agricultural science in a time of "population explosion." Even if we are temporarily ahead of domestic needs as far as agricultural production is concerned, the American farmer's problems of marketing are more perplexing than they were when livestock had to be driven across the mountains on the hoof.

Most of the land-grant colleges have become,

in fact, cosmopolitan multi-purpose universities, following faithfully the noble original purpose: " . . . without excluding other scientific and classical studies, and including military tactics, to teach such branches of learning as are related to agriculture and the mechanic arts . . . in order to promote the liberal and practical education of the industrial classes in the several pursuits and professions in life. . . . "[1]

The interest of the national government has extended far beyond the land-grant system to include all higher education, with emphasis on financial aid to the student without regard to what curriculum he selects or whether the institution he attends is public or private. Thus, the Depression brought about the student work program of the National Youth Administration (1935-42); and an aftermath of World War II was the vast program of student aid under the "G. I. Bills." More recently have come the student loan program for undergraduates and the fellowship program for graduate students, as well as various research and other programs under different titles of the National Defense Act of 1958.

The Depression of the 1930's also brought Federal loans and grants to the colleges and universities for the construction of buildings; and this practice, in frequently modified forms, has continued somewhat intermittently ever since.

During the past decade, a significant form of Federal partnership with universities and colleges, public and private, has mushroomed enormously. This is the practice of several major Federal agencies, mostly but not all concerned

---

[1] From Section 4 of the Morrill Act of 1862.

with defense activities, of using portions of the money appropriated to them by Congress to finance contracts (and, in some instances, grants) for research services to be performed at selected institutions of higher education.[2]

Among the agencies are the Atomic Energy Commission, the Department of the Army, the Air Force, the Office of Naval Research, the National Institutes of Health, the National Science Foundation, and the Office of Education. The regulations of the various agencies regarding the adjustment of "overhead charges" due the universities have constituted a continuing problem; and complaints sometimes are heard that the program is too heavily concentrated in the larger universities, that it endangers their integrity in the planning and management of their own research programs, that it is concerned too much with application and too little with theory, and that it produces a plethora in the physical sciences and a famine in other fields, particularly the humanistic.

During the short history of the program, there has been a substantial tendency to ameliorate the causes of these grievances. At least one Federal agency (the National Science Foundation) has a special program for the particular purpose of encouraging research in small colleges; some of the agencies are tending to favor transactions with reputable or promising researchers "without strings" rather than the narrowly defined "project" type of research; and it does not appear that any of the other sources of dissatisfaction are necessarily incurable.

It is impossible to name in brief space, let

[2] Charles V. Kidd, "American Universities and Federal Research" (Cambridge: Harvard University Press, 1959).

alone describe, all the types of partnership between the Federal government and higher education that have come into existence since 1862. One can summarize by saying the drift always has been upward, though often in tall waves rather than in a straight line, and that the year 1862 is only a benchmark in a trend which is older than the U. S. Constitution itself. It may seem unlikely that 1962 will be a landmark year, but few can doubt that other and broader forms of Federal support for higher education in the American states will be forthcoming in our time, for now higher education unquestionably has become, in addition to its other roles and not necessarily in conflict with them, an instrument of national policy.

State Legislation. Prior to the Civil War period, the few state universities that had come into existence were generally regarded in much the same light as private colleges. Regular annual or biennial appropriations of state tax funds for their support had not become the custom. Occasionally a state would make a small appropriation to tide over a crisis, or perhaps make a loan to the university, or authorize it to conduct a lottery to raise funds.

After 1865, regular state support soon became a habit. No doubt, the Morrill Act of 1862 played a considerable role in stimulating this development, as did also the inception and growth of the state normal schools (later to become teachers colleges and eventually multipurpose colleges and universities), only a few of which had been established before the Civil War. Soon after substantial state support of public universities and colleges became accepted practice, many of the states began to provide a backlog of annual income for the institutions by enacting a "mill-tax" on all taxable property in the state, with the proceeds earmarked for that purpose. This continued over a long period which probably had its mid-point somewhere near the turn of the century. By 1940, it had all but disappeared, though it still persists in a very few states. Indeed, property taxes now have become of minuscule importance in the picture of state revenues.

Even before the confirming of the habit of state support, the question of whether a state university should properly be a part of the state bureaucracy or, instead, should be an independent corporation operating autonomously had been encountered. The great decision that the Regents of the University of Michigan should be an autonomous corporation had been made by the people of Michigan in the constitution of 1850 and repeatedly was confirmed and implemented in decisions of the state supreme court through ensuing decades and up to the present.[3] When Michigan revised its constitution in 1908, the same independence was extended to the Michigan Agricultural College (now Michigan State University); and in 1959, when the state acquired full control of Wayne State University, it, too, was accorded constitutional status.

The Regents of the University of California were given a high degree of constitutional autonomy by the California constitution of 1879, and this has been maintained to the present with comparatively little controversy. The Min-

---

[3] *Sterling v. Regents of the University of Michigan*, 110 Mich. 369, 68 N. W. 253, 34 L. R. A. 150 (1896); *Board of Regents of the University of Michigan v. Auditor General*, 168 Mich. 444, 132 N. W. 1037 (1911).

nesota constitution of 1858 contained unmistakable language providing independence for the Regents of the University of Minnesota, but this apparently was largely misunderstood or ignored until a state supreme court decision of 1928 unequivocally declared that the regents rightly had exclusive control of the expenditure of university funds and their decisions were not subject to the scrutiny and approval of the state board of administration and finance.[4]

Later decisions of the Minnesota court have strengthened the autonomy of the regents, placing them substantially in the same high category as their counterparts in Michigan and California. Discriminating persons know that each of these three states has one of the nation's topmost state universities, each of which is, indeed, one of the greatest universities in the modern world. It deserves to be more widely known that each of these universities has constitutional autonomy, repeatedly sustained by the supreme courts of the respective states.

Somewhat similar status, not to be technically detailed here, is enjoyed by the state universities in Colorado, Idaho, Nevada, and Arizona, as well as by the Regents of the Agricultural College System in Oklahoma and the Regents of the University System of Georgia. The constitutionally independent universities are, however, only a minority. The Minnesota case of 1928 is an instance in which an "administrative reorganization act" of the type which has swept almost every state since 1910 (and some of them two or three times) collided with the constitution and came off second best. In many another state, similar acts have subjected the universities

---

[4] *State v. Chase,* 175 Minn. 259, 220 N. W. 951 (1928).

to detailed control and harassment by various non-educational central fiscal and administrative authorities of the state; and in some states, especially in New England and the northeast, the authority of their governing boards has been eroded to the vanishing point and their faculties have virtually become functionaries in the classified civil service.

This movement, proceeding in disregard of the nature of a university, was scarcely hindered by the justified outcries of university presidents and governing board members until about a decade ago, and only within recent years has it been halted and, in some instances, reversed. An influential event, already widely felt and of undoubtedly great future impact, was the publication in 1959 of the forthright report of the Committee on Government and Higher Education headed by Milton Eisenhower.[5] Since that date, the California Survey Team has recommended and secured the adoption of 1960 statutes providing substantially greater freedom for the California state colleges;[6] and even in conservative New York, the Governor's Committee on Higher Education reported in November, 1960, that the Trustees of the State University should be given such independence of non-educational fiscal and administrative agencies as would enable them to discharge their responsibilities "in the spirit and style of the nation's

[5] "The Efficiency of Freedom" (Baltimore: Johns Hopkins Press, 1959); Malcolm Moos and Francis E. Rourke, "The Campus and the State" (Baltimore: Johns Hopkins Press, 1959).

[6] "A Master Plan for Higher Education in California, 1960-1975" (Sacramento: California State Department of Education, 1960). See especially p. 30.

great public universities."[7] Many other examples of the trend are occurring.

Somewhat different evidence that the public university will be given leeway to develop and operate with the flexibility and adaptability that the nature of a university requires can be observed in the recent history of the consolidation of governing boards. From 1896 to 1948, a dozen states (none of which has a really top-ranking university) abolished all the governing boards of each of their several institutions and created one state-wide governing board for all their state institutions of higher education. This measure, in the name of efficiency and economy, is naive, harsh, unsophisticated, abrupt, futile, and self-defeating. For 14 years no state has adopted it. The trend — if it can be called that — is apparently outmoded, stopped in its tracks, defunct.

A more recent tendency of the past 20 years has been the creation in 10 states of a superimposed "coordinating board" or "commission of higher education" having, in a few instances, almost plenary authority over the governing boards, and in others only advisory responsibilities. A glance at their history shows that the older of these are the power-laden ones (such as the Regents for Higher Education in Oklahoma, created in 1941), and the newer ones have little or no coercive authority, but only responsibility to provide liaison among the institutions, to study the state-wide picture and make recommendations, and to perform only advisory functions. This is explicitly true, for example, of the California Coordinating Council for Higher Education, created in 1960.

---

[7] "Meeting the Increasing Demand for Higher Education in New York State" (Albany: New York State Education Department, 1960), especially pp. 19, 20.

This trend bodes well for the autonomy of state universities and colleges, without which they may degenerate to the status of mere appendages of the state bureaucracy. And let us mark the fact that in such great states as Michigan, Minnesota, Indiana, Ohio, Missouri, and Colorado, among others, the successful co-ordination of the several institutions in the state-wide system is wholly voluntary, through a central agency created by the institutions themselves, and with no additional layer of officialism created by statute. Voluntary state-wide co-ordination of autonomous institutions provides the climate for healthy development of public higher education.[8]

The States and the Private Colleges. In all states, the private institutions traditionally have had a wide sphere of freedom in the management of their own affairs, both fiscal and academic. Generally, they have been subjected to scarcely more than nominal surveillance for the maintenance of standards. In fact, the responsibility of detecting and suppressing "diploma mills" and of upgrading substandard facilities and faculties has been largely left to voluntary accrediting agencies. These have grown up to positions of great influence largely within the present century. Fortunately, their activities are aimed more largely at stimulating improvement than at rigid standardization or regimentation.

It is true, of course, that the laws of the states provide for the revocation of the charter of a fraudulent corporation by a court of law in an appropriate case; and fraudulent mail or other

[8] "Voluntary State-Wide Coordination in Public Higher Education" (Ann Arbor: University of Michigan, 1961).

solicitation across state lines may fall within the punitive or preventive statutes touching the U. S. postal system or the Federal Trade Commission. In all states, too, the courts of equity have a jurisdiction embracing the "superintendence" (not too explicitly defined) of charitable corporations — a classification covering most private colleges.

The practice of making appropriations of public money directly to private institutions, once common in the northeast, nearly has disappeared. More than 40 state constitutions now prohibit it. Pennsylvania is the only state which continues it on any substantial scale. Maryland and Vermont continue it in a more nearly negligible volume. All states permit exemption from taxation of nonprofit educational institutions, and the changes of a century have not been of sufficient consequence to be detailed here. The various types of exemptions from Federal income and estate taxes, designed to encourage private gifts to charitable corporations, are, however, a development of the present century and are factors of importance in the support of colleges and universities.

Within the past 15 years, gifts from business and industrial corporations to private colleges have grown considerably in volume and bid fair to increase. The tendency was given impetus by a 1953 decision of the New Jersey supreme court holding in effect that the directors of such a corporation are acting within their proper powers in thus disposing of appropriate fractions of the assets or income of the corporation entrusted to their control; that is, the making of such a gift in good faith and for purposes deemed sound does not automatically subject the directors to personal liability for misuse of funds belonging to the stockholders.[9] Prior to this case and some others which followed it, the question had been somewhat obscure.

The century, then, has seen the private institutions gain somewhat from statutory and judicial encouragement of private gifts, one of their principal sources of income. On the other side of the ledger, at least for those holding substantial endowment funds, there was a great and perhaps permanent decline in productivity of invested funds from 1930 to 1955, due in part to Federal statutes and administrative regulations, accompanied by a considerable inflation of prices and wages. The practical effect was that the real productivity of endowment funds was cut by more than half; and the effort to accumulate invested funds is no longer regarded with the favor it once had in college finance.

Removing Barriers to Higher Education. In the area of racial discrimination in higher education, the "equal but separate" doctrine of the famous *Plessy v. Ferguson* decision of the U. S. Supreme Court had begun to crumble a bit before the great *Brown v. Kansas* case of 1954, which legally abolished segregation in public schools. As early as 1938, the unanimous Supreme Court, led by Chief Justice Charles Evans Hughes, declared that Missouri must afford equal law school facilities for a qualified Negro applicant *within its own borders* and could not satisfy the law by offering to pay his tuition in

[9] *A. P. Smith Mfg. Co. v. Barlow* et al., 13 N. J. 145, 98 A. 2d 581; appeal dismissed, 346 U. S. 861, 74 S. Ct. 107, 98 L. Ed. 373 (1953).

any out-of-state law school that would admit him.[10]

In 1950, deciding two cases which had come up for argument together, the high tribunal, again unanimously, and this time through the voice of Chief Justice Fred M. Vinson, held that "the Equal Protection Clause of the Fourteenth Amendment requires that petitioner (a qualified Negro applicant) be admitted to the University of Texas Law School." Regarding a Negro who had been admitted to the Graduate School of the University of Oklahoma but required to occupy only designated seats in classrooms, library, and dining room, which in effect segregated him, the Chief Justice ruled, "Appellant, having been admitted to a state-supported school, must receive the same treatment at the hands of the state as students of other races."[11]

Subsequent cases in other states have now virtually cleared away all legal barriers to the admission of qualified Negro students to public professional and graduate schools. It is a sad commentary that a century has not fully sufficed to eradicate all racial prejudice and discrimination, even at the level of higher education; but progress continues.

One other development of the century is of great concern. If history is read correctly, the state universities and land-grant colleges established in the 19th century were generally intended to be tuition-free and to be the capstones of great free public school systems. In some of

[10] *State of Missouri ex rel. Gaines v. Canada* et al., 59 S. Ct. 232, 83 L. Ed. 207 (1938); rehearing denied, 59 S. Ct. 356 (1939).

[11] *Sweatt v. Painter et al.*, 339 U. S. 629, 70 S. Ct. 848, 94 L. Ed. 1115 (1950); *McLaurin v. Oklahoma State Regents for Higher Education* et al., 339 U. S.637, 70 S. Ct. 851, 94 L. Ed. 1149 (1950).

the midwestern states, they still are required by law to be free of tuition, though all have followed for some time the practice of charging some more or less nominal fees for such incidentals as laboratory supplies, health service, and the like. A shocking trend of the post-World War II period has been the repeated boosting of student fees in public institutions, and so the policy of free public higher education seems about to be forgotten and abandoned. This, of course, is urged and abetted by all who wish to see higher education curtailed and restricted to those who are able to pay fees and thus made a special privilege of the affluent or of those who are able to "beg or borrow."

In some instances, there is the spectacle of legislatures bargaining with university governing boards, threatening to cut appropriations unless student fees are raised. In some quarters, it is insisted that scholarships and loans are ample answers and that students who cannot pay the cost of their education should "learn now and pay later" by mortgaging their future earnings. Peculiarly incomprehensible is this recent trend toward high fees when one understands that every other nation in the world today is proceeding in the other direction. University fees are low, decreasing, disappearing, or already nonexistent in Britain, Europe, and Latin America. In the Soviet Union, some 80% of university students are not merely free of fees, but are paid stipends equivalent to at least a meager living wage.

High fees are cruelly discriminative against girl students, most of whom have neither present nor prospective earning power equal to that of boys. Thus, we bar them from college at a time when more women are urgently needed in scientific pursuits and the professions, especially the health professions, teaching, and social work. Scholarships are never sufficient for more than a small fraction of worthy applicants; they go mainly to those of very superior capacity and serve mainly to enable them to attend a more expensive college than otherwise; they involve invasions of personal and family privacy that many excellent people will not countenance; they type education as a charity rather than as a right; and they are of little use in getting more people into college than would be there in any event. In New York City, the Midwest, Far West, and the South, influential voices are calling for a halt in the continual raising of student fees in public institutions and for an eventual return to the historic principle of free public higher education.[12]

The value in a retrospection of the last century is in what we gain in comprehension of the issues that confront higher education in the U. S. at the present time. The lawmakers and the judges of the past century have something to contribute to those of the present. Much more than ever before, more and better higher education for more people is an imperative of our day.

The fostering of academic freedom is explicitly recognized in the words of many opinions of Federal and state courts as an obligation not to be overlooked by legislatures and institutional governing boards. Again and again, judges have attested its primacy as a foremost essential in higher education. There have been fluctuations, however, in the climate of popular tolerance of

[12] "The Campus and the People" (Danville, Ill.: Inter-state Printers and Publishers, 1960. Especially pp. 55-62, on "Where Will the Money Come From?"

unorthodox ideas and in prevailing attitudes of confidence or suspicion toward academicians. Each of our wars in the 20th century has had an aftermath of "witch-hunting" which involved some tendency to demand the application of unnecessary and ill-considered methods of screening college and university faculties and student bodies for supposedly disloyal elements.

In the early 1950's, a California statute requiring an elaborate "loyalty oath" of all state employees was construed to include all teachers in the state university and colleges and was sustained by the state supreme court in a divided vote.[13] At the same time, a similar Oklahoma statute, its validity having been appealed to the U. S. Supreme Court, was declared invalid unanimously and called forth three eloquent opinions from Justices Clark, Black, and Frankfurter—all in support of academic freedom. The tenor of the decision can be savored in a few of Frankfurter's words: "Teachers . . . must be exemplars of open-mindedness and free inquiry. . . . They must have the freedom of responsible inquiry, by thought and action, into the meaning of social and economic ideas, into the checkered history of social and economic dogma."[14]

There have been other litigated controversies regarding the liberty of teaching in other state and Federal courts, the intricacies of which we cannot go into here. The general trend over a

---

[13] *Tolman v. Underhill; Pockman v. Leonard; Fraser v. Regents of University of California,* (Cal.), 249 P. 2d 267, 280, 283 (1952).

[14] *Robert M. Wieman v. Paul W. Updegraff,* (U.S.S.Ct.), 21 U. S. Law Week 4057 (1952), reversing *Board of Regents of Oklahoma Agricultural Colleges v. Updegraff,* 205 Okla. 301, 237 P. 2d 131 (1951).

long period is unquestionably toward the weakening of prejudices and the strengthening of reliance upon reason; but the trend has its occasional setbacks and its intervening high points; and its upward direction needs to be continued. This is equally true of many of the other tendencies noted herein. The legal context of higher education is continually developing; and the past century has witnessed many more changes than can be encompassed in the foregoing brief catalogue.

3

A Century of the Liberal Arts College

GEORGE P. SCHMIDT

*I*F A VISITOR to a modern American university campus were to look for the undergraduate college of liberal arts, he might have trouble finding it. Overshadowed by imposing professional schools, glittering science buildings, and sprawling field houses and stadiums, the original college building seems no longer of much importance. Yet, 100 years ago, this plain, unassuming structure, alone or flanked by one or two equally plain dormitories, contained the entire college establishment: it *was* higher education. An occasional embryonic professional school only served to emphasize this salient fact.

The unique American four-year college of liberal arts was the result of circumstance, not design. When, in 1636, the General Court of Massachusetts "agreed to give 400£ toward a schoale or colledge,"[1] the college they were authorizing was presumably to be followed in due time by others, after the manner of the colleges which

[1] Samuel E. Morison, "The Founding of Harvard College" (Cambridge: Harvard University Press, 1935), p. 168.

made up the universities of Oxford and Cambridge. But any lingering memories of a larger university concept were dissipated gradually by 3,000 miles of ocean. Neither Massachusetts nor any of the other struggling British colonies had the means, the leisure, or the continuous contact with the sources of their culture necessary to build and maintain complete universities. The single autonomous college thus became the standard unit of higher education in America and remained so until the centrifugal forces of the New World reversed direction late in the 19th century. At that time, the European university came to the U. S., but even then with a difference.

By 1860, the nine colleges founded before the Revolution had increased to perhaps 200, the survivors of a precarious and often intensely competitive infancy. The exact number is difficult to ascertain, for records then were inadequate and the term "college" was one of hopeful ambition rather than precise definition. In these colleges, founded by churches and kept alive by religious zeal and community loyalty, some 10,000 young men and a handful of young women were being exposed to the then current version of a liberal education. The institutions varied considerably in size and quality. Yale and the universities of Virginia and North Carolina, with over 500 students each, were the largest; but Harvard, though fourth in enrollment, had the largest faculty—24—and a library twice as large as that of Yale and four times that of Virginia. Costs varied, too. At Harvard, for example, or Princeton, or Virginia, or South Carolina, expenses of more than $500 a year were not unusual, while at some of the more modest church colleges like Bowdoin, Oberlin, or Davidson, the thrifty student, so the catalogues announced, could keep his total annual costs under $100.[2] Yet, all these colleges, large and small, rich and poor, had a family resemblance: each would have recognized the course of study and the campus problems of the others.

The intellectual fare at all of them was an Americanized version of the so-called liberal arts and sciences which, as the indispensable intellectual equipment of the educated free man, had come down from its original Aristotelian formulations, via Oxford and Cambridge, to the first three colonial colleges: Harvard, William and Mary, and Yale. By that time, it had come to include Greek philosophy, made palatable for the Christian world by the medieval schoolmen; polite letters, both Latin and Greek, the contribution of the Renaissance; and mathematics, a reflection of the 17th century's increasing preoccupation with science. The actual course of study constructed out of these materials, and which every student was required to take, shaped up about as follows. Freshmen and sophomores spent most of their classroom time translating Latin and Greek classics and acquiring, it was fondly hoped, a disciplined mind and a free spirit in the process. The remainder of the two lower years was given to mathematics, rhetoric, and natural philosophy (lectures on the rudiments of physics and chemistry). In the junior and senior years, the classics tapered off to give way to logic, metaphysics, ethics, and polemical lectures on the evidences of Christianity. Smatterings of modern languages, history, zoology, and geology rounded out the program.

[2] This information comes largely from the catalogues and the histories of the colleges mentioned.

52

This course of study, inflexible and irreducible, remained in force against mounting opposition, but with little actual change, until past the middle of the 19th century. The purpose of it all, in the words of the Harvard charter of 1650, was "the advancement of all good literature, artes and Sciences" in the framework of eternity: "The maine end . . . is, to know God and Jesus Christ."[3] In proclaiming these goals, the charter was speaking not only for Harvard, but, as it turned out, for the old-time college in general. Two centuries later, a president of Columbia College was to rephrase them: "Here in college is to be fashioned, in the highest attainable perfection, the scholar, the citizen, the good man, the Christian gentleman."[4]

If the colleges failed to attain that highest perfection, there were extenuating circumstances. Provincialism and inbreeding became inevitable as contact with old-world academic centers, fairly well maintained in colonial days, broke down in the little freshwater colleges that marked the westward movement. The course of study in these newer institutions was, with few exceptions, a replica of those eastern colleges, usually Yale or Princeton, at which their presidents and professors had studied: copies of copies. Life was narrow and monotonous. With 100 or 200 boys— college students averaged about two years younger than now—cooped up in a campus at the edge of a small town, far from the worldly temptations of cities, the regime tended to be legalistic and mechanical. Rules governed every waking hour from the rising bell at 5:30 or 6:00 a.m. to lights out at 9:00 or 10:00 p.m. Student response to these cramping regulations varied from ex-

---

[3] Morison, *op. cit.*, pp. 248, 434.
[4] Pres. Charles King, in his inaugural address (1849).

uberant horseplay and childish pranks to open insubordination and rebellion. Punishments ranged from admonitions, private or public, to suspension and expulsion. Widely used, also, were money fines, graded according to the magnitude of the offense, from perhaps four or five cents for cutting chapel to $4.00 or $5.00 for getting ostentatiously drunk or beating up a professor.

At its best, the old liberal college gave a fairly thorough grounding in a limited field—classical literature—and provided a casual acquaintance with several other segments of the organized knowledge of the times. What was expected in the better colleges appears, for example, in the final examinations given to the senior class of Princeton in 1871, a time when the Eliot reforms at Harvard, which brought the ascendancy of the classical college to an end, were getting under way. In that year, the Princeton seniors, having disposed of mathematics earlier, were examined in Latin and Greek literature and composition, in ethics and metaphysics, in chemistry, political economy, history, problems of science and religion, and, for the first time, in English literature from Shakespeare to Tennyson.[5]

At the zenith of its power and influence 100 years ago, the single-minded college was, before the end of the 19th century, to lose its position of pre-eminence to the multi-purpose university. The vigor and prestige of its golden age were derived from its clear purpose and simple philosophy and the acceptance of both by its constituency. But, in the second half of the century, the economic organization of American life was transformed, and the intellectual and moral

[5] The questions are listed in the "Calendar of the College of New Jersey, 1871-72."

foundations of the western world were severely shaken. Not all college leaders were hospitable to these changes or even aware of them. Many a venerable campus rumbled on as though nothing of importance had happened since Caesar found all Gaul divided into three parts. But in trying to hold back the tide of change, the conservative colleges succeeded no better than King Canute. The flood that engulfed them came from three main sources: the new western state universities, German scholarship and higher criticism, and the philosophy of evolution. The first was a native product, while the other two were imported and marked the re-entry of Europe into American academic life.

State universities had existed, in name, since the late 18th century. Georgia had chartered a state institution in 1785 without doing much about it for another 20 years; Vermont authorized one in 1791; the University of North Carolina was in actual operation from 1795 on. But these state colleges differed little from the private and church-sponsored institutions with which they competed. The University of Virginia, with its separate schools and unconventional curriculum, pioneered in a new direction, but it was one of the most expensive schools in the land and did not reach the common man. The state universities west of the Appalachians were reared, by contrast, on the assumption that public higher education was a responsibility of society and must be made available to everyone who qualified. This meant, at least in the opinion of the first president of the University of Oklahoma, "any young man or woman who . . . will work."[6] Similar claims, to be sure, had been made for

[6] Ray Gittinger, "The University of Oklahoma" (Norman: University of Oklahoma Press, 1942), p. 16.

church and community colleges, but these had not done the job. Their narrow classical curriculum seemed an unrealistic answer to the needs of a rapidly changing pragmatic society. Unedifying denominational rivalries had kept most of them small and had disillusioned many of their former supporters.

The beginnings were humble enough, but the growth of these western state universities was phenomenal, and soon after the Civil War they were challenging the supremacy of the older eastern colleges. Their costs were lower and their appeal was wider. Catering to the wishes of the farmer, the merchant, and the mechanic, they set up departments and schools for technical training and vocationally useful information. Departments of agriculture, engineering, business, and secretarial studies offered opportunities that the older colleges could not or would not match. The liberal arts also were taught, but they no longer dominated.

Horizontal expansion was accompanied by a deepening of the intellectual experience, and the impetus for this came from Europe. The surge of philosophical speculation and scientific research, which characterized the 19th century, was beginning to affect America and to demand recognition and appraisal. For this purpose, a new channel of communication was opening to American students: the German universities, whose prestige was at an all-time high. Between 1815 and 1915, it is estimated, nearly 10,000 Americans studied in Germany, the migration reaching its height in the last two decades of the 19th century. What impressed the Americans most in Germany was the rigorous insistence on scientific and rational criteria for all knowledge, the wide range of subject matter, and the high

degree of academic freedom. Equipped with the coveted Ph.D. degree, which gave them entry to virtually any college position in the country, the returning scholars introduced such educational devices as the formal lecture, the laboratory, and the seminar, by means of which they hoped to bring higher education to maturity. The universities which now took shape were by no means exact replicas of the German, for the liberal arts college on which they were based was not the German *Gymnasium*. The American answer was the graduate school, grafted onto the college of arts and sciences and then finding a place, somehow, among or above the various vocational schools.

Third among the forces of change was the philosophy of evolution. Cautiously advanced as a biological hypothesis by Charles Darwin, expanded into a universal philosophy by Herbert Spencer, and carried directly to the lecture-loving and magazine-reading American public by eloquent popularizers, it gained an influence that was soon all-pervasive. The evolutionary thesis provided the rationale that raised the scientists to the position once held by the classicists. It offered a fresh point of view in other fields as well and called for a reappraisal of the entire curriculum. It introduced the organic approach to history and literature and speeded the emergence of the social sciences as a separate division of teaching and research.

Under this triple impact the old-time college crumbled. The intellectual authority of the classical curriculum and the moral authority of a theologically oriented faculty now gave way to the claims of science and the critical norms of professional scholarship. When Charles W. Eliot, Daniel C. Gilman, William R. Harper, and other innovators had completed their work, the university with its wide range of offerings and freedom of choice had taken the place of the college as the capstone of American higher education. But, though reduced in importance, the autonomous four-year college was by no means eliminated. The university modified but did not destroy it. Even today, colleges granting only the bachelor's degree far outnumber those institutions that carry a full complement of graduate and professional schools. And new ones continue to appear, in country and in town.

Are they still colleges of liberal arts? They certainly are not what they were a century ago. For one, the course of study has changed almost beyond recognition. The classical languages, once the heart of the matter, almost have vanished, and literature is studied through the medium of English, French, German, and Spanish, with Russian coming on fast. The sciences have come a long way since the day, in 1862, when the faculty of a prominent eastern college grudgingly permitted one of America's foremost botanists to give a lecture course in his subject "at such hours as will not interfere with the regular studies of the undergraduates."[7] Today, science buildings and laboratories often consume the largest share of the annual budget. Perhaps the greatest expansion has come in the social sciences, which were not even known by name in the old college and appeared, if at all, only in embryonic form in the senior course in moral philosophy. In short, most of the subjects that now are accepted as the core of the liberal curriculum were recognized only unwillingly 100 years ago or were entirely without the pale.

[7] "Annual Catalogue of Columbia College, 1862-63."

As subjects and departments multiplied, virtually all colleges broke away from the rigidity of one required course of study and adopted, or adapted, the principle of free electives introduced by Pres. Eliot at Harvard. This in turn necessitated quantitative measurements of achievement and led to the credit-point system, which, originating at the University of Michigan, became an inevitable part of college bookkeeping.[8] Henceforth, when a student amassed the prescribed number of credit points, properly distributed among required subjects, a field of major concentration, and free electives, he graduated.

Other features distinguished the modern college from its prototype. Concessions have had to be made to the vocational demands of constituents to such an extent that, in many colleges today, the students in the vocational and pre-professional departments outnumber those in the liberal arts. There also has been a tremendous proliferation of extracurricular activities, resulting in a fragmentation of campus life. All that the old college had of such activities were a few fraternities where the faculty allowed them, vigorous literary and debating societies, and sporadic and largely unorganized outdoor play. That play has mushroomed into the present, highly organized and commercialized intercollegiate athletics. Debating societies still exist but rarely flourish. Fraternities and sororities have created new interests—and problems. All of these, plus musical and dramatic societies, student publications, and various other interests or pres-

[8] Dietrich Gerhard, "The Emergence of the Credit System in American Education Considered as a Problem of Social and Intellectual History," *AAUP Bulletin,* vol. 41, Winter, 1955.

sure groups, make up the kaleidoscopic campus of today.

What of the future? With such powerful forces threatening its integrity, can the liberal arts college survive? The question applies to form as well as content. In form, it would seem, the four-year college will continue very much as we have known it for some time to come. Changes, no doubt, will occur. Some already are under way, such as the 11-month academic year and other forms of speed-up and the expanded community college program of some states. But these are variants within the established framework. There is little likelihood that our system will be re-organized completely along European lines, with secondary school extending to about the sophomore college level and graduate and professional schools superimposed on that. This has been tried, by prominent educational leaders, and thus far it has failed. Of most recent memory is the now-defunct plan of former Chancellor Robert M. Hutchins to make over the University of Chicago. By contrast, such new colleges as are established tend to conform to the four-year pattern, and so do the former teachers colleges, which, in state after state, are being converted into four-year institutions of general education and aspire to become genuine colleges of liberal arts.

But, though the form may not change, the content inevitably will. Today, as has been pointed out, while colleges continue to confer the A.B. and occasionally the A.M. degree, as their proto-types have been doing since the 13th century, the work and achievements represented by these degrees are far from what they were then. They will continue to diverge. Changes are not likely to be uniform, however, nor will they proceed

everywhere at the same pace. As a result, several distinct types of institutions may emerge, all variants of the present college.

The first will include the overwhelming majority of colleges whose students will devote—as most of them already are doing—the two lower years to a series of largely required and variously organized courses in the humanities and sciences and then will move, with few exceptions, into one of the vocational or pre-professional departments. The traditional liberal majors in English, history, Romance languages, or philosophy will shrink in numbers and perhaps vanish altogether. Increasing co-operation can be looked for among colleges of the same neighborhood or region which are aiming for more efficient use of resources and avoidance of wasteful duplication—in imitation of such current examples as the Claremont Colleges in California, the New College of the Connecticut valley, and the group of church-related liberal colleges in the upper Mississippi valley.

A different course is indicated for the larger universities, both state and private. These will have to maintain, somewhere within their complex organization, at least one school of liberal arts with a full roster of academic majors. Respect for traditional scholarship as well as the prestige of the university will require this. Even here, however, the liberal arts college is likely to decline in relative size and to be linked more closely with the graduate school; its majors will increasingly be those students only who intend to go on to graduate study and themselves become university professors and research specialists.

There is a third possibility. A handful of colleges whose established position, distinguished clientele, and impressive endowment give them greater freedom of choice may decide to continue the liberal tradition in all its vigor, spurning the popular trend, maintaining the most rigorous intellectual standards, and restricting themselves to a highly selective student body.

If, then, with the exceptions noted, vocational interests can be expected to put an end to the historic liberal college, will this mean the end of the liberal philosophy in higher education? Not necessarily. For one thing, enrollments have increased so tremendously that, in spite of the inroads of vocationalism, a larger percentage of the young people of the nation is exposed, even if only in the freshman and sophomore years, to the arts and sciences today than 100 years ago when the latter presumably were in their prime. Furthermore, liberal values are not confined to the traditional self-styled liberal subjects, which, as demonstrated, have changed over the centuries and will change again. A liberal education is not necessarily bound up with a fixed curriculum or major or a prescribed accumulation of credit points. Liberal subjects can coexist with vocational. The latter, if taught by competent, philosophically oriented instructors, can enlarge the understanding, while traditional academic subjects, in the hands of unimaginative pedants, may be narrowing and illiberal. The much-quoted *bon mot* of Pres. John Gardner of the Carnegie Corporation bears repetition here:

An excellent plumber is infinitely more admirable than an incompetent philosopher. The society which scorns excellence in plumbing . . . and tolerates shoddiness in philosophy . . . will have neither good plumbing nor good philosophy. Neither its pipes nor its theories will hold water.[9]

[9] "Excellence" (New York: Harper, 1961).

62

Though the liberal tradition is in serious difficulties, none of them need touch its essence or destroy its permanent values. To state exactly what these values are has always proved difficult, for a liberal education is not a matter of precise definition, like a chemical formula or a proposition in geometry. The literature of the subject is voluminous and, as one prominent scholar has put it, "slops over with effusions about sentimental purposes."[10] Yet, despite extravagant clichés and vaguely defined goals, the hundreds who have written about it and the hundreds of thousands who have experienced it are convinced there is *something* there and *that* something is priceless. A liberal education—to state the consensus—means knowledge of the world of nature and of men. It means a disciplined mind, and this includes the effective use of language and the ability to think critically and to judge intelligently among alternatives. It means examination of moral values and appreciation of the products of man's imagination, whether displayed in painting and music, in poetry and drama, or in mathematics and astronomy.[11] A liberal education is something like that. To one who never has experienced it, this attempt to define the indefinable will be meaningless; to one who has, it is superfluous. Both groups will include bachelors of art and doctors of philosophy, as well as men and women who have never set foot in a college.

Yet, the liberal colleges are the historic guardians of this heritage of civilized man. To remain so, they will have to set their houses in order.

---

[10] W. H. Cowley of Stanford University.

[11] This formulation owes much to the exposition of liberal values in Huston Smith, "The Purposes of Higher Education" (New York: Harper, 1955), chapters 8, 9, 10.

And they might begin by resolving an internal conflict in the academic family itself. The term "arts *and* sciences" suggests the rift. Too often, the exponents of a liberal education base their claims exclusively on the humanities, ignoring or even deprecating the central role of science. Too often, humanists view the scientist with deep suspicion as one who substitutes formulas and statistics for the human spirit and offers up man's free imagination on the altar of the electronic computer. Scientists, in turn, tend to despise the humanist for his fuzzy sentimentality, which would seem to have nothing useful to offer to this tough and dangerous age. Both are wrong; neither the scientist nor the humanist can deal effectively with the issues of the day without the aid of the other. The arts and sciences stand and fall together.

There are other cluttered corners on the modern campus. Sooner or later, the colleges will have to deal firmly with what Woodrow Wilson years ago called the side shows, which have grown so formidable in some institutions as almost to crowd out the main show and which create everywhere a conflict of values. When undergraduates are more concerned with election to the right club or fraternity than with attaining excellence in their studies, something has gone askew. A similar scrambled sense of values would seem to prevail in that university which is reported to have provided its marching band, in addition to a regular uniform, with "blue blazers, a red and white candy-striped blazer, a red blazer, bermuda shorts, a tuxedo, and a red nightgown—for pep rallies."[12]

Pep rallies suggest the most reprehensible of the side shows—namely, commercialized athletics

---

[12] United Press Dispatch, Oct. 30, 1961.

with all its deleterious by-products. If the academic integrity of our athletic-minded colleges is to be maintained, administrations and faculties will have to end their connivance at the widespread practice of beefy bonecrushers and gangling giants in high school graduating classes who sell their football or basketball skills to the highest bidder in a competitive collegiate market. It is time to face this issue honestly and to stop toying with palliatives. Above all, the alumni will have to curb the chronic adolescents in their midst and create the public opinion necessary to put an end to this major scandal. As for those institutions that are too deeply involved in the commerce to extricate themselves, let them hire their players openly and pay them what they are worth as professional entertainers without requiring them to attend classes or giving them a degree. This would be honest, the university would clear its conscience, and the talented young athletes would be spared the embarrassing pretense that they are scholars trying to preserve *mentem sanam in corpore sano.*

Many colleges have cleaned house, with gratifying results, and their number is growing. For American higher education is alive to its dangers. There is no severer critic of today's college than the college itself. Campuses currently abound in programs of critical self-analysis, pilot projects, and new departures of many kinds. These include reorganization of the course of study, changes in class structure and teaching methods, better articulation with the secondary schools, and adjustment—without surrender of integrity—to the demands of the community, the nation, and the world. Students, too, are alive to the issues. On many a campus, to cite but one example, paperback books have wrought a minor revolution in the reading habits of undergraduates, freeing them from the tyranny of the textbook— a truly liberalizing move. As long as it continues to demonstrate such awareness and concern, we may be confident that the college of liberal arts will continue as a vital force in American life.

4

A Century of the State University

JOHN S. BRUBACHER

*I*N THE SPRING of 1908, the commencement speaker at the University of Wisconsin
was the British ambassador to the U. S.,
Lord James Bryce. Few foreigners have been such
astute students of American institutions as was
Lord Bryce. On this occasion he took American
state universities as his theme. They are, he said,
"the newest, the most peculiar, and the most
interesting product of American educational
zeal. They are a remarkable expression of the
spirit which has latterly come to pervade this
country, that the functions of government may
be usefully extended to all sorts of undertakings
for the public benefit which it was formerly
thought better to leave to private enterprise. . . .
In committing yourselves to the principle you
here in the West have abandoned that *laissez-
faire* doctrine generally held seventy years ago.
. . ."[1]

In its heyday during the 19th century, the sup-

[1] James Bryce, "University and Historical Addresses"
(New York: Macmillan, 1913), pp. 161-162.

porters of *laissez-faire* looked to the state principally for the maintenance of civil order within its boundaries and defense against attack from without them. Provision for social progress was left to the guidance of natural forces—that is, to private self-interest. Consequently, during the colonial period and for some time into the early national period, the founding and maintenance of institutions of higher education were left to private initiative, an initiative largely exerted by the churches. The long-run result, however, was insufficient. On the one hand, the private church-dominated colleges too long favored a curriculum serving the limited intellectual interests of the learned professional classes. They failed to respond to the development of new vocations in the 19th and 20th centuries. In an even larger sense they failed to conceive of themselves as instruments of governmental policy whereby social institutions, instead of being left untended, deliberately could be taken in hand and molded to a more just pattern. On the other hand, the private church-dominated colleges served too narrow a clientele. Left free to exert their own initiative, they provided no outlet for the energy and independence of vast numbers of American youth. To give these numbers their fair chance, too, it was necessary to reverse the policy of *laissez-faire;* it was necessary to realize that for the state to take the initiative in making provision for higher education was not an interference with, but an enhancement of, the freedom of the individual.

The first true state university to reflect this reversal of policy was the University of Virginia, when it opened its portals to students in 1825. This statement may occasion some surprise to those who may reflect that Virginia was by no means the first state to bear the name of a state university. This is true, but on close inspection it will be seen that these earlier state universities like Vermont, Georgia, and North Carolina were really more private than public institutions. True, they were chartered by the state and bore the state's name, but actually they closely resembled the conventional private foundations of the day. Thus, the first trustees of these institutions held office as private individuals rather than public officials. Furthermore, these early state universities were left to fend for themselves financially except for an occasional largesse from the state.

If these early state institutions were not truly state universities, neither were the colonial colleges after which they seemed to be modeled. It would be a grave mistake to think that institutions like Harvard and Yale, because they were sired by colonial governments and intermittently received financial nourishment from them, were forerunners of state higher education. Not only were the colonial colleges not state institutions, but they energetically resisted becoming such institutions. The high watermark of this resistance, of course, occurred at Dartmouth. Originally, Dartmouth derived its charter from the British sovereign, George III. When the State of New Hampshire stepped into that sovereign's shoes as a result of the American Revolution and tried to make Dartmouth a state institution, John Marshall and the United States Supreme Court refused to sanction such an alteration of the Dartmouth charter on the ground that Dartmouth was not a public corporation.

In the same vein, it was the final refusal of William and Mary to become a state institution which led Thomas Jefferson to enter on the long gestation of the University of Virginia, America's first true state university. In large part, it became America's pioneer university because it was, as Jefferson intended it to be, a "revolutionary" university. The University of Virginia revolutionized the standards and practices of American higher education at five principal points.

In the first place, Jefferson saw to it that from its inception the University of Virginia took form under public auspices. Thus, its board of visitors, which was to exercise all the powers conventionally vested in private boards of trustees, was appointed by the governor of the state and approved by its legislature. Not only that, but the state put up public funds for the physical plant of the university and assured it annual appropriations for its maintenance. The University of Virginia, consequently, was unmistakably a state university. In the second place, reflecting its public origin and its public responsibilities, the university put forward a program of study which, in tune with the times, tried to catch the revolutionary spirit of the 18th-century "enlightenment." Most notable here was the new breadth of studies offered. Instead of the narrow and often decadent scholasticism of the conventional colleges of the day, Virginia offered an array of modern science—chemistry, physics, geology, botany, zoology, among others. To the senior professions of law and medicine it added such studies as architecture, mining, manufacturing, legislation, and diplomacy.

This catalogue of studies, in the third place, was made elective. In the face of the prescribed curricula of the day, this was another revolutionary innovation. On second thought, however, it was quite in keeping with a fourth point. Not only did Virginia offer this enlarged scope of studies, but it hoped to pitch instruction in them at an advanced level, a truly university level. To insure the success of such a program, Jefferson hoped to staff his university with leading scholars. Believing local American scholarship not yet ripe enough to produce the quality of professors he had in mind, he explored the possibility of enticing European savants to these shores. And lastly, the University of Virginia struck the modern note of a state university by being strictly nonsectarian. In a day of powerful religious tides, this struck many a denominational ear as a distinctly discordant note. Nevertheless, if the new state university was to achieve the maturity expected of it, it would have to be beholden to none in its pursuit of the truth.

Unfortunately, the outreach of the University of Virginia was greater than its grasp. The secondary schools of the day were not of a quality which could feed into the university the well-prepared students necessary for its advanced program. This was a shortcoming for which Jefferson himself was not without blame. Looking at the whole span of elementary, secondary, and higher education, he had recommended that public resources be directed toward improving elementary and higher instruction, leaving the secondary to private effort. Not only were the students not up to hoped-for standards, but it turned out, too, that it was impossible to attract the high-grade faculty necessary to their maintenance. Besides these obstacles there was much denominational strife which delayed the progress of the university toward the stature for which Jefferson's academic blueprints called. But, nonetheless, the design, short of its embodiment, had its effect on the subsequent development of American higher education. Fellow laborers in the academic vineyard, like Philip Lindsley at the University of Nashville, Horace Holley at Transylvania University, and even George Ticknor at Harvard, were in close touch with what was taking place at Charlottesville. There is also convincing evidence that the founding of Michigan's "Catholepistemiad," the forerunner of its state university, felt the personal influence of Jefferson's ideas.

Whatever the success of the University of Virginia, it yet remained to make the state university a popular one. It obviously could not become more popular till it became more accessible. More than anything else, it was the dedication of large sectors of the public domain on the frontier which brought the state university within reach of the people. Strategic in this achievement was the policy initiated by the Northwest Ordinance in 1787 which required the new states carved out of the public domain to set aside extensive tracts of land for the erection of a state university. So successful did this policy prove that by the middle of the 19th century, 4,000,000 acres of land had been earmarked for some 15 state universities. Such a handsome endowment kindled men's imaginations. Thus, Indiana's first constitution directed its legislature "as soon as circumstances will permit" to "provide by law for a general system of education; ascending in regular gradation from township schools to a State University, wherein tuition shall be gratis and equally open to all." The Morrill Act of 1862 continued the policy of distributing Federal lands for the promotion of higher education in the states. Indeed, it was by this Act that state universities finally gained lodgment in the older eastern states.

Both the Morrill Act and the Northwest Ordinance apparently expected institutions of higher education not only to be erected, but to be maintained through their landed endowment. With real estate values what they were on the frontier, optimistic schemes like that of Indiana were difficult to realize without further regular subsidies. Even the leading state of Michigan, whose state university took its origin from the second decade of the 19th century, did not support it with an annual appropriation till the seventh decade, 50 years later. The second Morrill Act in 1890 improved this situation by providing annual financial appropriations and encouraging state legislatures to adopt similar measures.

The forces promoting the state university were not without opposition. Sectarian influences, as in the case of Virginia, generally were arrayed against it. Not only did they oppose a Godless secular public university, but they feared its eminence would dwarf their own private church-related institutions. Others, holding belatedly to the theory of *laissez-faire,* took a stand against public taxation for higher education because it was socialistic. Not a few on the frontier, where many lived on a bare subsistence economy, insisted that their hard-earned tax dollars be spent on the provision of elementary schools for the masses rather than of higher institutions for the few.

Establishing the popularity of the state university was more than a matter of making it financially viable. It was also necessary to convince the mass of the people that its curriculum could be identified with their interests. In spite of Virginia's "revolutionary" university, the stereotype of higher education in mid-19th century was anything but popular. Composed principally of Latin, Greek, and mathematics, the college curriculum seemed to have a waning appeal. Failure to meet the needs of farmers, mechanics, and industrialists, Pres. Francis Wayland of Brown University pointed out, was resulting in a deplorable decline of college enrollments. The antidote for this decline subsequently was found in curricula which drew their spirit from the state universities, especially the land-grant institutions fathered by the Morrill Act.

The pioneer in this direction was Cornell, which, due to the combined genius of Ezra Cornell and Andrew Dickson White, enjoyed the unique distinction of being a private institution to which the State of New York had awarded the state's Morrill benefactions. It thus was neither wholly private nor wholly public. In setting up this university, both men agreed that it was to be a place where anyone could learn anything. An echo of this all-purpose character of the state university was heard in the next century at the University of Minnesota, where its president, Lotus D. Coffman, claimed that there was nothing intellectually too undignified to teach at the university. There would be no narrow or preferential curriculum for these seats of learning, but all studies were to enjoy a plane of equality. The equivalence of studies received a strong assist from Charles William Eliot's popularization of the elective curriculum, a reform advocated by Jefferson at the University of Virginia.

At Wisconsin, the all-purpose university took on the function of social service as well. There the state university not only conserved and disseminated knowledge, but it also became an agency for social amelioration. It came to the full flower of this function in the early decades of the 20th century, when "Fighting" Bob La-Follette was governor of the state and when the "progressive" political movement was in full swing in the country. In driving his program through the legislature and into practice, he continually sought counsel from experts at the university in agriculture, economics, and political science. It might not be amiss to describe these university experts as the forerunners on the state level of Franklin Delano Roosevelt's "brain trust" on the national level a few decades later. So, it is not surprising that this "Wisconsin Idea" gave rise to the quip that Wisconsin had not a state university, but a university state. One can well imagine, therefore, the appropriateness of Lord Bryce's remarks which opened this whole discussion of the state university.

The point of this curriculum development is that, when the American people began to realize there was another kind of curriculum besides the conventional scholastic or humanistic one, which was concerned with their daily life in all its complexity, the state university became established as a popular institution. Not only have mounting waves of students sought entrance to it till they almost inundated it in the 20th century, but the larger public has taken it to its heart with ever increasing outlays of tax monies.

Although this advance had encouraged all classes in the U. S. to prize and desire higher education, there were many who thought the advance had been purchased at a price. The increasing number knocking at the portals of the state university not only had brought an increased portion of mediocre minds to the campus, but it had adulterated the curriculum so that the mediocre would find it profitable to stay out their term. Not a few regarded these marks as signs of the decay of the state university. As enrollments in the 20th century moved from four per cent of the college-age population to over 30%, state universities along with others seemed to be bursting at the seams. Increasingly were heard questions like, "Who should go to college?" and "What is higher education for?"

Analyzing the situation in his "American State University," Norman Foerster spoke for many when he condemned the humanitarian, sentimental impasse to which he thought democratization had brought the state university. The equivalence of studies, he believed, had destroyed standards of intellectual endeavor and standards of admissions. Even such an iconoclast as Herbert Spencer had set up a hierarchy of studies when he addressed himself to the question, "What Knowledge Is of Most Worth?" Moreover, in endeavoring to teach the average and even the inert, Foerster believed the able student had become the "forgotten man" on the academic campus. Such a situation was hardly one which Jefferson envisioned when he first started to draw up the specifications for a state university. Rather, it was his idea that higher education should be selective.

Much as the state university has scrambled from its inception to the present to become a popular institution, it has become, as a matter of fact, increasingly concerned with quality as well as numbers in the 20th century. Before World War II, the University of Minnesota took the lead in one direction by organizing a so-called "General College," whose curriculum was suited to those unable or unwilling to attempt the rigors of the traditional liberal arts curriculum. This device saved worth-while human resources from being thrown on the academic scrap heap and, at the same time, saved the more academically inclined from having their studies and standards impeded by their less competent fellows. The University of Wisconsin pioneered in a different direction with its "Experimental College," where an advanced interdisciplinary curriculum was designed to give exacting intellectual discipline to a selected body of undergraduates. After World War II, and especially after the ascent of Sputnik, state universities began to stress various honors programs already well advanced in private colleges and universities like Swarthmore, Princeton, and Harvard.

It would be a mistake to conclude from these measures that the state university was altogether belated in aiming at advanced standards of scholarship. In designing the University of Virginia, it will be remembered, Jefferson earnestly hoped to pitch its curriculum distinctly above that of the conventional institutions of higher education of his day. And Henry Tappan, when he came to the presidency of the University of Michigan in the mid-19th century, had the same high hopes. It is interesting that Tappan, unlike Jefferson, had in mind a German university as a model. Neither man was successful, but not for want of vision. Each was too far in advance of his time. As everyone knows, it remained for Daniel Coit Gilman to make the first successful graft of the German university idea on the American educational system, when he was called to organize privately founded Johns Hopkins. Nevertheless, it was the efforts of state universities, though abortive, which were first in this field. In the 20th century, of course, graduate schools became essential parts of all major state universities.

As research became one of the leading purposes of the American state university, the question became more and more insistent whether the public would interfere with professors whose inquiries led to unpopular conclusions. It is worth noting that one of the first ringing defenses of academic freedom was made at the University of Wisconsin just before the turn of the century. It was very heartening to many to see the regents of that great university refuse to censure one of its leading professors of economics, Richard T. Ely, for advanced views which he held on labor.

No space remains in which to recount many other points at which the history of the state university in the past century has been coincidental with that of private universities. But we know at least that public state universities shared with the private ones the exploration of the elective curriculum which was first projected in the 19th century. So, too, if they did not initiate the graduate school, they did share in its development. Also, the campus of the state university was just as much a battleground for academic freedom in the 20th century as was the private one.

Enough should have been said by now, however, to show the pluralistic role of state higher education in the past century. An exceedingly complex society like that of the U. S. demands for its successful operation many kinds and grades of higher education. Although only half of that century had elapsed when Lord Bryce spoke at Wisconsin's commencement, what he said at that time is still just as appropriate 50 years later at the conclusion of that century. "Whereas the universities of Germany," he declared, "have been popular but not free, and those of England free but not popular, yours ...

are both popular and free. . . . Nor is it only that your universities are accessible to all classes. They have achieved what has never been achieved before—they have led all classes of the people to believe in the value of university education and wish to attain it. They have made it seem a necessary part of the equipment of everyone who can afford the time to take it."[2]

[2] *Ibid.*, pp. 161-162.

5

A Century of the Church-Related College

ALLAN O. PFNISTER

$\mathcal{T}$HE CHURCH-RELATED COLLEGE in America faced in 1962 a world vastly different from that in which it lived a century ago. American higher education in 1862 was essentially Protestant church-related higher education. Of the 182 permanent colleges established before the Civil War, 175 had been established under religious auspices, and the vast majority had retained their denominational affiliations.[1] At the outbreak of the Civil War, there were only 17 state institutions, although the state governments had in the cases of three or four additional institutions established some rather tenuous connections. While the pioneer Roman Catholic higher institution, Georgetown,

---

[1] While many of these early colleges represented a mixture of public, "private," and church support and control, in the absence of a clearly defined group of public colleges, they were essentially church-related. As a matter of fact, denominational politics also were much felt in the development of the early "state" institutions. *Cf.,* John S. Brubacher and Willis Rudy, "Higher Education in Transition" (New York: Harper, 1958), p. 144.

had been established in 1789, the great development of Catholic higher education took place after the 1860's, with the most significant movement occurring during the 20th century. Yeshiva University traces its origin to 1886 and to Etz Chaim Yeshiva, the oldest Orthodox Jewish Theological Seminary in the U. S., but Jewish efforts to establish broadly based institutions of higher learning other than seminaries awaited the 20th century.

By way of contrast with 1862, in 1962 Protestant church-related colleges constituted only somewhat over one-quarter of the higher institutions in the U. S. and probably claimed only 15% of the total degree-credit enrollments. These figures are only estimates, because at present it often is difficult to determine at what point a college is "related" to the church and at what point it should be classified simply as private, non-sectarian.[2] On the basis of the fall, 1960, degree-credit enrollment in 1,975 institutions, liberal arts colleges represented 39% of the total number of institutions, but enrolled only 28% of the total number of students. While the majority of these liberal arts colleges are church-related, a sizable number may be classified as independent, non-sectarian institutions. Whatever the precise figures, it is clear that the church-related college, from occupying the dominant position, has moved into an uneasy second

---

[2] Guy E. Snavely, in "The Church and the Four-Year College" (New York: Harper, 1955), sets the following limits in his definition of church-related: "When a college loses its church connection and its presidents cease to be clergymen, its destiny will be no longer recorded here" (p. 9). Whether within this limitation or not, some of the colleges listed by him as church-related are listed simply as "private, non-sectarian" in the most recent Directory of the U. S. Office of Education. The lines are hard to draw.

or third position among American higher educational institutions. Moreover, "church-related college" at present is not restricted to Protestant-related; approximately one-third of the colleges now classified as church-related are Roman Catholic institutions, and the colleges of other religious groups, while small in number, also must be taken into account.

The story of the church-related college during the past 100 years is not, however, simply the story of a dwindling share in the American higher educational enterprise. It is the story, rather, of change and realignment that parallels the story of the reorganization of all of American higher education. Let us review in a limited way the major developments among Protestant, Catholic, and Jewish collegiate programs.

For the Protestant church, the decades immediately preceding 1862 had witnessed an enormous expansion of denominational colleges. Tewksbury's well-known study[3] documents the establishment of 516 colleges in 16 states. While the mortality rate for these ventures was high—over 80%—the Protestant college still dominated the scene in 1862. The establishment of colleges on the frontier was viewed as part of the missionary outreach of the church. Such agencies as the American Home Mission Society, established in 1826 to unite Christians of several denominations in comprehensive planning and action, fostered the development of "seminaries of learning." In 1837, the Society for the Promotion of Collegiate and Theological Education at the West was founded to bring order to the

[3] Donald G. Tewksbury, "The Founding of American Colleges and Universities before the Civil War" (New York: Bureau of Publications, Teachers College, Columbia University, 1932).

solicitation of funds in the East for the support and development of colleges on the frontier.

The efforts begun by the Protestant churches during the first part of the 19th century continued through the final years. According to Snavely's listing,[4] 60% of the colleges currently related to Protestant denominations were established *after* 1860. (The process slowed down after 1900, however, for only 12% of these colleges were established after that date.) But, in spite of these advances, new forces were being brought into play that were to challenge the position of the church-related college.

The first challenge came in the form of the rapid development of other kinds of higher institutions. Before the Civil War, the establishment of state colleges had been slow and sporadic. Even those colleges organized by the states received minimal, if any, direct support from the state treasuries. It took the Morrill Act of 1862, coupled with the after-effects of the Civil War and the beginning of American technology, to provide new stimulus. The land-grant funds helped create Cornell University, a combination private and public institution, with the beginnings of a new curriculum. Land-grant funds helped to resurrect the University of Minnesota and to give new life to Wisconsin, Georgia, and North Carolina. While subsequent aid under the Hatch Act of 1887 and the Smith-Lever Act of 1914 was required to implement fully the intent of the Morrill Act, the development of non-denominational and public institutions was clearly under way. Perhaps more significant than the amount of financial support given to the institutions was the fact that a clear distinction

---

[4] Snavely, *op. cit.*, pp. 66 ff.

was being made between public and denominational colleges.

The last quarter of the 19th century also saw the establishment of the American university—Johns Hopkins in 1876, Clark in 1888, and Chicago in 1892. Consciously playing down the undergraduate program and teaching, the new institutions emphasized research and service. Pushing forward the frontiers of knowledge, they fostered the multiplication of disciplines and specialties and opened up entirely new worlds of speculation and investigation. Growing rapidly, they have come to dominate the American higher educational scene. In 1962, the 10 largest universities in the U. S. enrolled 10% of all degree-credit students. While constituting only seven per cent of the total number of higher institutions, universities enrolled over 40% of the students. Some of the early Protestant colleges have developed into universities, but in the process of doing so they either dropped or lost their church affiliation. Today, less than a dozen complex multi-purpose universities claim affiliation with a Protestant denomination.[5] The Protestant college has remained essentially a single-purpose, liberal arts institution.

The new universities challenged not only the position of the liberal arts college, but also the

[5] Although the lineal descendant of a Baptist institution established in 1857 and until recently, at least, listed as affiliated with the Board of Education and Publication of the American Baptist Convention, the University of Chicago from 1892 on could hardly be considered a church-related institution. Harvard, Yale, and Princeton had long since ceased considering themselves church-related institutions. Currently, such institutions as Syracuse University and Northwestern University are listed by the U. S. Office of Education Directory as "private" rather than "Methodist."

concept of knowledge upon which these colleges had been built. As "liberal arts college" and "church-related college" became more firmly identified, at least among Protestant groups, the challenge of the university was to the church-related college as well. As Richard Hofstadter points out:

The old-time college, with its intimate linkage with the church, had doubtless been limited. . . . But it had been based upon the notion that a man's education and his intellectual life were fundamental parts of his character and his spiritual being; now, in all too many institutions, education was to be neither intellectual nor spiritual but practical, accumulative, and indeed acquisitive.[6]

The development of the teachers colleges and junior colleges in the 20th century added further complications, and in little more than half a century the Protestant colleges found themselves in competition with rapidly growing institutions of new form and outlook.

But a second, and perhaps even more significant, challenge faced the church-related colleges. Whereas the mood of America during the early 19th century had been strongly charged with religion, the mood of the waning years of the century was strongly secular. The publication of Darwin's "Origin of Species" in 1859 set in motion a new period of free inquiry and more extensive scientific research. In this changed climate, the church-related college faced the challenge to remain faithful to a conservative theology and yet to maintain contact with a rapidly shifting world of knowledge. At the same time, the churches began to experience a general decline in reforming zeal. By the end of the 19th century,

---

[6] Richard Hofstadter and C. DeWitt Hardy, "The Development and Scope of Higher Education in the United States" (New York: Columbia University Press, 1952), pp. 36-37.

denominational zeal was clearly flagging. The new science, the higher criticism, and increasing wealth and physical comfort all contributed. More and more professors were becoming specialists in their subjects, while fewer were ministers. Wealthy alumni in ever increasing numbers with larger and larger contributions to dangle before the trustees demanded more voice in the control of their alma mater, often at the expense of the church. Whatever the causes, it no longer seemed quite so important that the college be Presbyterian, or Methodist, or Baptist.[7]

As a matter of fact, such a development as the pension plan of the Carnegie Foundation for the Advancement of Teaching sorely tempted many a college to deny that it was Presbyterian, or Methodist, or Baptist.

The announcement of the Carnegie plan to pension retired professors put great strain on denominational bonds because professors of denominational colleges were excluded from its largess. Yet the terms on which this much-needed security was offered professors were so generous that it is no wonder that a number of church-related colleges went through elaborate contortions to convince the officers of the fund that they were not really related after all.[8]

On other fronts as well, battles were being fought to determine the meaning of "related" in "church-related." One of the more dramatic battles was that involving the trustees of Vanderbilt University and the General Conference of the Methodist Episcopal Church South. Because of differences of opinion between the General Conference and the board of trustees regarding authority for electing new trustees and after rejection by the trustees of the findings of a lay commission regarding the authority of the church over the university, the bishops of the church brought suit against the trustees in 1910. The case ultimately went to the Supreme Court of Tennessee, and while the decision of

---

[7] George P. Schmidt, "The Liberal Arts College" (New Brunswick, N. J.: Rutgers University Press, 1957), p. 41.
[8] Brubacher and Rudy, *op. cit.,* p. 347.

the court gave some measure of victory to both sides, the General Conference passed a resolution which in essence severed the relations between the church and the university.[9] Similar to Vanderbilt, which was allowed to drift free from the church, numerous other institutions also experienced the same separation.

As the last years of the 19th century and the opening years of the 20th century saw church and college drift apart, the second quarter of the 20th century witnessed attempts at re-establishing stronger ties—stronger in that sounder bases were being sought for the relationships. Denominational boards for higher education had been established as early as 1819 (the Presbyterians), but the majority of the boards came into existence in the decades before and after the turn of the century. The authority and services of these boards now expanded. Seeking increased financial support from the churches for the colleges, the boards also sought to define more clearly the nature of the commitment of the colleges to the denominations.[10]

In the meantime, the colleges themselves

---

[9] *Cf.*, Samuel P. Capen, "Higher Education," Chap. VII in Report of the Commissioner of Education for the Year Ended June 30, 1914 (Washington: Government Printing Office, 1915), pp. 159-190.

[10] Colleges were asked to agree to certain regulations, sometimes minimal, sometimes substantial, depending on the denomination. This was also the time for major surveys of denominational colleges. Witness such publications as: R. J. Leonard, E. S. Evenden, and F. B. O'Rear, "Survey of Higher Education for the United Lutheran Church in America" (New York: Teachers College, Columbia University, 1929); Floyd Reeves and John Dale Russell, "College Organization and Administration" (Indianapolis: Board of Education, Disciples of Christ, 1929) —survey of Disciples institutions; Floyd Reeves, *et al.*, "The Liberal Arts College" (Chicago: University of Chicago Press, 1932)—survey of Methodist institutions.

sought new ways of exploring the meaning of their identity as church colleges. In 1914, the Association of American Colleges was launched with a membership of 204 Protestant colleges. As the association expanded its functions and invited into membership other Protestant colleges, Roman Catholic and Jewish institutions, and later the college departments of independent and state universities, the National Conference of Church-Related Colleges was formed. In 1944, this conference became a semi-autonomous commission of the AAC, the Commission on Christian Higher Education. With the establishment of the National Council of Churches of Christ in 1950, there also was set up under its Division of Christian Education a Commission on Christian Higher Education. In 1954, the first quadrennial convocation of Christian colleges convened, the theme of which was "What is a Christian College?" Out of this conference came a rather detailed position paper outlining the characteristics of a Christian college. The third quadrennial convocation was scheduled for June, 1962, with the theme, "The Mission of the Christian College in the Modern World."

The movements toward organization and study have been accompanied by the development of a considerable body of literature directed toward the church and higher education.[11]

---

[11] Attention is directed to such volumes as the following, and these are only a small sample of the literature published in the last two decades: Harold H. Ditmanson, Howard V. Hong, and Warren A. Quanbeck, editors, "Christian Faith and the Liberal Arts" (Minneapolis: Augsburg Publishing House, 1960); Edmund Fuller, "The Christian Idea of Education" (New Haven: Yale University Press, 1957); John Paul von Grueningen, "Toward a Christian Philosophy of Higher Education" (Philadelphia: Westminster Press, 1957). Witness also the beginning in 1953 of the new journal, *The Christian Scholar*.

As minority institutions, faced with problems of financing and staffing, the church-related colleges no longer may take their role for granted. In 1962, they were engaged in serious study of their position in American higher education and in American society. Within the various denominations there is, hopefully, a reawakening of the necessity for strong backing for the colleges. Earl McGrath observed at the 1961 meeting of the Council of Protestant Colleges and Universities that "a reaffirmation of an institution's religious affiliation and the consequent shaping of its entire life in accordance with its declared religious purpose will give new meaning and clearer features to its program."[12] He also pointed out that "until these colleges clearly reestablish their peculiar mission, they will have no *unique* service to perform. In the intensifying competition, without a unique service, they will not be able to survive as church-related liberal arts colleges."[13]

Although the first permanent Roman Catholic higher educational institution in the U. S. — Georgetown — was founded in 1789, there were by 1860 only 14 permanent Catholic colleges in America. As Brubacher points out, in the early years of their development, Catholic institutions, expanding with the increase of Catholic immigration, often "had to contend against deep-seated religious antagonisms. American nationalism had long been identified with Protestantism, and a particularly bitter anti-Catholic agitation expressed itself in the nineteenth centry. . . ."[14]

[12] Earl J. McGrath, "The Future of the Protestant College," *Liberal Education*, 47:1, March, 1961, p. 48.
[13] *Ibid.*, p. 47.
[14] Brubacher and Rudy, *op. cit.*, p. 73.

Using Snavely's listings[15] as a basis, it is apparent that the period of greatest development for Catholic higher education has been during the 20th century. Over 60% of the listed colleges were founded after 1900, only 25% were established between 1860 and 1900, and 14% prior to 1860.

Until the beginning of the 20th century, little attempt had been made to separate secondary and collegiate programs. Under the lead of St. Louis University, a plan for the reorganization of collegiate education (called the St. Louis Plan), requiring a clear separation between high school and college, was adopted by many Catholic institutions between 1890 and 1920. Lay faculty were employed in Catholic colleges before 1860, but the use of lay teachers probably has received greatest currency during the last decade. The initial excursion into coeducation was during the special summer session at Marquette University in 1909. In 1914, DePaul University in Chicago admitted women on an equal basis with men, but it was not until the late 1920's that the woman in the erstwhile man's college could expect to receive the full status of a student.[16] Of the 84 colleges for men in 1955, only 15 admitted women on an equal basis. Coeducation in reverse was in effect among Catholic women's colleges, however, where in 1950 some 2,618 men were in attendance.

Regulations applying to the master's degree were announced by St. Louis University as early as 1838, but the first doctoral programs in Cath-

[15] Snavely, *op. cit.*, pp. 115-125, for listing of Catholic colleges.
[16] Edward J. Power, "A History of Catholic Higher Education in the United States" (Milwaukee: Bruce, 1958), p. 143.

olic colleges must be credited to Georgetown (1895). Catholic University opened in 1889, but during the first years it was essentially a professional school of theology, an advanced seminary, not a university.

Faced with the same cultural developments previously mentioned in relation to the Protestant colleges, Catholic colleges maintained much more clearly their connections with the churches. In the beginning, Catholic colleges were established largely under diocesan control, but subsequently a large part of the development was carried on under the various religious communities. The year 1962 found Catholic colleges also restudying their roles, experimenting with new curricula, but not facing the same pressures of defining their relations to the supporting constituency that characterized the Protestant institutions.

Jewish educational programs in the 19th century were almost exclusively at the elementary level, with limited excursions into the secondary field. The product of successive waves of immigration, the 19th-century American Jewish community found its educational demands supplied for the most part in schools connected with the congregation and under the supervision of the rabbi.[17] There were, however, attempts as early as 1821 to establish higher institutions, the initial motivation for which was the need for rabbis, Hebrew teachers, and cantors. Hebrew Union College, a theological seminary representing the Reform point of view, was established

<hr />

[17] Israel Friedlaender, "The Problem of Jewish Education in America and the Bureau of Education of the Jewish Community of New York City," in Report of the Commissioner of Education for the Year Ended June 30, 1913 (Washington: Government Printing Office, 1914), p. 367.

in 1875. The Jewish Theological Seminary was organized in 1887 to serve Conservative Judaism. Two teachers' institutes subsequently were founded under the auspices of the respective seminaries, Gratz College of Philadelphia (1875) and Dropsie College for Hebrew and Cognate Learning (1907). Other training institutions followed. Representing a broader array of functions, Yeshiva University (1886) was the result of a merger of two other institutions and is now an accredited university with 17 schools and divisions providing both graduate and undergraduate programs. Brandeis University is a nonsectarian school established under Jewish auspices in 1948.

The establishment of the Bureau of Jewish Education in 1910 marked the turning point in Jewish education. Under its first administrator, Dr. Samson Benderly, the bureau "began to introduce the science of general education into Jewish education, without sacrificing Jewish content . . . [and set the pattern] for central coordinating agencies in Jewish education."[18] These central agencies are largely responsible for the extension of Jewish education beyond the elementary level.

One writer suggests that at mid-20th century the American Jewish community "is coming of age culturally as a group."[19] He points to more interest in graduate study with the development of graduate schools in all of the major seminaries and in some of the training schools. There also has been an increase in the number of de-

---

[18] Theodore Friedman and Robert Gordis, editors, "Jewish Life in America" (New York: Horizon Press, 1955), pp. 233-234.

[19] Samuel Dinin, "Trends in Jewish Education—1957," *Religious Education*, 53:27-28, January-February, 1958.

partments of Jewish Studies in the major universities of the nation, increased interest in Jewish scholarship, and wider dissemination of information about Jewish culture.

Indeed, the past century has witnessed some spectacular changes in the place of the church-related college in America. From occupying a dominant position in 1862, it has moved in 1962 into an uneasy second position, and it currently serves only approximately one-fourth of the degree-credit students in American higher institutions. While it is true that during the past 100 years the church-related colleges, especially those under Catholic auspices, have grown in number and enrollment, it is clear that private, non-sectarian, and public institutions have grown much more rapidly. The century has brought many challenges to the church-related colleges, and it also has brought numerous dire predictions of their demise. They emerged in 1962, however, still very much alive and still very much a part of the higher educational scene. At the same time, the mid-20th century has become a time for self-appraisal among these colleges. The kinds of answers now being formulated will have much to do with the kind of role these colleges will play in the century to come.

6

Contributions of Land–Grant Colleges and Universities to Higher Education

EARLE D. ROSS

*T*HE LAND-GRANT institutions of instruction and research, in their wide areas of subject matter and varied forms of organizations, have made the most original and characteristic American contributions to higher education. The term itself, as applied to the institutions founded or reorganized and expanded under the terms of the Morrill Act of 1862, is highly significant, since all of the colonial colleges and territorial and state universities were recipients of grants from the natural bounty. However, the departures in their avowed aims, their persistent growth and expansion, and their adaptations to social and economic changes have given a uniqueness to this group in the higher education of the western world.

Like other basic institutions—ecclesiastical, political, and industrial—New World education, at all levels, has drawn freely and heavily upon the Old. The English classical traditions, the French Enlightenment, the German zeal for new knowledge—however formal and meticulous, along with the periodic uprisings in behalf of the unprivileged masses—were all reflected in a country of unprecedented opportunity. At the same time, geographic and demographic contrasts resulted in profound and far-reaching alterations and adjustments. The emerging product was to be a uniquely American type of university system.[1]

The great shock to traditional education, as to thought and response in every area of life, was in the establishment and dissemination of basic science and its spectacular applications. Especially in a nation of vast undeveloped resources and rapidly increasing population, the old-time regimen of formalized drill and catechistic recitation in ancient languages, theoretical mathematics, and dogmatic philosophy, varied only by disputations in literary societies on abstract im-

---

[1] The fullest general survey of American higher education that relates the land-grant movement to background conditions is John S. Brubacher and Willis Rudy, "Higher Education in Transition: An American History, 1636-1956" (New York: Harper, 1958); Edward D. Eddy, "Colleges For Our Land and Time: The Land-Grant Idea in American Education" (New York: Harper, 1957), gives a general survey of the whole movement; Earle D. Ross, "Democracy's College: The Land-Grant Movement in the Formative Stage" (Ames, Iowa: Iowa State College Press, 1942), traces origins and establishments in considerable detail to 1890; and James L. Morrill, "The Ongoing State University" (Minneapolis: The University of Minnesota Press, 1960), has suggestive and stimulating addresses on various phases of state higher education. Nearly all of the land-grant colleges and universities have at least one history and many biographical and other special studies.

ponderables, was wholly out of contact with an era that was seeking agricultural experts, civil and mechanical engineers, and managerial talent in every field of enterprise, as steadily declining college enrollments indicated.

Realistic as well as devoted "old-time" college presidents were fully aware that their programs and methods were failing to meet the needs and interests of the day, and during the 1850's the leading colleges—the "ivy league" of their period —were offering the available sciences, with elemental applications, and modern languages on an elective basis. Enthusiastic young Ph.D.s from German universities were insufficient in number to meet the teaching needs. As early as the 1840's, scientific enthusiasts, eager to match the European graduate laboratories and experiment stations, had the chimerical scheme of a science graduate university to which the great master Liebig and other celebrities were to be joined. Obviously, at this stage, both funds and qualified students were hopelessly lacking. More directly utilitarian and, hence, popularly appealing were the early geological and agricultural state surveys—definite forward steps in research.

By 1860, vastly expanding supplies of food, fibres, timber, and minerals, the prevalence of the factory system, and the comparatively rapid succession of utilities in transportation and communication had made demands for technical training that existing facilities were unable to supply adequately. The Yale Scientific School with the Sheffield endowment of 1860 was by far the leading center in both general and applied science. The same year, the Lawrence School of Harvard finally got under way, as did the notable

M.I.T. Meanwhile, the U.S. Military Academy in its first half-century had educated in professional life more civil than military engineers. The Rensselaer Polytechnic Institute, founded as early as 1824 with the expectation of thorough training in all scientific subjects and professions, had found ample service in educating engineers within the existing branches.

With the commercializing and consequent mechanizing of the farm and plantation, there was the recognized need for improved and standardized cultivation and husbandry. Agricultural societies with exhibitional fairs, farm journals and books, and publications and exotic plants and seeds from the Federal Patent Office were providing more or less verified information. But in the two decades before the Civil War there was a growing conviction and agitation for agricultural colleges with experimental farms. It generally was assumed that such education for the nation's basic interest would be financed from the public domain, and numerous such designs, ranging from the realistic to the fanciful and from the theoretical to the strictly practical were submitted to Congress.

"The Industrial Movement" was a term applied to a very general and, at times, rather indefinite effort of reformers associated with a great variety of "causes" to combine both general and vocational educational opportunity at all levels and for all classes of society. In addition to supporting free schools, lyceums, manual labor academies, and proprietary agricultural and mechanical institutes, they had as their chief exhibits at the higher level the Farmers' College near Cincinnati and the Peoples' College at Havana, N. Y.; both were curious combinations of the classical and vocational, and both were dependent on the uncertain support of the benefactors.[2]

After two decades of agitation by influential individuals and organized groups of considerable economic and political weight, the time seemed opportune to Justin S. Morrill, an alert and observant representative from Vermont, with farming and mercantile background, to sponsor a grant act for the promotion of a range of higher education which, according to his observations and consultations, seemed suited to meet all reasonable demands by addition to, rather than substitution for, the time-honored content and control. If his motive had a considerable degree of political opportunism and was based on compromising generalities that would not alienate too greatly either the old-line classicists or the vocationalists, these considerations of the ways of practical legislation should not detract from his service in initiating the measure at this time and his loyal and continuous support for supplemental aid throughout his prolonged congressional career. And in any case, his abstention from hampering specifications and directives, whether due to nonacademic modesty or legislative finesse—no doubt something of both—made possible interpretations and achievements far

---

[2] The most convenient background references for the Land-Grant Act, in addition to the general ones given in the previous note, are: Elizabeth A. Osborne, editor, "From the Office-Files of S. W. Johnson" (New Haven: Yale University Press, 1913); George A. Baitsell, editor, "The Centennial of the Sheffield Scientific School" (New Haven: Yale University Press, 1950); Alfred C. True, "History of Agricultural Education in the U. S." (Washington: U. S. Department of Agriculture, Misc. Publication No. 36, 1929); A. C. True, "History of Agricultural Experimentation and Research" (Washington: U. S. Department of Agriculture, Misc. Publication No. 251, 1937).

beyond his most extended vision, then or later.[3]
In spite of impending national division, the bill
passed in both houses only to be lost by executive
veto. But it was soon to be revived with enlarged
grants as a measure of the Civil War agricultural
and industrial program.

In spite of the secession of the opposing states,
the organic act followed the precedents of general
purpose grants to the states, except that all states
were included on the basis of congressional representation. The choice of the one or more colleges and the particular subjects and methods of
carrying out the general objective were left to
the respective legislatures. Further, to insure support of the bill, all groups and interests concerned with this general type of education were
recognized. The "leading object" was "to teach
such branches of learning as are related to agriculture and the mechanic arts," but "other scientific and classical studies" were not to be
excluded. The education was to be both "liberal
and practical" and was to extend to "the several
pursuits and professions in life." While this inclusive range of higher education was to be for
"the industrial classes," that term was defined
nowhere and no class of students was excluded.
Again, sex, race, numbers, and preparatory standards were left entirely to the states to determine.

Inevitably there was keen and often bitter
rivalry between institutions and regions for what
was expected to be very substantial endowments.

---

[3] The most complete biography is William B. Parker,
"The Life and Public Service of Justin Smith Morrill"
(Boston: Houghton Mifflin, 1924). There has been a long,
heated, and rather futile dispute as to the originator of
the basic ideas of the act. The evidence is reviewed with
full documentation in E. D. Ross, "The 'Father' of the
Land-Grant College," *Agricultural History*, 12:151-86,
April, 1938.

The eventual choices ranged from existing or newly formed state colleges and universities to reorganized and expanded sectarian colleges. In general, the outlook for this high-purposed venture in state-Federal higher education was by no means promising. Income from land or scrip in most cases proved disappointingly inadequate, and states, especially in years of hard and uncertain financial conditions, were not willing to exceed the capital requirements of the Act. The manual labor requirement, a major tenet of the Industrial Movement, as in earlier experiences in academies and seminaries, proved instructionally and financially unsound.[4] There was a most disturbing lack of balance and of mutual understanding in subject emphasis. Universities tended to neglect the technical branches and, in several states, new separate A. and M. colleges were founded. Agriculture, even with limitations of teachable subject matter and trained specialists, sought by pressure of organizations with narrow or politically ambitious leaders to dominate the separate colleges, often disrupting programs and creating insecurity of tenure of administration and staff. In spite of the number of clerical presidents and staff members in the formative years, sectarian colleges and their supporters attacked the immoral influence of "godless colleges." Leaders of private universities, notably Eliot of Harvard and McCosh of Princeton, who were ardent champions of modernized education, contended vigorously that all higher education was a preempted right of endowed institutions.

Such limiting and delaying opposition and confusion was overcome gradually by the steadily

---

[4] E. D. Ross, "The Manual Labor Experiment in the Land-Grant College," *Mississippi Valley Historical Review,* 21:513-28, March, 1935.

increasing need for creative scientists, technical experts, and managerial directors and planners. Such services were essential not only for the industries and big business, but, as public service grew in size and complexity, for "big government" as well. And with these needs came the recognition that an unusually large proportion of such talent for the nation was coming from its own peculiar institutions of learning and research. The direct immeasurable services to the farms, the industries, and government at all levels could not be gainsaid. To be sure, such widely distributed institutions have contrasted greatly in nature and degree of service. Thus, in considering the contributions that the system as a whole has made to higher education, it is necessary to have in mind the varied regions, types, and periods under which these academic entities have arisen and grown to maturity. But whatever their differences in size and structure, in basic aims and objectives they have come to be increasingly in general agreement. The Association of State Universities and Land-Grant Colleges, which, under varied titles, has been functioning since 1887, has been influential, especially in more recent years, in defining and extending appropriate areas of work and in raising and standardizing instruction and research. And all, of whatever size and situation, have before them the idea of the true American university that the major prophets of the movement prevised in the crude, simple days.[5]

Basic and cardinal of land-grant contributions have been conscious and increasingly realistic efforts to adjust the relationships of the general

---

[5] For three of the outstanding leaders, see E. D. Ross, "The Great Triumvirate of Land-Grant Educators," *Journal of Higher Education*, 32:480-88, December, 1961.

and special, or liberal and technical, with the steadily increasing subject matter and rising standards in both realms. The ablest of the early technical leaders recognized the obligation for training for citizenship as well as for the vocation, and many of the early students who, from curricular or financial necessity, took their degrees in one of the technical divisions, found careers in many other "pursuits and professions." In recent years, both the general and technical colleges have been extending widely in subjects and methods, and the further and more rationally they have gone, the more they have come to recognize their interdependence. The leading state universities have been systematizing their technical curricula and the standard professional colleges are requiring from two to four years of general education for entrance. Similar preliminary study for the leading branches of technology is being seriously considered. At the same time, general education has pioneered in its realm no less notably than the technological. Achievements in the social sciences and modern languages have kept pace with those in the physical and biological realms. And as the former A. and M. colleges come, legally as well as functionally, as most of them have, to full university status, the general colleges, in co-ordinate position, should have no less essential appropriate values to provide.[6] In the ideas and aims of current education, intercampus feuding, which in some cases extended far into the present century, has become as out-

[6] Earl J. McGrath, "Liberal Education in the Professions" (New York: Teachers College, Columbia University, 1959); E. D. Ross, "Contributions of Land-Grant Education to History and the Social Sciences," *Agricultural History,* 34:51-61, April, 1960; and E. D. Ross, "History in the Land-Grant Colleges," *Mississippi Valley Historical Review,* 32:577-81, March, 1946.

moded as a state's alleged interinstitutional "encroachments."

No feature of the land-grant system of instruction and research has been more characteristic than the full "laboratory method": the direct participation in the fullest and latest equipped laboratory, shop, field, barn; observation trips of natural features, industries, and social institutions; economic and sociological surveys; plant and animal judging; and varied project designing. History and the social sciences have had something of their equivalent in statistical collection, analyses, and the study of documents with maps, charts, and physical survivals.

Ingenious colonial farmers and mechanics had tried new plants and methods of cultivation and tinkered with new devises, and later American students visited and, at times, worked in the laboratories and experiment stations in Germany, England, and Edinburgh which they sought to reproduce in a simple way on their return. From the beginning, the agricultural colleges conducted simple experiments, and several rudimentary stations were set up by state and private support before the Hatch Act of 1887 provided modest Federal funds for more systematic projects. Supplemental Federal, state, and local grants have greatly extended the scope and facilities for research in all branches of agriculture and home economics. Engineering has developed highly serviceable stations without benefit of Federal aid. The other colleges in fully developed universities have organized research institutes with projects appropriate to their division of courses. The most elaborate and, no doubt, eventually the most significant are the highly equipped and manned Federal atomic institutes, devoted mainly to the basic principles and productive utilization of this revolutionizing agency of power. The interrelations and cooperation of such realistic and serviceable investigation has provided an incentive to graduate work and a stimulus to the undergraduate.[7]

The possible careers resulting from such a range of general and applied subjects has brought markedly increased enrollment. More than any other influence, this type of education has brought complete freedom of opportunity in higher education to women. In addition to the wide offerings in general education, there has developed the special profession of home economics with varied branches and possibilities so attractive as to induce men to enter certain phases of the profession. At the same time, all lines of special training have been entered by women—even, in a few cases, engineering.

The supplemental grant of 1890 prohibited racial discrimination, but judicial decree permitted the resulting requirement to be met by founding or utilizing existing Negro colleges. Inevitably from background training and preparation, equipment, teaching, and research have been substandard. The range of subjects has been narrow and, of necessity, much of the emphasis has been devoted to teacher training. For the few adequately prepared in state and private colleges, the northern universities have been generally available, and the land-grant training, in its varied lines, has marked a step forward for the Negro. How the integration policy will affect this as it has other grades of education remains for the future to determine.

Meanwhile, the larger universities have been

---

[7] Bernard Berelson, "Graduate Education in the United States" (New York: McGraw-Hill, 1960).

peculiarly available for the technical education sought by the multiple races from the new countries of the Far East and Africa. As a matter of record, the cosmopolitan appeal of the better-known land-grant institutions always has been unusually strong.

In accord with the service motive from early days, non-degree short courses have been provided for special groups of trainees, varying from three months to two years. Homemakers, farm managers and operators, and special groups of mechanics have thus secured vocational competence. Most recently, these agencies that so largely have made automation possible have sought to alleviate some of its most unsettling problems by the training of special technicians.

Services to the states and nation by no means have been confined to the regular collegiate programs of instruction and research. In addition, thousands were reached through one of the most elaborate and inclusive systems of adult education ever devised. The co-operative agricultural-home economics extension services directed from the colleges and functioning in county organizations under the supervision of county agents and home economics specialists included problems of production, marketing, homemaking, and rural standards of living. Engineering extension, started earlier in a few colleges, found its great opportunity in World War I.

None of the prescriptive features of the organic act has had so marked an alteration and expansion as the rather casual inclusion of "military tactics." In the early years, there was considerable interest in such training and a few enthusiastic executives envisioned the colleges as centers of basic training for advanced work at the national academy. But both state and Federal concern reached a low ebb in the pre-war years of the present century. Sudden reversal of attitude and effort came with major involvement in World War I. So many students hastened to enlist that, to maintain the essential functioning of the colleges, state and private, and to provide special training for officers and technical experts, the Student Army Training Corps was introduced. The armistice came too soon to judge the effectiveness of the plan, but it led directly to the establishment of the Reserve Officers Training Corps. This program with various perfections and extensions was available in the vastly enlarged and prolonged struggle of the 1940's to transform the campuses and curricula with remarkable celerity and orderliness for the training of officers for the different branches of the services along with essential technicians.

In World Wars I and II, the full facilities of the stations and extension services were concentrated on production, fabrication, and economical utilization essential for military and civilian needs. Most spectacular and determined of the new investigations was the notable contribution of certain of the land-grant institutions to the fateful nuclear projects.[8] In the post-war years, systematic programs of instruction were established in all branches of the services.

In efforts to promote permanent stability and world peace there has been no little activity. In seeking to carry out programs of technical assistance to new and backward nations in all parts of the globe, under varied auspices, the services of well trained and understanding experts in

---

[8] James P. Baxter, "Scientists Against Time" (Boston: Little, Brown, 1946).

agriculture, engineering, home economics, social science, and education have been in constant demand.

Land-grant, along with kindred municipal, universities have been forced to bear the brunt of the mass enrollments, in size and complexity, that have confronted higher education at the middle of the century. Remarkable readjustment and ingenuity have been necessary in the reorganization of teaching matter and materials, such as skilled and attractive lecturing in capacity-filled auditoriums, patient and imaginative section leaders, improvised reading rooms and convenient library facilities, and appropriate utilization of visual, hearing, and computing devices. But with all the improvisation, certain states have been forced to set up regional branches, both along vertical and longitudinal lines.

Capacity enrollments of students with such varied origins, backgrounds, and aims and interests have involved intensified problems of social life, adaptability, and moral and religious standards. The first required a staff of specially trained counselors and understanding but impartially strict supervisors. The best solution for religious advice and ministration has proven to be the setting up of foundations by each of the leading faiths—the aim, essentially, of Jefferson's plan for such a feature of his model university, which in this as in most other respects was realized only in small part.[9]

The land-grant system of higher education, like the Constitution, has expanded from rudi-

<hr>

[9] A brief historical sketch of this highly involved and continuing controversial subject, with a remarkably wide and varied range of citations, is in E. D. Ross, "Religious Influences in the Development of State Colleges and Universities," *Indiana Magazine of History*, 46:343-62, December, 1950.

mentary organization and generalized authorizations by supplemental legislation, interpretation, and usage. But throughout the changes of the most changeful of centuries, the basic objectives of the movement have persisted and at their fullest attainment have realized the ideas and ideals of the true founding fathers in an all-purpose and all-service university. Captious humanists freely have derided and deplored this "degradation" of the university—this "service station" for the many rather than the training in the highest learning of the select few. Inevitably, because of pioneer ventures in new areas and methods of instruction and research, new types of organization, and new forms and combinations of governmental direction and control, there have been unfortunate misdirections in subject emphasis, methodology, public relations, and competence and adaptability in staff and leadership. Both teaching and research have been victims at times of political ambitions—local, state, and national—as well as jurisdictional feuds between state and Federal authorities. Colleges and university histories record all too many such untoward episodes, and many more, as every official historian is aware, remain unrecorded. Objectionable teachings or inconvenient findings for influential interests have led to abrupt ending of tenure or improper and humiliating concessions to economic and political pressures. To be sure, such interference with the regular and proper course of academic functioning has not been confined to public academic realm; the privately supported have had their "cases" of more or less general interest. Fortunately, too, the consensus of land-grant opinion has come to stand for complete objectivity in research, full freedom of teaching in areas of specialty, and expert advice to governmental agencies without participation and promotion in political policy-making. Thus, the land-grant institutions have come to be aligned with the forces of realistic and rationalistic academic freedom.[10]

All things considered, at the end of their first century of trial and error and amid the stress and strain of a transforming economic and social order, these unique and indigenous institutions of education and research have demonstrated a capacity to grow and a flexibility to adjust and change that, we may fairly conclude, afford the most hopeful potentialities for the future of American higher education.

---

[10] From the reports on this subject by various organizations, special case studies, and a great number of articles and books—general and special and more or less controversial—perhaps the following books, with their references, may be the most directly available: Robert M. MacIver, "Academic Freedom in Our Time" (New York: Columbia University Press, 1955), especially pp. 116-117 and index under "loyalty oaths"; and Charles M. Hardin, "Freedom in Agricultural Education" (Chicago: University of Chicago Press, 1955).

7

Historical Development of the Junior and Community College

TYRUS HILLWAY

*W*HEN THE GREAT educational reformers of the 19th century proposed the modernization of American higher education by abolishment of the traditional English pattern, imported from Cambridge University by Harvard in 1636 and imitated by nearly all of our institutions of higher learning, and by substitution of the German university pattern, they had no recognizable intention of introducing anything resembling the junior college into our system of education.[1] They mainly hoped, as William Watts Folwell carefully explained in his inaugural address as president of the University of Minnesota, that colleges could rid themselves of their problems with adolescents by refusing

---

[1] One of the earliest reformers was Prof. Henry P. Tappan, later president of the University of Michigan, whose "University Education" (1851) spelled out the steps by which American colleges might become universities.

to admit students until they had reached full maturity — until, in Folwell's words, they were old enough "to enter upon the work of a man."[2] The university under the proposed reform would concentrate its activities in advanced and professional studies and the production of able scholars — that is, experts in academic subject matter and research—while the secondary school, as in Germany, would assume responsibility for completing the student's general education and his preparation for admission to higher studies. This plan would impose an additional two years upon the curriculum of the American academy or high school and simultaneously lop off the freshman and sophomore years of college. Higher institutions would compensate for the loss by extending their programs at the top into more advanced and specialized areas of subject matter. Professors then would be freed from the onerous routine of teaching elementary courses and supervising the behavior of adolescents and could put their ability and learning to work more effectively in the discovery — so vital to national progress — of new knowledge through research and in the training of academic specialists.

Desirable as the proposal appeared and enthusiastic as its proponents obviously were, the German university plan, in its pure form, never actually achieved wide acceptance in the U.S. (except briefly at Clark University under G. Stanley Hall). Our universities installed graduate and professional schools but retained the undergraduate colleges. Public high schools in some places expanded their programs beyond the 12th

---

[2] William W. Folwell, "University Addresses" (Minneapolis: University of Minnesota, 1909), pp. 37-38.

grade;[3] yet, so few students were attracted that practically all these experiments had to be abandoned. Private academies with dormitory accommodations proved somewhat more successful than the public high schools in drawing students into programs on the 13th- and 14th-grade levels. During the last part of the 19th century and the first part of the 20th century, a considerable number of private academies, especially those for girls, began to add courses of what now would be called junior-college grade. Many eventually were to close down their secondary schools and, applying themselves exclusively to offerings on the collegiate level, to call themselves junior colleges.[4]

The particular two-year institution identifiable as the junior college did not make its entrance on the American educational scene until around 1900, when Pres. William Rainey Harper of the reorganized University of Chicago negotiated agreements with certain large high schools in the Chicago area to accept as university juniors any students of academic promise who had completed an extra two years of secondary-school studies equivalent to the first half of an undergraduate curriculum. Harper's principal interest, of course, lay in establishing his institution as a university of the German type, devoting its energies and facilities to advanced subject matter, professional training, and research. He believed — with Tap-

---

[3] Typical of these was the high school in Greeley, Colo., which advertised a 13th grade as early as 1883. Several Michigan schools offered five-year programs in the 1890's, their graduates being admitted to the University of Michigan as sophomores.

[4] Bradford Academy in Massachusetts, founded in 1803 as a coeducational secondary school, began giving work for girls beyond the 12th grade late in the 19th century and by 1932 had become Bradford Junior College.

pan, Folwell, Daniel Coit Gilman, and other outstanding educators of the day — that this object could best be accomplished by relegating the traditional freshman and sophomore courses to the secondary school or to a separate lower-division status within the university. Although he did not succeed in entirely subverting the well-entrenched pattern of the four-year undergraduate college, he openly advocated the formation of junior colleges throughout the U. S. as distinctive two-year institutions within the framework of our public educational system.

In reports to his trustees that received much currency among educators, Harper suggested three methods of setting up junior colleges.[5] Many strong high schools and academies, he said, might become six-year secondary schools (approximating the German *Gymnasium*) by adding the 13th and 14th grades; their graduates would be admitted to college with advanced standing as juniors. Weak and struggling four-year colleges, of which he believed there were some 200 in existence, might strengthen themselves by cutting off the expensive junior and senior years and applying their efforts to better programs for freshmen and sophomores. Finally, new two-year colleges might be founded in the more densely populated locations to serve as feeders for the universities. The total effect of these changes would be to make possible the elimination of lower-division work from the university program. If the steps he advocated could be taken, Harper argued persuasively, at

[5] See especially his decennial presidential report of 1902. Harper is customarily credited with having introduced the name "junior college" to identify lower-division studies and for this and other reasons has been called the "father" of the junior college movement.

least five advantages would accrue for American students: a student wishing to terminate his collegiate career at the end of two years would be able to do so conveniently and without a sense of surrender; the student hesitating to undertake a four-year program of studies might be willing to attempt the two-year course; with junior colleges accessible to more students, the professional schools would be justified in requiring a longer period of preprofessional preparation and thus obtain applicants of better calibre and background; greater economy in the financing of collegiate education would result; and students could live at home while attending junior colleges and reach maturity before entering universities.

While Harper with his brilliant intellect and powerful personality preached the gospel of the two-year college in order to further university reform, some of his ideas already were being tested in Texas and Missouri, where a handful of colleges reduced their programs to the freshman and sophomore years as a means of alleviating budgetary difficulties. The best known example is Decatur Baptist College in Texas, which became a junior college in 1897 with the understanding that its graduates would receive preference as transfer students at Baylor. Public high schools in and around Chicago, and some farther away, proved receptive to Harper's persuasions; by 1904, between 20 and 30 of them were six-year schools. At Joliet, Ill., the 13th and 14th grades were separately organized in 1902 and known as Joliet Junior College — the first public institution of its kind officially on record.

It is worth noting that almost all junior colleges appearing at the turn of the century offered courses aimed at exactly duplicating the freshman and sophomore courses in the traditional undergraduate college. The close association between university reform and the emergence of the two-year college is abundantly clear. An exception to the pattern may be seen, however, in the establishment in 1896 of Lewis Institute, a privately controlled school of technology in Chicago that later expanded its offerings to the full four years and then joined the Armour Institute in forming the Illinois Institute of Technology.[6] For the most part, the nearly 200 junior colleges that came into being between 1890 and 1920[7] displayed less interest in technical or vocational studies than in courses of a traditionally academic nature. When Frank Waters Thomas a few years later made his pioneering study of the functions claimed by the junior colleges of the 1920's, he found evidence of only minor interest in vocational or semiprofessional programs.[8]

If the transformation of American undergraduate colleges into universities with professional and graduate schools, which occurred between 1850 and 1900, constituted the chief influence upon the junior college during its formative period (1895-1920), other influences assumed increasing importance during the following two

[6] Lewis Institute has been called the first junior college. See Phebe Ward, "Development of the Junior College Movement," in Jesse P. Bogue, editor, "American Junior Colleges" (Washington: American Council on Education, 1952), p. 9.

[7] C. C. Colvert, "A Half-Century of Junior Colleges," *Junior College Journal*, 17:244, February, 1947.

[8] Frank W. Thomas, "The Functions of the Junior College," in William M. Proctor, editor, "The Junior College: Its Organization and Administration" (Stanford: Stanford University Press, 1927), pp. 11-25.

decades. From 1920 to 1940, the number of two-year institutions denominating themselves junior colleges rose from some 200 to 575, and their total enrollment grew rapidly from about 15,000 to nearly 200,000 students.[9] This remarkable growth was accomplished not merely by the formation of new junior colleges, both public and private, but also by the conversion of numerous institutions which previously had existed — some for an extremely long time — in various other forms. These included business schools, trade schools, evening courses, adult education programs, and many more. In addition, some junior colleges were established within the structure of certain large universities, particularly in urban centers. Growth during this period represents, then, diversification of type and some change in function for the junior college, with a decided inclination toward the aim of meeting vocational needs of students.

In California, where the development of two-year colleges has been more spectacular than anywhere else, economic factors played a significant role.[10] Not only did funds from the Mineral Leasing Act of 1920 supply a convenient source of support for the state's junior college program, but labor groups recognized in the new institution a means of keeping young people off the labor market for two more years after high school. Dean Alexis F. Lange of the University of California, the West's leading advocate

[9] See Ward, *loc. cit.*, and the annual "Junior College Directory," published by the American Association of Junior Colleges.
[10] See Frank B. Lindsay, "California Junior Colleges: Past and Present," *California Journal of Secondary Education*, 22:137-142, March, 1947; and H. A. Spindt, "Beginnings of the Junior College in California," *College and University*, 33:22-28, Fall, 1957.

of public junior colleges, regarded the two-year college largely as an institution which would fit students who lacked the ability to succeed in university work for positions of skill in business and industry. Both he and Pres. David Starr Jordan of Stanford believed in the extension of secondary education partly as a device for abolishing the lower-division courses from the university and partly as a refuge for the less capable student. California pioneered in state legislation when its enabling act of 1907 formally declared the right of public high school districts to introduce "postgraduate" courses approximating the work of the lower division in the university. Few successful junior college departments were established, however, until after 1917, when the legislature voted $90 per student annually to support these programs.[11] With state aid and the authority to add courses in agriculture, home economics, and industrial and mechanical arts, junior colleges in California began to spring up in large numbers. Their growth was further stimulated by legislation in 1921 permitting the organization of separate junior college districts.

In California and elsewhere during the 1920's, a number of districts experimentally combined the final two grades of high school with the junior college and thus produced a new four-year unit. George A. Merrill, director of the California School of Mechanical Arts in San Francisco, had proposed a similar plan in 1894 to begin vocational training for boys in the 11th grade instead of in the ninth. The 6-4-4 method of organization includes a six-year elementary

---

[11] Under the 1907 law, junior colleges were authorized and expected to charge tuition fees.

school for childhood, a four-year junior high school for early adolescence, and a four-year junior college for late adolescence. This pattern became a popular one during the decades of the 1930's and 1940's, when some three dozen public and private four-year junior colleges were in operation, and advocates began to speak of these institutions as representative of a "new American college."[12] Although logical in theory, the four-grade institution eventually proved unsatisfactory in practice, not only because of parental uneasiness over the elimination of the customary high school diploma at the end of the 12th grade, but also because of psychological incompatibility of students. Young people between 16 and 20 mature quickly, and the intellectual and social interests of those at opposite ends of the spectrum differ considerably. (They are unlikely, for example, to enjoy the same parties or play on the same athletic teams.) In view of these and other difficulties, the four-year junior college gradually has disappeared from the scene in favor of a return to the two-year institution.[13]

The President's Commission on Higher Education, in its report on the urgent educational problems facing young people and the nation immediately following World War II, found one of the chief desiderata of the hour to be the establishment of more tuition-free, public two-year colleges.[14] Every community of sufficient size in the U. S. was admonished by the Com-

[12] See John A. Sexson and John W. Harbeson, "The New American College" (New York: Harper, 1946).
[13] After the people of the Compton, Calif., union district voted in 1950 to abandon the 6-4-4 plan, other districts rapidly followed suit.
[14] President's Commission on Higher Education, "Higher Education for American Democracy," 6 vols. in 1 (New York: Harper, 1948).

mission to provide its youth with suitable opportunities to continue their education beyond high school in a locally controlled community college giving two years of instruction in courses adapted not to historical tradition, but rather to the actual needs of students and the community. Such community colleges, publicly financed and operated, also would serve, the Commission contended, as ideal centers for adult education. Speaking of conditions in modern education, the Commission stated:

"Only a few decades ago, high school education in this country was for the few. Now most of our young people take at least some high school work, and more than half of them graduate from high school.

"Until recently college education was for the *very* few. Now a fifth of our young people continue their education beyond the high school.

"Many young people want less than a full four-year college course. The two-year college — that is, the thirteenth and fourteenth years of our educational system — is about as widely needed today as the four-year high school was a few decades ago. Such a college must fit into the community life as the high school has done.

"Hence the President's Commission suggests the name 'community college' to be applied to the institution designed to serve chiefly local community education needs. It may have various forms of organization and may have curricula of various lengths. Its dominant feature is its intimate relation to the life of the community it serves."[15]

The Commission's nationwide survey of the postwar status and problems of American higher

---

[15] *Op. cit.,* III, 5.

education encouraged many of the individual states to conduct similar studies within their own borders. Several, like New Mexico and California, made special investigations dealing with junior college education; others, like New York and Minnesota, considered all phases of their systems of higher education; a few, like Connecticut, surveyed the educational program from top to bottom. In 1955, Florida undertook progressive and broad-scale planning for a coordinated system of two-year community colleges to serve all sections of the state and placed these institutions under the control of county boards and the state department of education. A Community College Council designated 31 areas in which two-year colleges were needed and, by 1959, had brought about the establishment of more than half of this number. Leland L. Medsker has reported that, of all Florida students entering college for the first time in 1958-59, three-fourths chose to enroll in local community colleges.[16] Mississippi, which had begun statewide planning for junior colleges as early as 1924, when its county agricultural high schools had been permitted to add collegiate programs, appointed a Junior College Commission to divide the state into suitable junior college zones and appropriated funds to extend free public education into the 13th and 14th grades for all resident students in the two-year institutions.[17]

Since about 1925, junior colleges under public jurisdiction have grown in size at a noticeably faster pace than private junior colleges — a strong indication of the effect of low tuition

---

[16] Leland L. Medsker, "The Junior College: Progress and Prospect" (New York: McGraw-Hill, 1960), p. 216.

[17] *Op. cit.,* pp. 245-246.

charges (or none) and geographical accessibility upon the development of this type of education.[18] Growth of enrollments in publicly supported community colleges from 1930 to 1955 exceeded that in private institutions by seven to one, and the trend is not only continuing but becoming more pronounced. Furthermore, growth has been most rapid in states (notably California) in which no tuition is charged. Public two-year colleges have the same advantages that the American high school had over the academy during the late 19th century: low tuition or none, adaptability to the requirements of a particular community, and ease of access (most students live at home rather than in a dormitory). While many states encourage their junior colleges to support their programs through tuition money collected from students, a few, such as New York and Illinois, limit the amount that may be charged against the students to not more than one-third of the cost of instruction. States like New Mexico, on the other hand, expect junior college students to pay substantially the same fees as those charged in state-supported four-year colleges and universities. Events appear to be moving slowly but inexorably in the direction of universally free, public junior college education, as recommended by the President's Commission. Even in such a stronghold of excellent private education as the New England region, pressures in this direction are beginning to be felt.

Junior or community colleges, associated at their origin with efforts to reform the universities and regarded by the early reformers as properly the capstone of secondary education,

[18] See Tyrus Hillway, "The American Two-Year College" (New York: Harper, 1958), pp. 16-20.

have created for themselves a place in the American pattern of education distinctly different from anything originally intended. Today they are neither an extension of the high school nor mere lower-division branches of the university. Community-serving, as the public high schools are, and university-paralleling in that they offer academically transferrable programs, they serve new and broad purposes. Flexible in curriculum, they adapt easily to changing community and national needs and extend educational opportunity to thousands who, without them, might never enter college.

Before World War II, neither the general public nor the two-year institutions themselves fully understood the junior college movement. Leadership in gaining public acceptance and in guiding the development of the movement has been provided largely by the American Association of Junior Colleges, organized in 1920. Under such men as Walter Crosby Eells, the association has given currency and respectability to the two-year institution and has maintained a forum for the discussion of its emergent aims. For years the pages of the official *Junior College Journal* have exhibited concern over the question of what the junior college is, what functions it can best serve, and what place it occupies in the American scheme of education.

In 1962, approximately one-third of the 2,000 approved institutions of higher learning in the U. S. are junior or community colleges, and these enroll over one-fourth of the nation's nearly 4,000,000 college and university students.[19]

[19] See the annual "Junior College Directory" of the association and the biennial reports of the U. S. Office of Education.

While marked variety exists among the two-year colleges (they include among their number technical institutes, adult evening schools, religious seminaries, university branches, and many other types, both public and private), the increasingly typical exemplar today is the publicly supported and locally controlled community college with a two-year program that offers (1) university-parallel courses transferrable for credit toward an academic degree, (2) vocational courses preparing for some of the semiprofessions, and (3) adult education of many kinds (depending on the community's needs) in late afternoon and evening courses. In the typical community college the student lives at home and pays little or no tuition. Now that its value has been tested and its functions defined, the junior or community college may be said to have achieved a permanent and important place in the American educational system.

8

Graduate Education, 1862–1962

EVERETT WALTERS

*I*N THE PAST 100 YEARS, graduate education in the U.S. has been conceived, born, reared, and acquired maturity. Today it is one of the major cultural facets of our society, a significant contribution to the well-being of our economy, and an important factor in the building of our national security.

Graduate work—courses and laboratory exercises taken after the baccalaureate degree—was offered at a handful of universities and colleges during the first half of the 19th century but not in regular programs leading to a higher degree. The first landmark in the development of graduate education was the granting of three Doctor of Philosophy degrees by Yale in 1861 to students in philosophy and psychology, physics and classics.[1] In the next decade and a half, the earned Ph.D. was awarded to a scattering of students at Harvard, Columbia, Michigan, Rutgers, Cornell,

---

[1] Ralph P. Rosenberg, "The First American Doctor of Philosophy Degree," *Journal of Higher Education*, 32:388, October, 1960.

Syracuse, and Pennsylvania; of course, honorary doctorates were granted widely and promiscuously.

Graduate education, as it is now known, began in 1876 with the founding of Johns Hopkins University. There the first clear-cut attempt in this country was made to offer education at a level definitely beyond the undergraduate; its inspiration and model was almost entirely Germanic. Pres. Daniel Coit Gilman, the great pioneer leader of graduate education, was thoroughly familiar with the great German universities. Like hundreds of Americans who had studied in Europe, he returned to his native country thrilled with the excitement of scholarship. He was fully aware, moreover, of the rapidly expanding body of knowledge, the pressures of the sciences on the classical curriculum, and the dissatisfaction with the level of contemporary collegiate instruction. From the beginning, Gilman recruited faculty and students to form an institution in which the chief emphasis was on advanced graduate study and research. In the words of Thomas Huxley, the inaugural speaker at Johns Hopkins, the university was designed "to increase the stock of knowledge by the investigation of truth." Yet, Gilman and his colleagues at Johns Hopkins stressed the direct application of university teaching and research to the needs of society; Gilman, from the first, spoke of the need for studies of man in his relation to society in such areas as political science, taxation, crime, geology, and the biological sciences.[2] These same

---

[2] W. Carson Ryan, "Studies in Early Graduate Education: The Johns Hopkins University, Clark University, The University of Chicago," Bulletin 30 (New York: Foundation for the Advancement of Teaching, 1939), pp. 30-31.

basic ideals of graduate education were established at the opening of Clark University in 1889 by G. Stanley Hall and at the University of Chicago in 1892 by William Rainey Harper, although each institution placed emphasis on particular aspects of their total effort. Harper's stress on research rather than teaching as the important factor in the promotion of young faculty members, his emphasis on university publications (including a university press), and his concern for freedom of speech were to have profound influence in the succeeding years.

Such was the success of these institutions and the interest they created that other universities began to offer or extend their graduate work and formulate specific programs leading to advanced degrees. Among these were Harvard, Yale, Columbia, Pennsylvania, Princeton, Cornell, and Michigan. These were closely followed by state universities, such as California, Illinois, Iowa, Minnesota, Ohio State, Virginia, and Wisconsin. Not all of these and the other institutions offering graduate degrees, however, fully accepted the basic principles of Gilman, Hall, and Harper; at the University of Minnesota, for example, the regents in 1906 approved the establishment of a graduate school "only on condition that it was not to cost anything."[3] Few of these institutions received adequate funds to carry on advanced work for several decades. At certain land-grant universities and colleges in the early decades of the 20th century, graduate degrees were given primarily for work of an applied nature.

Recognition of the growing importance of

[3] Edwin E. Slosson, "Great American Universities" (New York: Macmillan, 1910), p. 247.

graduate work in the academic community came in 1900 with the formation of the Association of American Universities. Organized for the "purpose of considering matters of common interest relating to graduate study and research," the association soon came to be regarded as the prestige group of universities which offered graduate work. For many years (1913-48) the association maintained an approved list of colleges whose qualified graduates were admitted to its graduate schools. The original association membership of 14 gradually was expanded; in 1962, there were 42 members. For several years the presidents of the AAU directed the affairs of this organization, but in time there were more graduate deans than presidents at the meetings. In 1949, the graduate deans broke away from the parent organization and formed the Association of Graduate Schools. This association represents those institutions which now grant over 60% of the Ph.D.'s, and, like its predecessor, it consistently has set the standards of graduate education. Other organizations of graduate schools devoted to furthering graduate study and research include the Division of Graduate Work (Association of State Universities and Land-Grant Colleges), the Deans of Southern Graduate Schools, the Midwest Conference on Graduate Study and Research, the New England Conference on Graduate Education, and the Western Association of Graduate Schools.

Since 1890, enrollment in the graduate schools approximately has doubled in each decade. It was 5,831 in 1900; 9,370 in 1910; 15,612 in 1920; 47,255 in 1930; 106,119 in 1940; 237,598 in 1950; and 314,349 in 1960. Similarly, the number of doctor's degrees awarded increased rapidly during each decade: 54 doctorates were awarded in 1880; 124 in 1890; 382 in 1900; 443 in 1910; 615 in 1920; 2,299 in 1930; 3,290 in 1940; 6,633 in 1950; and an estimated 10,000 in 1960. At the turn of the century, 1,583 master's degrees were awarded; 4,279 in 1920; 14,629 in 1930; 26,731 in 1940; 58,219 in 1950; and 65,614 in 1959.

The reasons for the growth of graduate education lay in the ever-increasing demand for persons with advanced degrees. Soon after the formative years of 1876-1900, it became generally accepted that college teachers should have earned the doctorate. Fewer and fewer institutions were willing to accept teachers holding only bachelor's degrees or, as had been the custom in hundreds of colleges, former ministers (with or without a degree). Regional accrediting associations soon began to use the number of doctors on faculty rosters as an important measure of appraising collegiate standards. The doctorate has increasingly become the virtual union card of the college teacher and the mark of academic respectability; today the prestige of the Ph.D. is higher than ever before. Similarly, school teachers and administrators have recognized the importance of graduate education, primarily that leading to the master's degree, and, indeed, in many school systems the possession of this degree will bring an automatic salary increment. In several states a master's degree in school administration is a requirement for school principals and superintendents.

In recent years, graduate schools have been called upon to train two groups of persons other than those in the traditional arts and sciences. The first of these includes those who wish graduate degrees to secure positions in industry, research organizations, state and Federal governmental agencies, and foundations. With the tremendous emphasis placed upon research, chiefly in the sciences and somewhat less in the social sciences, many college graduates now enter graduate schools to obtain the advanced training and degrees that will enable them to become research persons in industry or will help them to obtain promotions and salary increases. A second group consists of those who want a "professional" degree that will qualify them for particular positions. Typical of this group are those who earn the Master of Social Work degree (M.S.W.), the Master of Business Administration (M.B.A.), and the Master of City Planning (M.C.P.), and the number of these is growing rapidly. Course requirements for these degrees often are rigidly fixed and call for practical or on-the-job experience. There are a few "professional" doctorates; the Doctor of Education (at some institutions), the Doctor of Business Administration, and the Doctor of Nursing are a few examples of degrees now being offered, and several others are contemplated.

Requirements for graduate degrees, quite remarkably, have remained unchanged. From the earliest days to the present, the doctorate represents approximately three years of full-time academic work beyond the baccalaureate, a knowledge (more or less) of foreign languages, a general examination, and an acceptable dissertation (usually defined in the past as a contribution to knowledge). The master's normally requires one year of advanced work and a thesis, although the Master of Social Work requires two years (approximately one with on-the-job experience in a social agency) and the Master of Science at many graduate schools does not call for a thesis. All of these traditional requirements have been reviewed time after time by graduate deans and their graduate councils and by graduate deans' organizations. Bernard Berelson, in his comprehensive study of graduate education, pointed out that

there is hardly a topic active today that was not being debated then, and not infrequently in the same terms. Fellowships, the meaning of research, the character of the dissertation, the quality of the students, the foreign language requirement, the major-minor problem at the doctoral level, the proper examinations, the role of the Master's, preparation for college teaching, college-university relations, uniform statistics—all these topics came up in the first years of the AAU.[4]

Most graduate deans and graduate councils will regard these topics as old friends. One specific example: in the 70 years that Ohio State has been offering the Ph.D., the foreign language requirement has been reviewed formally on eight separate occasions. Although some modifications have been accepted at almost every institution, the traditional requirements have remained about the same.

World War II and the threat of Russian Communism probably have had a more profound effect on graduate work than on other areas of education. Most important, of course, has been the tremendous emphasis placed upon research. During the war, the Federal government went beyond its own laboratories, where most of its research and development had been carried on, and called upon academic institutions to conduct research, chiefly for such military purposes as nuclear energy, control systems, and communi-

---

[4] "Graduate Education in the United States" (New York: McGraw-Hill, 1960), p. 17. Berelson's review of the constant concern for the traditional requirements makes entertaining reading. Anyone concerned with the problems of graduate education must read Berelson's book.

cations. After the war, the government continued to support research both through direct grants and through contract research. Important in this development was recognition of the concept that science is a major national resource and that research is a vital aspect of national security. The year after the invasion of South Korea, Federal expenditures for research and development rose by 60%. There was a corresponding surge following the orbiting of the Sputniks and the realization of the Russian scientific achievements.

The effect of this governmental emphasis on research (a considerable part of it has been in the social sciences) was to increase greatly the demand for graduate students, especially in the sciences, engineering, and mathematics. In many instances it was these students who performed the research under the supervision of faculty members. Coupled with this was the demand for Ph.D.'s by industry, research organizations, and state and Federal governmental agencies. Almost every graduate student in the sciences and engineering was assured a lucrative position after obtaining the doctorate, all too often before he actually had received it. In an effort to relieve this situation, the National Science Foundation, later followed by the Atomic Energy Commission and the National Institutes of Health, sponsored extensive fellowship programs designed to encourage able young students to go forward to graduate degrees in the sciences.

Industry and the great foundations also supported the new effort in research. Many of the nation's largest industrial leaders such as Du Pont, International Business Machines, the Shell Oil Company, and General Electric, made outright grants for research to universities and colleges and underwrote the costs of industrial fellowship programs. These efforts were duplicated by such foundations as Ford, Rockefeller, and Lilly. The bright college graduate—in the sciences—could anticipate financial aid in graduate schools from fellowships, teaching assistantships, research assistantships, or a combination of these.

Another important development affecting graduate education in the last five years has been the increasing demand for the preparation of more college teachers. Predictions of future college enrollments clearly indicate that, at the present rate of Ph.D. production, there will be a great scarcity of doctors to teach the burgeoning college populations. Leaders in graduate education have attempted to stimulate a greater interest in becoming college teachers among undergraduates and graduates through specially devised local and state-wide conferences, fellowship programs, and active recruiting schemes— something that would have been regarded as *infra dig*. 30 years ago. More effective, however, has been the splendid Woodrow Wilson National Fellowship Program, financed by the Ford Foundation and primarily designed to encourage potential teachers, chiefly in the humanities and the social sciences. (In 1960, 17% of Woodrow Wilson Fellows were in the sciences.) This well-financed and effectively administered program has made it possible for thousands of young men and women to acquire a graduate education and look forward to satisfying careers as college teachers. The fellowship programs of the National Science Foundation, especially the Cooperative Program, similarly have provided support for hundreds of future teachers in the sciences.

The Danforth Foundation also has made an impressive contribution in its efforts to finance the graduate education of future college teachers.

Perhaps the most significant long-range fellowship program has been Title IV of the National Defense Education Act. Title IV of the Act, a landmark in educational legislation, provides that graduate schools which offer "new or expanded" doctoral programs may award a designated number of fellowships at their institutions to persons who plan to become college teachers. The stipends for the students have been set at a competitive level, and the institutions receiving the programs have been reimbursed for a considerable share of the expenses they incurred. Especially benefited by this section of the Act were the newly established graduate schools which had just embarked upon doctoral programs and the older, established graduate schools which could announce a "new" program. Clearly this fellowship program, which provided for 1,000 fellows in 1959 and 1,500 each in 1960 and 1961, should dramatically increase the number of college teachers within a few years.

Despite the increasing demand for persons with graduate degrees and the spreading prestige of the Ph.D., the halls of our graduate schools are not peaceful. Indeed, criticism is voiced concerning every aspect of graduate education, from the matter of admission standards to the power status of the graduate dean in the university community. Many of the criticisms are old, but intensified by the growing emphasis on science or the approaching need for college teachers; others are relatively new, such as the impact of the Federal government on fellowship programs and on research.

The sharpest criticism takes the form of the deceptively simple question, What is the purpose of the Ph.D. and the master's degree? Five years ago, four graduate deans maintained in a report for the Association of Graduate Schools that "current pressure forces us to examine our myth-enveloped Ph.D. with candor." Their examination provoked them "ruefully [to] conclude that the Ph.D. is tortuously slow and riddled with needless uncertainties. . . . The basic flaw is: we have never clearly *defined* this protean degree."[5] Their criticisms, and their recommendations for remedies, have been discussed widely and debated in speeches and in articles. Almost every graduate dean has commented on them in approbation or in disapproval. Dr. Berelson has used them *in extenso,* as have a string of other commentators on the status of graduate education. The four deans' suggestion for a "rehabilitated" master's degree, chiefly for college teachers, also has attracted wide attention and comment but thus far has not been accepted by any large graduate schools.

Closely related to these charges has been the criticism that graduate schools are slighting one of their major functions: they are failing to train properly future college teachers. Earl J. McGrath, the most recent proponent of this view, vigorously asserts that the graduate schools have stressed narrow specialization and vocationalism and thus have tempted the liberal arts colleges to place too much emphasis on research and on heavy "majors" for undergraduates. The gradu-

---

[5] *Journal of Proceedings and Addresses of the Fifty-eighth Annual Conference of the Association of American Universities and the Ninth Annual Conference of the Association of Graduate Schools* (Columbia, Mo., 1951), p. 35.

ate schools, Dr. McGrath believes, have led liberal arts colleges to abandon their chief purpose, which is to instruct "the young people in the Western European intellectual and spiritual traditions."[6] Other persons, inside and outside graduate education, have strongly backed McGrath's view; some, without necessarily agreeing that the liberal arts college has declined, have called for new programs which would ensure that prospective college teachers be given more specific training and experience in teaching. Others would add to this the provision that they should have broadly conceived courses in Western cultural traditions and in the role of science in today's world. There have been some advocates of new degrees—doctor's (Doctor of Arts) and master's (Master of Philosophy) —for teachers so prepared.[7]

Still another basic criticism revolves around the nature of graduate work and the function of the graduate school. At certain universities, the graduate school awards the Ph.D. only in the arts and sciences; at others, doctor's degrees in applied and professional fields are awarded through particular colleges and schools, such as the Doctor of Education in colleges of education and the Doctor of Business Administration in schools of business. Yet, in perhaps half of the nation's graduate schools, the Ph.D. is the only doctorate offered, and it is given in all subjects from accounting through animal science, home economics, education, German, nursing, nuclear

---

[6] "The Graduate School and the Decline of Liberal Education" (New York: Bureau of Publications, Teachers College, Columbia University, 1959).

[7] Cf., Oliver C. Carmichael, "Graduate Education: A Critique and a Program" (New York: Harper, 1961), chaps. 11-12.

engineering, physical education, and veterinary pathology to zoology. Advocates of the former practice protest against "stretching" the traditional Ph.D. principles and requirements to accommodate those in the applied fields whom, they believe, should have professional doctorates defined by their own professional needs. Proponents of the latter practice, however, believe that the Ph.D. has a well-established position in the academic community and that it can be made sufficiently flexible to accommodate the older disciplines as well as the applied and professional fields. Unquestionably, the number of professional and applied fields will continue to expand in the years ahead, but it is highly doubtful that there will be a "named" doctorate for each.[8]

At almost every meeting of graduate councils or of graduate deans' organizations there is some discussion of the traditional requirements for graduate degrees. Someone is certain to ask whether the residence and foreign language requirements are realistic, while another will question the need for the master's thesis. Perhaps the most compelling appeal of all: Why not substitute statistics for the foreign language requirements—and then, at the last stand, well, why not for *one* foreign language? Such discussions are, as has been pointed out, the perennials which bloom into rich prose—indeed, often into overripe threats to the graduate dean. It is safe to predict that the next few years will witness a sharp renewal of all these disputes.

A rapidly developing problem, not necessarily a criticism, is the extent to which the Federal

---

[8] For a recent discussion of this problem, see *Journal of Proceedings of the Thirteenth Annual Conference of the Association of Graduate Schools, 1961* (Columbus: Ohio State University Press, 1962), pp. 42-45.

government will influence graduate education. As we already have outlined, the volume of sponsored research and of grants has been increasing rapidly each year. And the Federally sponsored graduate fellowship programs are being expanded yearly. Will these handsome financial supports mean that graduate schools and, of course, universities soon will come to depend on the Federal government? Could our graduate schools continue without contracts from the Air Force or fellowships from the National Science Foundation, especially without the present overhead and cost-of-education contribution? What will be the effect of an expanded Title IV of the National Defense Education Act? These are sobering questions—questions which must be kept in mind by those charged with the direction of graduate education.

Whatever the outcome of these criticisms and debates, it is clear that graduate work will continue in almost the same patterns that now are established. It may be predicted quite safely that there will be only a few innovations and that, despite the pressures from a rapidly expanding population and from international tensions, the Ph. D. (and the other doctorates) and the various master's degrees will retain the same prestige they have today. The only appreciable change will be a considerably increased number of students in the well-established degree programs.

9

A Century of the Professional School

LLOYD E. BLAUCH

A MAJOR FEATURE of higher education in the U. S. is the preparation of men and women for the practice of the various professions. This has come about because one of the principal characteristics of a profession is the possession of a body of erudite knowledge which it applies to the service of mankind through an educated group of practitioners.

Broadly considered, the professions include the occupations which provide for mankind the highly specialized intellectual services. Inasmuch as no precise definition of a profession is altogether satisfactory, it is not possible to state exactly how many vocations should be included in this category. For purposes of this chapter, however, it is well to consider as professions those occupations for whose education and training the universities maintain schools or

---

* Lloyd E. Blauch, editor, "Education for the Professions" (Washington, D. C.: U. S. Government Printing Office, 1955), chap. 2. Some of the material is verbatim from this work, some has been changed to up-date it, and other new material is included.

faculties — a total of around 25. This number does not include the officers of the armed forces or the large numbers of persons (historians, scientists, sociologists, etc.) who receive the principal part of their specialized education in the graduate schools of the universities rather than in the professional schools.

Evolution of Professional Schools. The education of the professions in the U. S., except for the Christian ministry, originally was provided through apprenticeship or preceptorship. The next step was taken by a profession when a number of its members joined in establishing a school which they owned and operated. Such a school, generally known as a proprietary institution, represented an improvement over apprenticeship as a means of learning a profession, but it fell far short of serving the need for professional education. The next step was for the professional school to be incorporated as a nonprofit institution to be operated in the public interest. The final step in the evolution of professional education was to include it in the university as a major feature of its educational program. In some instances, the universities adopted independent schools previously established; in other instances, the universities instituted new professional schools of their own.

Today, most of the professional education in the U. S. is provided through the universities, but there are some independent (apart from universities) professional schools which offer approved educational programs. The education of ministers is done mostly through independent theological seminaries, and for a few burgeoning professions, such as optometry and podiatry, most or all of the education is outside universities. Some of the professional schools are maintained under public auspices and others are under private, nonprofit auspices. There are no approved proprietary schools for the professions.

Early Development in Particular Fields. The first professional instruction in the U. S., other than in theology, which was provided was in medicine, that subject having been offered at the College, Academy, and Charitable School of Philadelphia (now the University of Pennsylvania) as early as 1765; at King's College (now Columbia University) in 1767; at Harvard University in 1782; and at Dartmouth College in 1798. The enrollments were small; it was reported that the number of graduates in medicine from those institutions at the close of the American Revolution was only 51.

During the colonial period and the Revolutionary and Post-Revolutionary eras, sporadic attempts were made in several colleges to provide instruction in law, but these feeble beginnings were born out of time and came to nothing. The first law school in the U. S. was a private venture which a judge in Litchfield, Conn., conducted in his office from 1784 to 1833. But the first permanent instruction in law by the universities came with the establishment of the law faculty of the University of Maryland in 1816, the opening of the law school at Harvard University in 1817, the adoption of a private law school by Yale University in 1824, and the opening of the law school at the University of Virginia in 1826.

In the field of technology, the first professional school to be established was the U. S. Military Academy at West Point, N. Y., in 1802, but the first civilian institution was the Rensselaer

School (later changed to Rensselaer Polytechnic Institute), founded in Troy, N. Y., in 1824.

Instruction in some other professional fields also was begun before the Civil War by institutions. Instruction in pharmacy as a supplement to apprenticeship was established by the Philadelphia College of Pharmacy (an association of pharmacists) in 1821, but the first university school was opened at the University of Michigan in 1868. The Baltimore College of Dental Surgery began instruction in 1840, and the first university school was established by Harvard University in 1867.

More Recent Progress. There was a great increase in professional schools after the Civil War. Many of these were proprietary institutions operated on a low educational plane. The universities took increasing interest in professional education and either established professional schools or absorbed schools already established. Some of these university endeavors were on a high plane, but others were little better than the proprietary schools. With some notable exceptions, education for the professions near the close of the 19th century was in a sad state. Most of the schools were wretchedly housed. Their only income was from student fees, out of which were paid the costs of instruction and a profit for the owners. The entrance requirements were low and few, and the instruction was almost entirely didactic.

A turn for the better came early in the 20th century, and in the last 60 years there has been a remarkable development in professional education. The schools have at their disposal and have assisted in developing a great body of scientific and technical knowledge which they have organized in extensive curriculums. They have recruited thousands of students whom they have prepared for professional service. And they have found large philanthropic and public funds running into many millions of dollars to provide the facilities and sustain the costs of instruction.

In this evolution, the schools have undertaken and developed their functions beyond that of providing the initial professional education of their students. Many offer graduate education for those students who wish to pursue formal study beyond the first professional degree. A considerable number offer "continuing education" whereby practitioners renew their contact with the organized knowledge in their fields and keep abreast of new developments. A goodly number of professional schools engage in research and thus extend the frontiers of scientific and professional knowledge. The collection, organization, and interpretation of knowledge for instructional purposes, together with the reporting on research, lead to the production of a sizable body of scientific and professional literature. Therefore, the professional schools have become centers of light and learning whose inspiration reaches the farthest recesses of the professions. They hold aloft the highest professional standards, renew their personnel, and continually infuse the professions with fresh dynamics. Their position is central in the evolution of the professions in the U. S.

Collective Action for Improvement. The low state of professional education in the last quarter of the 19th century became a concern of some associations of professional practitioners, and they devoted a good deal of attention to it.

During this period, associations of professional schools were formed, which usually adopted standards and admitted to membership only those schools whose practices conformed to these standards. Through such means and through discussions of and actions on educational matters at their meetings, these associations exerted strong influence. Today, there is a national association of educational institutions in every field of professional education.

Accreditation of professional schools and curriculums has been another means of collectively promoting improvement. This practice — setting up standards and criteria for educational institutions and according recognition to those that conform to the standards and criteria — is found in all fields of professional education. Accrediting agencies may be associations which undertake accrediting as a part of their extensive activities, or they may be organizations especially established to carry on accrediting functions. The latter are commonly known as councils, but sometimes other names are used. As examples, for architectural education the agency is the National Architectural Accrediting Board; for dental education, the Council on Dental Education of the American Dental Association; for engineering education, the Engineers' Council for Professional Development; for medical education, the Liaison Committee on Medical Education of the American Medical Association and the Association of American Medical Colleges; and for Protestant theological education, the American Association of Theological Schools.

The educational survey also has been an important means of collectively promoting improvement in professional education. This procedure was developed in the early years of the 20th century. Its first noteworthy application in professional education occurred in 1908-10, when Abraham Flexner, under the auspices of the Carnegie Foundation for the Advancement of Teaching, conducted a survey of medical education in the U. S. and Canada.

The survey has been used in every field of professional education, and several times in the past half-century in some professional education fields. For example, it has been applied in dental education four times since 1920. Frequently the survey has been an educational landmark in the appraisals and recommendations it has made. It has provided a basis for self-criticism and evaluation by the professional schools, has informed the profession about the status of its educational institutions, and sometimes has established new ideals and goals for co-operative action through the associations concerned with the particular fields.

Admission to Professional Schools. Some years ago, gaining admission to a professional school presented no great problem for the student who was able to pay the fees. In general, all who met the established requirements, which frequently were quite low, were admitted, for the capacities of the schools exceeded the number of applicants. Indeed, the schools often found it necessary to send emissaries into the highways and byways to gather in those who could be induced to prepare for professional service.

Soon after World War I, this situation began to change. About 1920, the number seeking admission to medical schools exceeded the number who could be admitted. Such situations already had risen in some of the schools, but previously there always were places in other schools to which qualified applicants could go. In education for other professions a similar change occurred. The professional schools, particularly in some fields, then found it necessary to devise means for selecting the best applicants. Various criteria were adopted by selection committees, and test experts were asked to produce tests, scales, and inventories to evaluate applicants.

Attendance at professional schools is considerably limited by an economic barrier. Low family income and the very high cost of some forms of professional education prevent many young people with superior minds from preparing for professional careers. Currently, only limited financial assistance is available to students in professional schools, but such assistance is slowly increasing. Student loans under the National Defense Education Act are a great help.

Plans of Professional Education. Each profession has developed its own plan of professional education. These plans are being changed continually, principally by increasing the subjects of study and lengthening the period required to complete the education.

The first professional programs usually consisted of a few lecture courses for a period of a few months. As the programs were lengthened to two years, it was not unusual to repeat the same lectures for the second year. Very little was demanded by way of admission requirements. Over the years, as the high school became widespread, it became customary to require some high school education and, eventually, the completion of a course in an approved four-year high school. During the same time, the professional school curriculums were expanded to three years and later to four. The earlier curriculums emphasized technical and clinical study, but, as the sciences were developed, they assumed greater importance in the curriculums and professional education was largely transformed by placing it on a scientific foundation.

The education of professional personnel now includes a certain amount of education in the liberal arts and sciences on the college level, the purposes of which are to broaden the student's understanding and appreciation of the arts and sciences, to provide an intellectual foundation for specialized education, and to encourage and develop a social outlook that will enable a professional person to live responsibly and perform his duties as a good citizen. Indeed, the tendency is to place considerable emphasis on the liberal education of those who prepare for professional careers. Both the universities and the professions join in demanding that professional persons shall be well educated persons.

Currently, the plan of education for some professions consists of a four-year curriculum in a professional school, to which a student is admitted after he has been graduated from high school, and which ends with the attainment of a bachelor's degree. Some of these curriculums consist almost entirely of technical and clinical (or practice) subjects with related sciences, while other curriculums include also a fair proportion of more general subjects in the liberals arts and sciences.

There is a definite trend to require that, if a student desires to attend a professional school, he first must complete a stated number of years of study in a college of liberal arts and sciences.

It now is possible to make such a requirement in some professions because a large number of young people attend college and afterward apply for admission to professional schools. In several professions, education is available only to applicants who have received a bachelor's degree in the liberal arts and sciences.

The plans for education for the various professions and the degrees most commonly awarded are shown in Table 1.

There is no rigid uniformity in the plan of education in any profession. The accrediting agency for a profession sets minimum standards for the schools of that profession, and those standards usually include a minimum plan. Each individual school, however, establishes its own plan, which may exceed the required minimum. Thus, there is considerable variation among the schools of a profession with respect to the requirements for admission, the arrangement of subjects in the curriculum, and the requirements for graduation.

Despite this freedom of action, there is much similarity among the schools of a profession. As an example, the accrediting agency in medical education has set as a minimum for admission to an accredited medical school three years of study in an approved college of liberal arts and sciences, including courses in certain stated subjects, but a considerable number of medical schools require that before they will admit an applicant he must have obtained a bachelor's degree and have studied certain subjects in addition to those stated in the minimum requirements of the accrediting agency. All medical schools require four years of study in medicine and award the degree of doctor of medicine (M. D.).

TABLE 1

Plans of Education for the Professions and First Professional Degrees

Profession	Liberal arts and sciences (years)	Professional curriculum (years)	First professional degree most commonly awarded (some institutions award other first professional degrees than those named)*
4-year programs			
Agriculture	—	4	Bachelor of Science in Agriculture
Business administration	—	4	Bachelor of Science in Business Administration, or Bachelor of Business Administration
Education (Teaching in elementary and high schools)	—	4	Bachelor of Science in Education
Engineering	—	4	Bachelor of Science in Civil Engineering, Bachelor of Science in Electrical Engineering, etc.
Fine arts	—	4	Bachelor of Fine Arts
Forestry	—	4	Bachelor of Science in Forestry
Home economics	—	4	Bachelor of Science in Home Economics
Journalism	—	4	Bachelor of Arts in Journalism, or Bachelor of Science in Journalism
Music	—	4	Bachelor of Music
Nursing (college programs)	—	4	Bachelor of Science in Nursing
Occupational therapy	—	4	Bachelor of Science in Occupational Therapy
Physical therapy	—	4	Bachelor of Science in Physical Therapy
5-year programs			
Architecture	—	5	Bachelor of Architecture
Optometry	1	4	Doctor of Optometry
Pharmacy	1	4	Bachelor of Science in Pharmacy
Podiatry (Chiropody)	1	4	Doctor of Surgical Chiropody, or Doctor of Podiatry
Library science	4	1	Master of Library Science
Public health	4	1	Master of Public Health
6-year programs			
Dentistry	2	4	Doctor of Dental Surgery, or Doctor of Dental Medicine
Hospital administration	4	2	Master of Hospital Administration
Law	3	3	Bachelor of Laws
Osteopathy	2	4	Doctor of Osteopathy
Social work	4	2	Master of Social Work
Veterinary medicine	2	4	Doctor of Veterinary Medicine
7-year programs			
Medicine	3	4	Doctor of Medicine
Theology	4	3	Bachelor of Divinity

* Walter C. Eells and Harold A. Haswell, "Academic Degrees," Bulletin 1960, No. 28, U. S. Office of Education (Washington, D. C.: U. S. Government Printing Office, 1960).

148

Professional Education on the Graduate Level.

The large majority of the members of a profession are practitioners who devote themselves to rendering service to the largest number of consumers, such as patients, clients, and customers. They are prepared through the undergraduate programs of professional education described above. In addition to these men and women, a profession requires the work of other persons, such as research workers, teachers, and specialists, who need education beyond that afforded by undergraduate programs. To prepare them, provisions are made for graduate study.

Programs of graduate study run from one to three or more years. To gain admission to such study, an applicant must have acquired a bachelor's or the professional doctor's degree (the first professional degree). Graduate education leads to the master's degree or the degree of doctor of philosophy. At some universities the graduate professional degrees carry the designation of the fields, e.g., doctor of social work, doctor of jurisprudence, and doctor of sacred theology. In programs for the degree of doctor of philosophy, there is much emphasis on research, and a principal objective is to prepare research workers.

Graduate work in professional fields is usually conducted in the university under the general control and supervision of the graduate school, but most of the instruction is given by the departments in the professional schools. The students register in the graduate school, which sets admission requirements, approves the graduate courses offered, and establishes and enforces the requirements for the graduate degrees, particularly for the degree of doctor of philosophy.

The programs for graduate professional degrees with field designation, such as master of science in dentistry, doctor of social work, and doctor of sacred theology, are generally established and administered more largely by the respective schools.

One who desires to practice a specialty of medicine, such as surgery, usually learns the specialty through a "residency" in an approved hospital for a period of several years after he has obtained the degree of doctor of medicine. During that time, he observes the work of specialists in his specialty and participates in the service. In order to become a specialist, he must pass an examination given by a specialty board.

Enrollments and Degrees. Enrollments in the professional schools run into some hundred thousands. No one central agency collects and publishes enrollment statistics for all professional schools, and therefore, the precise totals are not available. An idea of the size of personnel being prepared for professional practice may be had from the number of professional degrees conferred. The data for the year 1959-60 are shown in Tables 2 and 3.

Conclusion. Professional education in the U. S., revolutionized in the last half-century, is now largely a university function. In general, it is characterized by a scholarly attitude, high standards of training, competent and dedicated faculties, capable students, and excellent physical facilities, including well-stocked libraries and well-equipped laboratories and clinics.

The professional curriculums rest on sound scientific bases and are sufficiently extensive to provide adequate foundations for beginning professional practice. General education, includ-

TABLE 2

Earned Degrees Conferred in Professional Fields by Colleges and Universities in the U. S., 1959-60

Professional field	First professional	Second level (master's except first professional)	Doctorate (Ph.D., Ed.D., etc.)
Agriculture	4,898	996	411
Architecture	1,801	319	17
Business and commerce	51,522	4,643	135
Dentistry (D.D.S., D.M.D)	3,247	—	—
Clinical dental sciences (advanced degrees only)*	—	185	—
Education (mostly teaching in elementary and high schools)	90,179	33,512	1,590
Engineering	37,808	7,159	786
Fine arts (exclusive of music)	10,178	1,721	173
Forestry	1,437	207	29
Home economics	4,450	484	40
Hospital administration	150	70	—
Journalism	2,272	261	8
Law	9,314	520	24
Library science	1,938	305	19
Medicine (M.D. only)	7,074	—	—
Clinical medical sciences (advanced degrees only)*	—	166	19
Music	2,988	1,171	119
Nursing	6,661	599	—
Occupational therapy	348	5	—
Optometry	339	2	1
Osteopathy	423	16	—
Pharmacy*	3,492	131	51
Physical therapy	439	26	—
Podiatry (chiropody)	160	—	—
Public administration	451	158	17
Public health	168	527	24
Social work, social administration	2,259	239	23
Theology (includes very few Jewish and Roman Catholic schools)	5,184	795	180
Veterinary medicine (D.V.M. only)	825	—	—
Clinical veterinary medical sciences (advanced degrees only)*	—	56	9

* Degrees in such basic sciences as anatomy, microbiology, biochemistry, biophysics, pathology, pharmacology, and physiology are not included.

Source: Summary Report on Bachelor's and Higher Degrees Conferred during the year 1959-60, U. S. Department of Health, Education, and Welfare, Office of Education, September, 1961.

TABLE 3

Earned Degrees Conferred in Professional Fields and in All Fields by Colleges and Universities in the U. S., 1959-60

Fields	First professional and bachelors'	Second level (masters' except when first professional)	Doctorate (Ph.D., Ed.D., etc.)
Professional	250,005*	54,273	3,675
Others	144,884**	20,224	6,154
Total	394,889	74,497	9,829
Per cent professional are of total	63.3	72.9	37.4

* First professional degrees include: (1) bachelors' degrees in fields where the bachelor's is the first professional, such as bachelor of science in agriculture, bachelor of architecture, etc.; and (2) the usual first degrees in other fields, as doctor of medicine, master of social work, etc.

** Mostly in liberal arts and sciences — bachelor of arts and bachelor of science.

ing the humanities and the physical and social sciences, is an accepted feature of the education of professional personnel. The findings of research, so widely carried on in the universities, are shattering old dogmatisms and transforming the education of the professions, thus making the professions increasingly useful in their services. That the citizens of the nation appreciate the great services of the professional schools is shown by the large support they provide for this form of higher education.

However, education for the professions is not without problems. At present, there are not sufficient numbers of capable applicants to fill the places in some of the professional schools and to prepare sufficient numbers of professional personnel to meet the needs of society. Many professional schools experience difficulty in recruiting sufficient numbers of competent and inspiring members of the teaching staffs. Although the educational programs are reasonably satisfactory, some often are criticized as not maintaining an appropriate balance between the basic and theoretical foundations and application in practice. Owing to the generally accepted time limits of the educational programs, it is not possible to include in many professional curriculums all the rapidly expanding knowledge that is desirable. This circumstance makes it necessary continually to select and adapt the curriculum content that is required for the undergraduate education of professionals. The relation between general or liberal education and specialized and professional education is a subject of perennial discussion. The development of graduate education for the professions is also a matter of widespread interest. Lastly, the financial problem is always present, and the professional schools and colleges keep calling for more and more support to enable them to fulfill their growing responsibilities for preparing professionals to serve the people of a rapidly advancing and increasingly complex civilization.

10

A Century
of Teacher Education

PAUL WOODRING

THE title of this historical chapter seems
to imply that the opening date should be
1862, but in that unhappy year the nation
was far too preoccupied with a bloody civil war
to give much attention to teacher education or
any other kind of education. The beginnings of
professional education for teachers may be traced
to a date a quarter-century earlier, when the first
American state normal schools were established
in New England, but it was not until after the
Civil War that teacher education, in the professional sense, became a part of higher education.

One hundred years ago there were no teachers
colleges; universities had not yet established
schools or departments of education; and the
subject of "education" would have been difficult
if not impossible to find in the course listings of
American colleges. Edgar Wesley has observed
that, in 1859, "Colleges, academies, and upper
schools of various kinds had existed for two cen-

turies in America without making any noticeable contribution to the training of teachers."[1]

After the Civil War, a few universities and colleges, mostly in the Middle West, established chairs of "pedagogy" or "didactics." Usually, these were found within the department of philosophy, which at that time also included whatever psychology was taught. But the state universities of Iowa and Michigan created departments of education during these years, and Teachers College became a part of Columbia University in 1892. Most of our university schools and departments of education, however, did not come into being until after the close of the century.

Throughout most of the 19th century, it was the normal schools and institutes that carried the responsibility for teacher education and both focused their attention on preparing teachers for elementary rather than secondary schools. Neither was a part of *higher* education. The 19th century normal school usually accepted students with only an elementary education and institutes often had no admission requirements. Yet, both these institutions made very important contributions to teacher education and they set the pattern for much that was to follow.

Institutes offered short courses of a few days or a few weeks, taught by itinerant speakers or local school administrators who gave instruction in schoolkeeping and inspirational lectures. The poorest institutes were probably better than none at all because they brought teachers together for a discussion of mutual problems; and when a Horace Mann came to speak, or when William

---

[1] Edgar Wesley, "NEA: The First Hundred Years" (New York: Harper, 1957), pp. 79-80.

James came to deliver his "Talks to Teachers," as he did in many parts of the country in the 1890's, the institute must have reached a high peak of excellence.

Before the Civil War, normal schools were established in at least 10 states, but enrollments were small and it is doubtful that more than two or three per cent of the teachers had attended them. During the last third of the century, however, normal schools spread rapidly across the country and enrollments rose dramatically. The *National Education Association Proceedings* for 1876 reported that in 1874 there were 67 state normal schools and 54 private ones. The *Proceedings* for 1898 reported that the number had grown to 166 state and 165 private institutions. There were also county normal schools and several of the larger cities maintained such schools of their own, offering courses in the late afternoon and evenings for teachers on the job. Wesley estimates that normal school enrollments grew from 10,000 in 1870 to nearly 70,000 at the end of the century.[2]

The philosophy of the normal school shifted with the successive waves of educational theory which, during most of the 19th century, were of European origin. Brubacher says, "Not until the establishment of the state normal school at Oswego, N. Y., in 1860 did a wave of Pestalossianism sweep through American normal schools. . . . The second wave of educational theory to sweep American normal schools was Herbartian, toward the end of the nineteenth century. . . . The State normal school at Normal, Illinois, was the center from which Herbartian doctrines of

---

[2] *Ibid.*, pp. 82-83.

apperception and correlation radiated. . . ."[3] It was not until the 20th century that the views of John Dewey and the many varieties of Progressive Education came to be influential.

Since their founding, there has been a great deal of debate about the quality of education provided by the normal schools. Perhaps the reason is that there was a tremendous range in quality among the different institutions and the debaters were not talking about the same schools. At its worst, the normal school was a shabby little institution with a single teacher who taught courses in pedagogy with perhaps a little time for a review of the elementary subjects. At its best, however, it was a very substantial professional school, headed by an able educator who was assisted by a devoted faculty. In addition to courses in pedagogy and a period of supervised practice teaching, the best of the normal schools offered an academic curriculum comparable to that found in the better academies of the day and probably not greatly inferior to that found in the first two years of the liberal arts colleges. Henry Barnard reported in 1851 that the three normal schools in Massachusetts offered a course that included algebra, geometry, astronomy, natural philosophy, intellectual philosophy, natural history, a critical study of the English language, an outline of the history of English literature, the history of the United States, and historical geography.[4] This, plus a review of the common branches and some professional courses and practice teaching, sounds

---

[3] John S. Brubacher, "A History of the Problems of Education" (New York: McGraw-Hill, 1947), pp. 509-511.
[4] Henry Barnard, "Normal Schools and Other Institutions, Agencies, and Means Designed for the Professional Education of Teachers" (Hartford: Case, Tiffany & Co., 1851), Vol. I, pp. 59-61.

like a great deal to cram into a course of, at most, two years and we do not know how deeply the subjects were pursued, but at any rate an effort was made to provide a liberal as well as a professional education.

Although reliable statistics are hard to come by, it appears that by 1900 the majority of urban elementary school teachers had received at least a short period of normal school preparation. Rural schools, however, continued to employ many teachers with only an elementary school background plus a few weeks of attendance at a teachers institute.

After the turn of the century, the number of private normal schools declined because these institutions were unable to face the competition from publicly supported ones that charged no tuition. The number of state normal schools continued to increase until about 1920 and their enrollments grew rapidly. By 1900, the growth of public high schools made it possible for many normal schools to require a high school diploma for admission. This enabled them to reduce their attention to secondary school subjects and to take steps toward transforming themselves into four-year degree-granting teachers colleges. Nineteen state normal schools made this transition between 1911 and 1920, 69 between 1921 and 1930, and most of the others did so between 1931 and 1950,[5] by which time the normal school had become almost obsolete.

The state teachers colleges, however, had a short life. Within 20 years after they had emerged out of the normal schools, they began transforming themselves into general state colleges or state universities which granted liberal

[5] Wesley, *op. cit.*, pp. 88-89.

arts and other degrees, as well as the B.S. in Ed., which was usually the only degree offered by the teachers college. This change came first in the Middle West and the Far West; it came more slowly in the northeastern section where powerful private colleges and universities bitterly resisted the efforts of the teachers colleges to take on new responsibilities.

In California, the state normal schools became teachers colleges in 1921 and general state colleges in 1935. Ohio bypassed the teachers college stage altogether, as far as titles were concerned; the "normal schools" at Bowling Green and Kent (which, despite their names, actually had been degree-granting teachers colleges throughout the 1920's) became "state colleges" in 1930 and "state universities" only a few years later. But, in the neighboring state of Michigan, the normal school at Kalamazoo became "Western Michigan State Teachers College" in 1927, "Western Michigan College of Education" in 1941, and "Western Michigan University" in 1957.

One teachers college in California, one in Wisconsin, and one in Minnesota became branches of the state universities in their respective states, while others in the same states are now general state colleges. The three colleges of education in Oregon were incorporated into the Oregon State System of Higher Education in 1932, and two of them became general state colleges in 1957. In Washington, where the normal schools did not become "colleges of education" until 1937, they began granting liberal arts degrees only a decade later but delayed changing their names to "state colleges" until 1961. In New York, the normal schools did not become teachers colleges until 1942 and did not take the next step until 1961.

At the end of 1961, public teachers colleges were found in only 15 states.

The changes have not been in name only; a new kind of college has emerged which continues to prepare many teachers but also provides a general or liberal education at modest cost for many who do not plan to teach. The academic courses offered in these colleges and the professors who teach them have the same strengths and weaknesses as are found in other undergraduate colleges, both public and private.

Since 1900, universities have accepted a growing proportion of the responsibility for teacher education. During the first two or three decades of the 20th century, most of the major universities established schools or colleges of education and the others established departments of education. The number of professional courses offered for teachers and administrators in a typical university grew from two or three in 1900 to several hundred in 1960, and this led to charges that the courses had proliferated beyond the available intellectual content and that there was much duplication of content in courses with different titles and numbers. The reply that proliferation could be found in other departments, too, was true but was not accepted as a sufficient justification.

In 1958, 25.3% of all beginning teachers came from public universities and another 10.3% came from private universities.[6] Many of those who attended other colleges as undergraduates later went to universities for graduate work.

Today, all the major state universities and many land-grant colleges and municipal universities maintain large schools or colleges of edu-

---

[6] W. Earl Armstrong and T. M. Stinnett, "A Manual on Certification Requirements" (Washington: NEA, 1959).

cation. Most of them offer courses at both the undergraduate and graduate levels and grant bachelors' degrees for beginning teachers and masters' and doctors' degrees for teachers, supervisors, specialists, administrators, and college teachers of education.

In some state universities, all undergraduates planning to teach are encouraged to enroll as freshmen in the college of education. In many others, the college of education enrolls only those who plan to teach in elementary school and those who plan to teach physical education, home economics, agriculture, etc., in high school, while those who plan to teach the academic courses at the secondary level enroll in, and earn their degree from, the liberal arts college of the university, taking only such professional work in the school of education as is required for certification. But even when the prospective teacher is enrolled in the college of education, he usually takes the major portion of his academic work from professors in the liberal arts colleges; and if our teachers today do not know their subjects, or are not liberally educated, the responsibility must be accepted by the academic professors who failed to teach them properly.

Some large private universities maintain undergraduate and graduate schools of education similar to those found in state institutions. Many, however, including such renowned institutions as Harvard and Chicago, have graduate schools of education only, while Princeton and Yale have neither schools nor departments of education. Teachers College of Columbia University has become in recent years almost entirely a graduate school.

Today, American teachers are prepared, to the

point of initial certification, in more than 1,100 different colleges and universities, and, inevitably, the range in quality among these varied institutions will be enormous. Unfortunately, the colleges with the highest entrance standards and the highest standards of instruction do not turn out their fair share of teachers because they draw their student bodies from socio-economic classes in which parents as well as students do not look upon teaching as a sufficiently satisfactory, remunerative, and "prestige" profession, particularly for men.

But, although the talents of the students and the quality of instruction varies greatly among the colleges that educate teachers, there is a fair amount of uniformity in the courses studied—a uniformity resulting in considerable part from state certification requirements.

Of the 52 certification authorities (50 states plus Puerto Rico and the District of Columbia), 51 now require the bachelor's degree for beginning high school teachers and 44 require it for elementary teachers as well. Nine states require high school teachers to complete a fifth year of college during the period of initial certification and three require a fifth year for beginning secondary teachers.[7]

The required course nearly always includes a period of general education approximately two academic years in length, plus two more years during which the time is divided between a major in an academic discipline (or, in the case of elementary teachers, a "field" major which may include several disciplines) and a sequence

[7] W. Earl Armstrong and T. M. Stinnett, "A Manual on Certification Requirements for School Personnel in the United States" (Washington: NEA, 1961).

of professional courses. For elementary teachers, the professional requirements range from 16 to 36 semester hours in the different states, with a median of 21 hours. For secondary teachers, the range is 12 to 29 hours, and the median is 18.[8] Many colleges, however, require more professional hours than the state requirement for certification.

In some colleges, particularly those with a teachers college background, the required professional sequences begin in the freshman or sophomore year and continue through the undergraduate program. In liberal arts colleges and universities, it often does not begin until the junior year and may be restricted to the senior or the first graduate year.

An important departure from the standard or conventional program for teachers is that which leads to the Master of Arts in Teaching degree. This newer program was originated at Harvard in 1936 at the suggestion of James B. Conant, who then was president of the university. Dean Keppel of the Harvard Graduate School of Education estimates that today "at least thirty AMT (or MAT) programs are known to be in existence, plus fifty other programs that award different degrees but try to solve the same problems in the same way."[9]

The MAT program selects liberal arts graduates who have strong majors in the academic disciplines and offers them a year (or more) of instruction at the graduate level. In a typical program, the student takes a summer's work in educational psychology and educational philosophy, followed by a semester's internship in

---

[8] *Ibid.*

[9] Francis Keppel, "Master of Arts in Teaching," *Saturday Review Education Supplement,* June 17, 1961, p. 64.

a public high school. During this semester, he takes part in a weekly seminar on the methods and materials for teaching his subject and his teaching is closely supervised; in some cases he participates as a member of a teaching team. During the second semester, he returns to the university for graduate-level courses in his teaching field and, sometimes, an additional course or semester in education. Many of those who have worked with this program are convinced that it should and probably will become the standard program for the preparation of secondary teachers of the academic subjects.

None of the various programs for teacher education found in normal schools, teachers colleges, liberal arts colleges, or universities ever has been evaluated adequately in terms of the ultimate criterion—the effect of the program upon the learning experiences of the children whom the teachers will teach. The variables are too complex; the results cannot be fully known until the teacher has taught for many years; and there is insufficient agreement about the proper goals of education. Such evidence as we have is based upon the professional judgments of people who have worked with the various programs and of those who have employed the teachers coming from them. On the basis of such evidence, each program has both its vigorous supporters and its critics.

Today, however, there is widespread agreement that any sound program for teacher education must include: a substantial program of general or liberal education, representing not less than two years of work beyond high school; a knowledge of the subject or subjects to be taught, which, in the case of the secondary school teacher, should be provided by a strong academic major at the undergraduate level plus some graduate work in an academic discipline; a knowledge of the contributions of philosophy, history, psychology, and the other social and behavioral sciences to an understanding of the place of the school in the social order and the processes of learning; and a period of practice teaching or an extended internship during which time the prospective teacher tries out various methods of teaching under competent supervision.

There is still, in 1962, widespread disagreement about the proper organization and content of professional courses for teachers and about the place of these courses in the curriculum. There is also disagreement about whether the internship should come during the undergraduate years or after the student receives the baccalaureate. It seems clear, however, that, in the years ahead, teacher education will not be a thing apart, provided by separate institutions for teachers, but will be a part of the mainstream of higher education in America.

165

11

The Higher Education of Women, 1862–1962

SAUL SACK

*C*ONTEMPORARY SOCIETY, unlike its predecessor of 100 years ago, has come to regard the higher education of women as a commonplace phenomenon. This does not mean that higher education for women was non-existent during the years prior to the Civil War. Women in small numbers were getting the beginnings of a college education. But these were feeble beginnings beset by doubts as to the propriety of extending higher educational opportunities to women, doubts as to their capacity to pursue advanced studies, and misgivings as to the effects of such pursuits on women, on men, and on society as a whole.

Although the prejudice against advanced education for women had somewhat abated by the opening of the Civil War, the hoary conception of woman's proper sphere as the maker of the home and the educator of her children[1] served to perpetuate an atmosphere which militated against her entry into the existing colleges of the period and which inhibited the movement towards the establishment of separate institutions of higher education designed for her exclusive use. Further, many of those who espoused the cause of the higher learning for women conceived of such learning largely in utilitarian terms and along lines consistent with woman's historic and predestined role. A college education would serve to produce better mothers for the family and competent teachers for society.[2]

Coupled with this narrow view of woman's place in society was the equally circumscribed estimate of her mental powers. The female mind, it was held, was of an inferior order, incapable of penetrating the subtleties of complex disciplines and of ascending to the Aristotelian heights of pure reason. To educate such a mind, therefore, required separate facilities and special programs of studies. It was not surprising, consequently, that a convention of educators should conclude "that as an all-wise Creator has ordained that the spheres of man and woman should be different, so their education must be pursued separately, otherwise neither can be brought to the highest point of perfection."[3]

Such notions of the mental inferiority of women did not go unchallenged. Caroline Davis, in addressing a meeting of the Allegheny Teachers' Association (1853), asked:

[1] A. B. Clark, "Woman's Proper Sphere," *Pennsylvania School Journal*, 3:27-29, July, 1854; see also Thomas Woody, "A History of Women's Education in the United States" (New York: Science Press, 1929), Vol. 1, pp. 92-106; Lucius H. Beebe, "Inaugural Address," *Allegheny College Catalogue* (1875-76), p. 51.
[2] Saul Sack, "The Higher Education of Women in Pennsylvania," *Pennsylvania Magazine of History and Biography*, 83: 29-34, January, 1959.
[3] *Pennsylvania School Journal*, 3: 211-213, January, 1855.

Should one half of the world be educated as though they had minds and the other half as though they had not? And if so, why?—Should it be because, as it is said, woman is not endowed with faculties equal to those of man?—But is it true that her powers are more limited, or that there is a point in intellectual advancement to which man is capable to attain and woman not?—We are not of those who admit that man enjoys any such superiority, or that woman is his inferior in any other respect than in physical strength. . . .[4]

There were still others who maintained that the intellectual capacities of women were as yet unknown. To deny them equal educational opportunities on the basis of such uncertainty was not only unscientific, but undemocratic. Caroline Dall expressed this point of view in 1861:

We have already said, that the coeducational rights of women are simply those of all human beings, namely, "the right to be taught all common branches of learning, a sufficient use of the needle, and any higher branches, for which they shall evince either taste or inclination; the right to have colleges, schools of law, theology, and medicine open to them; the right of access to all scientific and literary collections, to anatomical preparations, historical records, and rare manuscripts."

And we do not make this claim with any particular theory as to woman's powers or possibilities. She may be equal to man, or inferior to him. She may fail in rhetoric, and succeed in mathematics. She may be able to bear fewer hours of study. She may insist on more protracted labor. What we claim is, that no one knows, as yet, what women are, or what they can do,—least of all, those who have been wedded for years to that low standard of womanly achievement, which classical study tends to sustain. Because we do not know, because experiment is necessary, we claim that all educational institutions should be kept open for her; that she should be encouraged to avail herself of these, according to her own inclination; and that, so far as possible, she should pursue her studies, and test her powers, in company with man. . . . We claim for women a share of the opportunities offered to men, because we believe that they will never be thoroughly taught until they are taught at the same time and in the same classes.[5]

---

[4] Caroline Davis, "Female Education," *Pennsylvania School Journal*, 1: 431-432, May, 1853.

[5] Caroline H. Dall, "The College, the Market and the Court" (Boston: Rumford, 1914), pp. 6-8.

Moreover, there were many who predicted the impairment of female sensibilities which was presumed to result from exposure to higher education, particularly of the coeducational variety. The Pennsylvania State Educational Convention of 1862 declared:

> We know of no instance of a graduate or alumna of a regular Female Seminary, presenting her papers at a College gate for matriculation. Such a spectacle, perhaps, would be admired by some as a noble specimen of female heroism. But by the general sentiment of our American society, it would rather be regarded as unwonted effort to gain the eclat of special strong-mindedness, and at a sacrifice of what, we hope, our country women will ever prize above,—even the highest reputation for literary attainments,—the gems of unsullied delicacy of thought, taste, and manners, and a sense of propriety, undimmed by the slightest divergencies, that college intercourse might possibly induce.[6]

Furthermore, it was contended that a college education would render a woman either unfit for marriage or less willing to enter that blissful state. Neither argument has been substantiated by available facts. David S. Jordan stated: "There is not the slightest evidence that highly educated women are necessarily rendered sterile or celibate by their education. . . ." And Horace A. Hollister insisted that "educated women are not shunning marriage or maternity. . . . It is simply wrong wedlock which they are avoiding."[7]

In large measure, the arguments presented against higher education for women on the grounds that desirable feminine attributes would be damaged by exposure to its influences were middle-class arguments. And it was from this class that the bulk of college women would be drawn. Society already was becoming accustomed to the spectacle of women leaving the

---

[6] *Pennsylvania School Journal,* 11: 94; September, 1862.
[7] Quoted by Woody, *op. cit.,* Vol. II, p. 210.

cloistered shelter of the home to enter the burgeoning factories of the nation in increasing numbers. In fact, it was not unusual in certain industries, like the textile and shoe industries, for women to outnumber men. In 1845, there were more than 75,000 women and less than 56,000 men employed in the textile industries. At Lynn, Mass., in 1850, there were 6,412 women as compared with 3,729 men working in the shoe factories.[8] Taking manufacturing as a whole, at the mid-point of the 19th century, there were 732,-157 men employees and 225,922 women.[9]

The entry of women into the industrial world was further accelerated by the onset of the Civil War. Women occupied posts and competently performed tasks that hitherto had been regarded as outside their proper sphere and alien to their natural capabilities. And once having tasted of this newly found freedom, they were frequently reluctant to return to household drudgery.

As long as the skills required for the operation of uncomplicated machines were relatively simple, women in industry had little need for education beyond the rudimentary schooling. However, there were women, particularly of the middle class, who were entering professions that demanded greater intellectual attainments. The spreading common schools and female seminaries of the country were increasingly being staffed by larger numbers of women. In fact, by 1870, three out of five teachers were women.[10] Preparation

[8] Arthur W. Calhoun, "A Social History of the American Family" (Cleveland: Arthur H. Clark Co., 1918), Vol. II, p. 175.

[9] "Ninth Census" (1870), Vol. III, "The Statistics of the Wealth and Industry of the United States" (Washington: Government Printing Office, 1872), pp. 392-393.

[10] Mabel Newcomer, "A Century of Higher Education for Women" (New York: Harper, 1959), p. 15.

for teaching, particularly in the seminaries, required advanced education which the colleges of the country could best supply.

It was precisely here, in a few of the colleges that were operating as coeducational institutions, that women first tasted of the hitherto forbidden fruits of the higher learning. Oberlin College admitted women to its regular classes in 1837. But this pioneering institution remained virtually the sole oasis in a desert of indifference until the 19th century had passed its mid-point.[11] New institutions emerging after 1850, less inhibited by the forces of custom and tradition, were inclined from the outset to be coeducational. Antioch College, for example, opened its door in 1853 dedicated to the idea of fulfilling Horace Mann's promise "to secure for the female sex equal opportunities of education with the male, and to extend those opportunities in the same studies, and by the same instructors. . . ."[12]

Perhaps the most influential forces in promoting the spread of coeducation — forces which received added impetus with the passage of the Morrill Act of 1862—were the state universities. Iowa (1856) and Washington (1862) pursued a coeducational policy from the beginning. In the main, the western state universities were the leaders in the movement. Even they were by no means uniform or unreserved in their adoption of coeducation. At the University of Wisconsin, the regents, as early as 1850, had proposed the

[11] Hillsdale College in Ohio, opened in 1844, admitted women from the beginning. It was not until 1852, however, that a woman was graduated from the classical course with a bachelor of arts degree. See Woody, *op. cit.,* Vol. II, p. 247.

[12] Henry Barnard, "American Teachers and Educators" (Syracuse, N. Y.: Bardeen, 1906), p. 396.

establishment of a normal or teachers department to which both men and women would be admitted and in which they would share the educational offerings equally. But it was not until 1860, however, that women attended the normal classes. With the beginning of the Civil War, their numbers increased until they constituted the total enrollment in the normal department during the academic year 1864-65.[13] A somewhat similar trend was observable at the University of Michigan. Despite petitions to admit women (1857-58), the authorities did not grant them the privileges of the university until 1870.

The stronghold of conservatism, however, lay in the older and better known eastern colleges and universities. Designed exclusively for the education of males and with a long tradition of such exclusiveness, they were loathe to disturb the course of history by the injection of a new and alien influence. Even they, however, could not withstand indefinitely the insistent demands of women clamoring for admission. When they did succumb, it was at first but a partial yielding, limiting women to graduate study, as at Yale, or to an occasional course, as at the University of Pennsylvania. Later, a new form was devised, designed both to still the voices of male opponents and to satisfy the petitions of women for equal educational opportunities. This was the co-ordinate college.

Despite the original intention to maintain separate facilities and to avoid the pitfalls that were presumed to accompany the indiscriminate intermingling of the sexes, the co-ordinate colleges, particularly where they were housed on the same campus with the parent institutions,

---

[13] Woody, *op. cit.,* Vol. II, pp. 239-240.

became virtually indistinguishable from the avowedly coeducational colleges. Thus, Radcliffe and the College for Women of the University of Pennsylvania are little more than administrative devices. In time, they, too, may follow the course adopted by the University of Rochester when it merged its two colleges, in 1952, for the sake of "coordination and efficiency."[14]

Because of the obvious resistance to the admission of women on the part of the long-established privately controlled universities of the East, like Harvard, Columbia, and the University of Pennsylvania, and because of statistics issued by the U. S. Commissioner of Education (1873) purporting to show that, of 97 institutions reporting women in attendance, five were in New England, eight were in the middle Atlantic, 67 in the western, and 17 in the southern states,[15] it has been concluded that the New England, central, and eastern states were conservative in their approach to coeducation.[16] While there is little question that the newer western states were freer and more liberal in their attitude, it is doubtful whether the older states were as backward and as conservative as they have been painted.

Recent research in Pennsylvania alone has revealed that, between 1850 and 1869 (four years before the Commissioner's report cited above), no fewer than 14 coeducational colleges were chartered, each with the power to confer degrees. Furthermore, Allegheny College opened

[14] Newcomer, *op. cit.*, p. 45.
[15] "Report of the Commissioner of Education for the Year 1873" (Washington: Government Printing Office, 1874), p. lviii.
[16] See Woody, *op. cit.*, Vol. II, p. 252; Newcomer claims that "Coeducation was almost unknown in the East." *Op. cit.*, pp. 19-20.

its doors to women in 1870 and conferred the bachelor of arts degree on one woman three years later. Similarly, the Agricultural College of Pennsylvania (now Pennsylvania State University) admitted women in 1871, and in 1873 granted the bachelor of science degree to five graduates, one of whom was a woman. While some of these institutions never survived the trauma of birth, at least 10 were functioning in 1873 (two more than the Commissioner's report attributed to the whole of the middle Atlantic states), and seven still grace the present scene.[17] There is no reason to believe that Pennsylvania was unique in this respect or that more intensive research in other states would not alter the picture appreciably.

So rapid was the growth of coeducation after the Civil War that, by 1880, more than half the institutions of higher education admitted women. Ten years later, the coeducational colleges and universities constituted 65.5% of the total; and by the turn of the century, they comprised more than 71% of the whole number.[18] This trend has persisted to the present day. The U. S. Office of Education reports that, of 2,028 institutions of higher education, 1,533, or 76%, are coeducational.[19]

Despite the emergence of coeducational insti-

[17] Sack, *op. cit.,* pp. 37-39.
[18] "Report of the Commissioner of Education for the Years 1889-90" (Washington: Government Printing Office, 1893), Vol. II, p. 764; "Report of the Commissioner of Education for the Years 1899-1900" (Washington: Government Printing Office, 1901), Vol. II, p. 1880; "Report of the Commissioner of Education for the Year 1902" (Washington: Government Printing Office, 1903), Vol. II, pp. 2388-2389.
[19] "Education Directory, 1960-1961, Higher Education" (Washington: U. S. Department of Health, Education and Welfare, 1961), p. 13.

tutions after 1850, the new colleges were not so numerous or so highly regarded as to satisfy the growing demand of women for a higher education comparable with that afforded men. This fact, coupled with the inertia of the older and more reputable institutions, stimulated the movement to found separate but equal colleges for women. A beginning already had been made in 1839, with the opening of Georgia Female College, empowered by charter provision "to confer all such honors, degrees, and licenses as are usually conferred in colleges or universities. . . ."[20] But the mere right to grant degrees was by no means a sufficient reason to characterize an institution as a college. If the contrary were true, women had no cause to complain about the dearth of higher educational facilities available to them even prior to 1850. Between 1838 and 1842, Pennsylvania alone had incorporated 38 female seminaries and had invested each of them with the legal right to confer the same kinds of degrees as were granted customarily by the existing colleges and universities of the country.[21] However, the right to the designation "college" depended upon the possession of characteristics other than the *de jure*. When the institutions for women are compared with the men's colleges of the same period, with respect to admission requirements, curriculum, facilities, and staff, neither the female seminaries nor the Georgia Female College were worthy of the name.

After 1850, the colleges for women began to make significant progress toward realizing the objective they had set themselves. Mary Sharp College (1851) was the first to require a modest

---

[20] Woody, *op. cit.*, Vol. II, p. 161.
[21] Sack, *op. cit.*, p. 47.

amount of Latin and Greek in the four-year course leading to the B.A. degree — a requirement which was universal in the colleges for men. As the century advanced, Elmira College (1855) and Vassar College (1865) established standards which were fairly comparable with men's colleges. With the establishment of Smith College (1875), the goal finally was reached to found "a college, like a man's . . . to teach them all that men are taught."[22]

Though successful in achieving their objective, colleges such as Smith, Vassar, Bryn Mawr, and others equally esteemed were by no means equally successful in stemming the tide of criticism. Such criticism varied in accordance with the individual preferences of the critics as to the nature of the curriculum proper for women's colleges. Those who were committed to a belief in the essential goodness of humanistic studies decried the tendency to transcend the circumscribed boundaries of the time-honored disciplines. For such critics, the curriculum of the women's colleges should be indistinguishable from the offerings of the best colleges for men. Contrariwise, those who would abandon the single-track conception of the liberal arts program argued that the women's colleges were failing to subserve the legitimate and singular interests of women. To the "liberal" studies they would add the practical and the useful. Thus, *Godey's Lady's Book* (1866) urged: "To that *half* education which our countrywomen now receive—the education in science and ornamental arts—add the education in useful arts and domestic knowledge necessary to fit them for the duties of their proper sphere, and they will not merely be, as at present, the 'queens of society,'

[22] Woody, *op. cit.,* Vol. II, p. 184.

but will be far better, the adored rulers of well-ordered and happy households."[23] Others insisted that a college education should prepare women for the professions of law, journalism, industrial branches of the fine arts, education, architecture, medicine, and the sciences.

Women, it already has been noted, were entering the teaching profession in increasing numbers. But the professions of law, theology, medicine, and teaching beyond the secondary school level required the kind of preparation that the professional schools and the graduate schools afforded. The former, with rare exceptions, were closed to women; the latter, again with few exceptions, emerged late in the 19th century. Z. C. Graves, in speaking to his graduates of Mary Sharp College (1855), described the world into which they would enter:

Having completed it [this course of study]—how different is your situation . . . from that of the young man in the same condition? The schools of Law, Theology and Medicine open their doors to him, inviting his entrance. They offer to him a thousand inducements to use all his natural and acquired abilities in appropriating to him their garnered truths. . . . But the doors of these schools are barred to your entrance. No public institution offers to you the means of ascending higher. Society has no inducements to offer in any of the learned professions, if we except that of teaching.[24]

Elizabeth Blackwell was the first to breach the wall of separation when she gained admission to the Geneva Medical School in 1848. But hers was an isolated case and by no means heralded the beginning of an enlightened policy. With the chartering and the opening of the Female Medical College of Pennsylvania (1850), a few more women were afforded the opportunity to

---

[23] *Godey's Lady's Book*, 72: 278-279, March, 1866.
[24] "Z. C. Graves and the Mary Sharp College, 1850-1896" (Nashville, Tenn.: Mary Sharp College Club, 1925), pp. 70-72.

obtain a medical education. However, the possession of the degree in medicine did not carry with it a corresponding recognition and acceptance on the part of the medical profession or signify a willingness on the part of the public to avail themselves of the services of the female physician. In 1867, the Philadelphia County Medical Society resolved "That, in conformity with what they believe to be due to the profession, the community in general and the female portion of it in particular, the members of this Society cannot offer any encouragement to women becoming practitioners of medicine, nor, on these grounds, can they consent to meet in consultation with such practitioners."[25]

Women met with opposition of a similar nature when they attempted to enter the fields of theology and law. Antoinette Brown Blackwell was the first woman to graduate from a theological school in the U. S., when she completed the three-year course at Oberlin College in 1851. The first woman to graduate from a law school was Ada Kepley, who took her degree from the Union College of Law, Chicago, in 1870.[26] Again, these were virtually isolated cases. Not until the turn of the century were women entering the schools of theology and law in sufficient numbers to warrant their inclusion in the statistical reports of the U. S. Commissioner of Education. In 1900, the Commissioner reported 181 women out of 8,009 students in attendance at schools of theology and 151 women as compared with 12,365 men students in the law schools of the country.[27]

---

[25] Sack, *op. cit.*, p. 33.

[26] Woody, *op. cit.*, Vol. II, pp. 368, 373.

[27] "Report of the Commissioner of Education for the Years 1899-1900" (Washington: Government Printing Office, 1901), Vol. II, pp. 1967-1968.

The 20th century has witnessed a relaxation of the barriers erected against women's participation in the professional life of the country — a relaxation which was accelerated by the experiences and contingencies of two world wars. Women practice and take degrees in engineering, science, theology, medicine, veterinary medicine, dentistry, law, forestry, architecture, and pharmacy, as well as in the traditional fields of social work, education, library science, and nursing, in which they far outnumber men. The time is rapidly approaching when choice, not social disapproval, will determine the extent of women's participation in those professions that hitherto have been considered the exclusive province of men.

The experiences of more than 100 years have placed a quietus on the objections to the higher education of women raised by our predecessors. Women, themselves, have demonstrated their determination to partake of its benefits by entering the halls of advanced institutions in increasing numbers. The fears, expressed by some, that now that the college doors are open, women are less eager to enter them, are not warranted by the facts.[28] While it is true that the proportion of women to the total college student population declined from a high of 47% in 1920 to a low of 30% in 1950, it is not true that this unfavorable balance has persisted. In fact, the trend has been reversed. The U. S. Office of Education reports: "Since 1955 there has been a general trend among the 4-year institutions and the junior colleges toward greater relative in-

[28] See Newcomer, *op. cit.*, pp. 45-47, 50.

creases in women's degree-credit enrollment than in men's."[29]

What does the future portend for the higher education of women? What will be the fate of the segregated college? While no definitive answer can be given to these questions, the signs point in the direction of the elimination of separate colleges for women. Certainly, they cannot be justified on the grounds of affording women equal educational opportunities with men. On the contrary, there are more colleges open to women than there are to men. Of the 2,028 institutions of higher education in the U. S., 259 are for women, 236 are for men, and the rest are coeducational.[30]

Is there anything unique in the curriculum offerings of women's colleges that would warrant their separate existence? Mabel L. Robinson stated in 1918 (and her words are equally true today) that "the growth of the curriculum of the women's college has been marked by no particular originality; that is the woman's college cannot be pointed out as the source of any single tendency in the American college today. . . . Able from the beginning to take advantage of the hard won experience of the older colleges, they have incorporated into the American colleges as yet little which could be designated as their original contribution."[31] Even the proponents of the separate colleges for women will

[29] Edith M. Huddleston, "Opening (Fall) Enrollment in Higher Education, 1960: Analytic Report," Circular No. 652 (Washington: U. S. Department of Health, Education, and Welfare, 1961), pp. 24-25.

[30] "Education Directory, 1960-1961, Higher Education" (Washington: U. S. Department of Health, Education, and Welfare, 1961), p. 13.

[31] Mabel L. Robinson, "The Curriculum of the Women's College," Bureau of Education Bulletin, No. 6 (Washington: Government Printing Office, 1918), p. 108.

have to agree with Mabel Newcomer's conclusion: "I am convinced that the usual case that is made for them has no validity today."[32]

Finally, although the two situations are by no means analogous, separate colleges for women, like segregated schools for Negroes, tend to perpetuate the fiction of separate but equal education. By comparison with their brother institutions, colleges for women have suffered the privations accompanying financial poverty.[33] That some have maintained high standards of excellence is a tribute to the sacrificing devotion of the men and women who have staffed them rather than to the quality of the facilities with which they have had to function. The conclusion is inescapable: the continued existence of separate colleges for women, in 1962 (or, for that matter, for men), constitutes an anachronism.

[32] Newcomer, *op. cit.*, p. 255.
[33] Woody, *op. cit.*, Vol. II, p. 188; Newcomer, *op. cit.*, pp. 150-152.

12

A Century of Negro Higher Education

HORACE MANN BOND

TO SET A DEFINITE DATE at which
the higher education of Negroes began in
North America is as difficult as the task of
dating the beginning of the Reformation or the
Renaissance. This is because the movement had
its roots in the eternal soil of mankind's highest
aspirations; like all of western culture, it flows
from constantly receding epochs—to the University of Glasgow, to Cambridge, to Oxford, to
Paris, to Bologna, to the Moorish University at
Cordova, to monasticism, to Rome, to Greece,
to the Temple in Jerusalem—and beyond.

A man becomes a fit subject for higher education when his higher capacity is acknowledged
by those who control his life. Hence, one might
select the year 1676 as a first beginning of Negro
higher education in the Northern Americas. In
that year, according to Cotton Mather, John
Eliot, a graduate of Cambridge's Jesus College,
and in Massachusetts Colony the gentle Apostle
to the Indians,

. . . had long lamented it with a Bleeding and Burning

Passion, that the *English* used their Negroes but as their Horses or their *Oxen* . . . that any wearing the *Name* of *Christians* should so much have the *Heart of Devils* in them, as to prevent and hinder the instruction of the poor *Blackamores*.[1]

He therefore proposed that neighboring slave owners send their slaves to him so that he might "catechize them, and *Enlighten* them." But Mather added, ". . . he did not live to make much *Progress* in this Undertaking."

Out of Cotton Mather came Jonathan Edwards; and out of him, Samuel Hopkins, who mingled his pastoral duties in Newport, R. I., the capital of the northern slave trade, with a passionate hatred for slavery and a deep faith in higher education and in the endowment of all men with equal capacity. Discovering two African seamen, originally from the Gold Coast, domiciled in Newport and members of his Congregational church, Samuel Hopkins arranged with his fellow-pastor, Ezra Stiles (later president at Yale), to send Bristol Yamma and John Quamine, in 1774, to the College of New Jersey, at Princeton, there to be given the highest education under the tutelage of John Witherspoon; and, once armed with knowledge, to return to their native Africa to redeem their fellows to the certain Glory of God. The Calvinists were committed to the idea of higher education and a learned clergy. John Knox was himself a Glasgow man, and from University of Paris-trained John Calvin had learned that a proper theocracy required university-educated pastors who also would be village dominies for the careful catechetic and general instruction of the humblest child in the parish.

The Scotch and Scotch-Irish in America and

---

[1] As quoted in G. W. Moore, "Notes on Slavery in Massachusetts" (New York: Appleton, 1866), p. 37.

the university-trained English dissenters from Jesus and Emmanuel Colleges at Cambridge brought with them to America the spirit of Knox's noble 1561 "Ordinance for Education in Scotland." As Knox had demanded, they believed in a university-trained pastorate; they planted "academies" everywhere in the wilderness and founded colleges in profusion. Bristol Yamma and John Quamine left Princeton in 1776 with the other students when the institution was wrecked by war and they never returned. But, in 1816, the Presbyterians of New York and Pennsylvania established a "School for Africa" at Parsippany, N. J., intended to be a higher institution for Negroes.

The Calvinists believed also in Divine Providence; they believed that God's providential hand was in everything; it was involved patently in the enslavement of Africans and in their transportation to America. Surely, they providentially were designed to be stolen in order that they might be baptized, evangelized, educated, and eventually restored to the "ancestral continent." The Negro was divinely ordained to be the instrument by which the continent could be evangelized. The Parsippany venture failed; but, in 1854, the Presbyterians chartered Ashmun Institute in Pennsylvania (renamed Lincoln University in 1866), dedicated to the "Glorification of God by Africa."

The theme has run through every effort designed to provide a higher education for Negroes: the early frightful mortality of white missionaries in Africa, before malaria and antibiotics, confirmed the faith. Even when the religious groups split on the slave issue, this faith persisted. The Calvinists who were radical abolitionists held to this faith; those in the North who were "gradualist" colonizationists adhered to it; and, in the South, southern Baptists and Presbyterians looked for, and found, the best educated Negroes available to staff their Congo and Nigerian missions. The ultra-radicals, Arthur and Lewis Tappan, held to the ultimate African providential mission. They proposed to establish a college for Negroes in New Haven in 1831; they were rebuffed when the townspeople and Yale University officials objected that such a college would embroil the prospective students with southerners at Yale and upset the town. In 1837, the Tappans induced the trustees of Oberlin Institute to accept their pastor, Charles Grandison Finney, as a professor, and to warrant that their pledge of four professorships in return for an institution pledged to co-education of the races would be fulfilled. In 1839, the Tappans joined a defense committee on behalf of the refugees of the slave-ship *Amistad*. The African slaves, in transit from West Africa to the West Indies, overthrew and killed most of the Spanish crew and ended a zig-zag journey bound back to Africa off the coast of Long Island, where they were taken in tow by an American naval cutter and turned over on charges of piracy on the high seas. John Quincy Adams took the case to the U. S. Supreme Court and won freedom for the Africans; the defense committee turned into a rehabilitation and repatriation committee, and one of the girls from the ship was sent to Oberlin; and there finally emerged the anti-slavery, radically abolitionist organization, the American Missionary Association, loosely attached at first to the Congregational Church.

By 1862, perhaps as many as 15 Negroes had graduated from American colleges, most of them from Oberlin. John Russwurm, Bowdoin '26, was long thought to have been the first American Negro college graduate; but Hugh Hawkins recently has pointed out[2] that an Edward Jones preceded Russwurm by 11 days in taking his A.B. from Amherst in the same year. Both men became missionaries in Africa.

An index to the frequency of college attendance by ante-bellum Negroes is provided by an inspection of the educational background of the 22 Negroes who were members of the U. S. Congress from 1869-1901. Ten had attended college and five were college graduates; one had attended Knox college; and James M. Langston graduated from Oberlin in 1857. Among other notables educated before the Civil War, James McCune Smith took an A.B. and M.D. from Glasgow, and Francis L. Cardoso, South Carolina Secretary of State during Reconstruction, and an Alabama congressman, James T. Rapier, had attended that university. The gifted minister and missionary, Alexander Crummell, took a degree at Queens College, Cambridge. Martin R. Delany took a medical degree at Harvard in 1852, and other Negroes are known to have graduated from Wesleyan and from Washington and Jefferson before the Civil War.

Yet, the century ending in 1962 has a claim to centennial honors in the higher education of the Negro; for this was the year when the co-ordination of efforts to bring relief to Negro refugees set adrift by the Civil War was placed on a national basis by the organization of the National Freedmen's Relief Association. The association undertook a task no less than that of assuring "the relief and improvement of the

---

[2] H. Hawkins, "Edward Jones: First American Negro College Graduate?" *School and Society*, 89:375-376, Nov. 4, 1961.

freedmen of the Colored race, . . . to teach them civilization and Christianity, and to elevate them in the scale of humanity, by inspiring them with self-respect."[3] Similar enterprises were a Freedmen's Aid Commission, a Contraband Relief Society, the Sanitary Commission, and other agencies. The various denominations organized relief agencies that became principally educational after the war. The American Missionary Association of the Congregational Church was earliest in the field; scarcely had the Confederates abandoned the town of Hampton, Va., under the guns of Fortress Monroe, than a school was set up on Sept. 17, 1861, for the hordes of children brought by their families within the security and freedom of the Union lines. The first teacher was a well-educated, free colored woman of the vicinity, Mrs. Mary L. Peake. Eventually this school grew into the Hampton Institute (chartered in 1867), with an endowment in excess of $20,000,000 in 1961—most substantial for any of the Negro institutions.

Once the war was concluded, each of the major denominations set out on a vigorous program of providing educational institutions for the Freedmen, establishing networks of elementary, secondary, and collegiate institutions throughout the South. The founders of these institutions named them "colleges" and "universities," although most of the students were scarcely literate. It has become a historical fashion to regard their titles as pretentious; rather, they tell us that the founders took emancipation seriously, believing that the Civil War had settled, indeed, the issue of human inequality in the nation; they also tell us that the founders were applying, to

[3] Francis G. Peabody, "Education for Life" (Garden City, N. Y.: Doubleday, Page, 1919), p. 42.

the newly freed population, the ancient faith in the efficacy of higher education to elevate a people.

One variation from the usual form of these institutions appeared; it was to become, for a period, the dominant force in the education of Negroes. Most of the institutions patterned themselves in objectives and curricula after the Calvinist education of New England and the midwestern extension of New England's educational system: rigid academic standards, emphasis on subject matter, and a classical education at the top. At Hampton, Va., the American Missionary Association wished to found a "college," as it had founded other colleges in Nashville (Fisk), Atlanta (Atlanta University), Talladega, Alabama, and Straight (New Orleans). To be its head, they invited a young ex-soldier who seemed to have the usual qualifications; he was the son of a missionary, he had studied at a New England college (Williams), and he was devoted to the uplifting of Negroes.

But Samuel Chapman Armstrong was, in fact, a very different person. This man was a son of no ordinary missionary and served in no ordinary heathen land. His father was Richard Armstrong, who had gone out to the Sandwich Islands in 1830, where the son was born. The father had risen to become Principal Advisor to King Kamehameha IV and his Minister of Public Instruction.[4] Richard Armstrong had established the Punahou School, the "School for Princes," where Samuel Chapman Armstrong was prepared for Yale. This school soon was frequented by the sons of the missionaries and the traders, who wanted to send their children back to the continent for college. Richard Armstrong and other missionaries were disappointed with the progress of the Hawaiians in the school, believing that its influence "spoiled" the simple natives, and established for them the Hilo Manual Labor School that eventually was attended exclusively by Hawaiians. Samuel Chapman Armstrong observed of the Hilo School that "it had turned out men less brilliant than the advanced schools, but more solid." While Cravath's students at Fisk and Ware's at Atlanta University were studying Latin, sometimes on the dirt floor of an abandoned army barracks, Armstrong set his pupils to work at "useful trades and occupations," feeling that what the Negro most needed to learn was the sense of the dignity of labor and the discipline of manual work. Quite openly, he advised his more brilliant students to go to schools like Howard University, where they could study the classics and prepare themselves to enter the professions. Hampton existed to turn out "solid men" who would work with their hands in skilled trades.

Out of Hampton Institute came Booker T. Washington and the "Tuskegee idea"—"industrial education"—which was, in fact, the idea Samuel Chapman Armstrong took from the adaptations Richard Armstrong had made in applying New England education in Hawaii to a "weak" race. By 1900, a violent controversy had arisen between the advocates of "industrial edu-

---

[4] James Michener's "Hawaii," although it makes no reference to American Negro education, appeals to me as a document that every one, hopeful of understanding the history of Negro education, should read. It is a beautiful account (however, "fictional") based on research of how a theory of education for an "under-developed" people came to vary from the Samuel Hopkins-Arthur Tappan-American Missionary Association line. A scholarly account of the same development may be found in Merze Tate, "The Sandwich Island Missionaries Lay the Foundation for a System of Public Instruction in Hawaii," *Journal of Negro Education*, 30:396-406, Fall, 1961.

cation" and those who advocated a higher, liberal arts education. Unfortunately, it became an "either . . . or" argument. The chief protagonists were Armstrong-educated Booker T. Washington of Tuskegee Institute and Fisk- and Harvard-educated W. E. B. DuBois.

For a quarter of a century—until 1925—Booker T. Washington's views clearly had won the day. Gifts to Negro liberal arts colleges declined to a starvation level and the endowments of the "industrial schools" mounted. State and private institutions, founded as "colleges" and "universities," were re-christened with names designed to reflect their adaptation to a "practical" education.

But the "colleges" and "universities" persisted, although with diminished means. Aging relics of the Reconstruction missionary zeal plodded on stubbornly, preserving even within decaying walls the curriculum *they* had studied 40, even 50, years before at Oberlin, or Bates, or Yale, or Bowdoin. And their graduates were the ones who became the college presidents and teachers, the writers, the physicians and lawyers, the founders of the National Association for the Advancement of Colored People, the heads of social welfare agencies, the pioneers scaling the heights of state and national civil services. Michener's account of Hawaiian education comes remarkably close to the reality of Negro Education:

Hewlett Hall [the Manual Labor School for Hawaiians] was limited by the vision of the great families who dominated its board. They sent their own sons to Punahou and Yale. It never seriously occurred to them that Hawaiian boys had exactly the same capacities as haoles; consequently, they consciously forced Hewlett Hall into a trade-school mold; its directors, with the greatest love in the world, rationalized: "The Hawaiians are a delightful, relaxed race. They love to sing and to play games. They make wonderful mechanics and chauffeurs. Let us encourage them to do these things even better." . . .

Now in the old days when a brilliant Chinese boy had fallen under the wing of preposterous Uliassatu Karakoram Blake, he was told daily: "You are as great a human being as I have ever known. There is nothing of which you are not capable." And these boys grew into doctors, political leaders and bankers. When outstanding Japanese boys like Goro Sakagawa crammed themselves into McKinley High—called locally Mikado Prep—they invariably found some inspired woman teacher imported from Kansas or Minnesota who told them: "You have a mind that can accomplish anything. You could write great books or become a fine research doctor. You can do anything." So the Chinese boys and the Japanese battled their way to proficiency, but the Hawaiians were not so goaded. They were given everything free and were encouraged to become trustworthy mechanics, and no society has ever been ruled by trustworthy mechanics and loyal schoolteachers.

The pattern changed rapidly after 1925. Perhaps it was the mass migration of Negroes from the South that prompted a second-thought on the part of the public; or perhaps the slow extension, throughout the South, of the notion that wars could be fought for democracy, at home as well as abroad; or perhaps the section was beginning to reap the first fruits of industrialized wealth. Probably all of these factors resulted in a renewed interest in Negro education in the 1920's. The city of Atlanta, for example, had no public high school education for Negroes until 1924. Negroes, before, had to find a local high school education in the "preparatory department" of one of the four private "colleges" in the city, where the enrollment generally ran 10 high school students to one collegian.

The Morrill Land Grant Act of 1862 provided no benefits for Negroes in the South until 1891, when it was amended to require states maintaining segregated institutions to provide one for Negroes. Like the private colleges, the institutions so designated were principally elementary and high schools; and practically the only financial support came from the Federal grant, since little supplement of appropriated state funds ever was given. Few gave degrees, and those given were generally of poor calibre. Promising students attended the private colleges after high school or frequently went North for a higher education.

In the new atmosphere, after 1925, institutions were elevated from "normal schools" to simple "colleges." Substantial state appropriations began to be made, and donations, principally from large foundations and church-supporting groups, grew tremendously. High schools began to be founded in profusion, and the colleges started to discard their high school departments. Howard University, Washington, D. C., long a changeling of the Federal government, received the assurance of definite inclusion in the Federal budget; and a small number of institutions that always had maintained excellence in miniature began to emerge as distinguished members of the national small college fraternity. Simultaneously, in the North, restrictions and discriminations that had barred Negroes entirely from many institutions, or restricted their admission by the application of microscopic quotas, or made them outcasts even after admission, were being relaxed.

The number of Negroes attending northern institutions has grown enormously. A 1940 census of 47 Pennsylvania institutions showed only 75 Negroes attending institutions other than Lincoln University and Cheyney State Teachers College; in 1957, there were more than 1,100 attending Temple University alone.

In 1936, Charles S. Johnson reported that academic degrees had been granted to 31,090 Negroes from 1826 to 1936.[5] He further estimated that 25,697 of these degrees had been granted by southern Negro colleges and 5,393 by northern institutions. While cautioning that "extrapolating beyond 1940 is a dubious procedure," he still made the attempt and arrived at a minimum annual figure of Negro colleges alone: from 5,000 to 6,000 by 1950, and a maximum figure of 9,000 graduates in 1950.

The maximum figure proved to be too low, as matters turned out. Negro colleges enrolled more than 60,000 persons in 1950, and their graduates exceeded 10,000. The annual report of Negro college attendance appearing in the August-November, 1961, issue of *The Crisis* magazine reported 68,000 students enrolled in 50 Negro colleges out of 134 in existence. The failure of such large institutions as North Carolina A. & T., the Tennessee State A. & I. University, the Alabama State College, the Arkansas A. & M. College, and four North Carolina State Teachers Colleges, among others, to report suggests that the number of Negroes enrolled in all Negro colleges now must exceed 100,000. The 50 reporting institutions recorded 6,708 baccalaureate degrees.

The number of Negroes enrolled in northern and southern, formerly "white," colleges now must be in excess of 50,000. There are said to be more than 1,200 Negroes enrolled in formerly "all-white" colleges in Louisiana alone. It is interesting to note, however, that the ratio of bachelor's degrees granted to total undergraduate enrollment in the 50 reporting Negro institutions was at the low figure of 11%—a sure sign of a college population with an extremely poor

[5] "The Negro College Graduate" (Chapel Hill: University of North Carolina Press, 1938).

economic background and a limited tradition of college graduation.

Within the century, the number of living Negro college graduates has grown from scarcely a dozen to perhaps as many as 125,000. The comparative recency of extensive college-going by members of the race is shown by the fact that perhaps 117,500 of this number have taken their degrees since 1930.

This growing supply has led in turn to more persons qualifying as professional graduates—and on the highest academic levels. In addition to the several thousands of persons employed in Negro colleges, Negroes are now to be found in the faculties of the nation's foremost institutions. The "industrial education" movement has become technological and even has approached the structure of liberal arts institutions.

As individual institutions, at least several are distinguished. After long years of total neglect, indifference, and grudging toleration, 57 are now full members of the Southern Association of Colleges and Secondary Schools. In their corporate organization as members of the United Negro College Fund, the private colleges pioneered cooperative fund-raising for colleges in 1944, and the credit for this contribution to American higher education deserves wider recognition.

Currently, the great problems of the "Negro" college arise from "integration" and its implications. In fact, a number of these institutions, even in the deepest South, quietly have enrolled white students for several years. In the border states of West Virginia and Missouri, state institutions that were formerly all-Negro in the composition of the student body are rapidly approaching the day when they will have a majority white student body. The private institutions universally have inter-racial faculties. Perhaps, because of the shortage of available personnel, many of these schools have what must be the most catholic faculties in America, including black and white native Americans, Catholics, Protestants, Jews, non-believers, Chinese, Indians, and assorted Europeans.

The recent and novel aggressiveness of the southern Negro in the face of racial segregation has created an impossible situation for the administrators of southern Negro colleges. In an undemocratic system where all controls are in the hands of the white majority, the Negro administrator finds himself in the middle of a situation where his immediate clients expect sympathy for their struggle for what they regard as legitimate human rights, while his employers expect him to conduct an institution within the local customary framework of acquiescence to segregation. It is a sign of the times, however, that Negroes now are enrolled in private or public higher institutions formerly "white" in all states, with the exception of Mississippi and South Carolina, and in state higher institutions in all states but these two and Alabama. Even in the latter, one Negro has been enrolled, though later forced to leave the University of Alabama by mob violence.

By contrast, the administrations of private Negro colleges have been obliged to align themselves with protest movements, either through conviction or policy. The private Negro college always has been a bright spot of equalitarianism and interracial freedom; it is much more so today. These institutions have kept alive more than an echo of the great humanitarian tradition exemplified by John Eliot and Samuel Hopkins and Arthur Tappan and Charles G. Finney; within the last century, they have been among the brightest illuminations the American educational scene displays.

13

An Appraisal of American Higher Education

ROBERT M. HUTCHINS

*B*EFORE the second world war, higher education was thought of as a decorous occupation for the children of those who could afford to have them take a few years off from the serious business of life and as a way of advancement to higher social and economic levels for the specially bright and industrious offspring of the less fortunate. They could "work their way through." Research had achieved little standing. In those days, we used to go around vainly trying to convince industrialists, through profuse historical examples, of the practical value of "pure" research. Money was hard to come by. The Great Depression had put a temporary end to the American Dream. I remember serious discussions in the finance committee of the University of Chicago of the question whether it ever would be possible to raise funds for higher education in America again.

At that epoch, higher education in America had considerable accomplishment to its credit. It had a larger proportion of the relevant age groups in colleges and universities than any other country, and it kept them there for a longer time. Students who aspired to careers in science, pure or applied, were beginning to see that the preparation offered at home did not fall below what they could get in Vienna or Berlin. American scholars in all fields were not without honor in other countries. The best colleges and universities professed devotion to academic freedom and made good their claim in times of crisis.

Yet, American higher education was ill-prepared for the hurricane of social change in which we have been living for the last 15 years. The hurricane, with its bewildering new problems, hit an educational system that already was confused, and confounded the confusion.

American higher education never has faced seriously the question of purpose. If one asked, "What are you trying to do?" the answer was, "Anything we can get anybody to pay for." The purposes of American higher education were not its own, but those of individuals, groups, and sections of the population who wanted something from it and from whom it could get something.

The standards of a practical activity are supplied by its purpose. A purpose is a principle of allocation and a principle of limitation. If you do not know what you are trying to do, you do not know what you ought to do or what not to do. You go where the pressures push you. In default of standards of your own, you accept those currently popular, even those which are obviously false.

The popular American standard is numbers: numbers of students, numbers of dollars, numbers of buildings, numbers of Nobel prize-winners. Any numbers will do, even numbers of courses. A college president once told me that it would take me 25 years to go through all the courses offered at his college. I asked, "Is that good?" He replied, "You know it is!" He was stating a self-evident truth.

The numbers game has been going on for a long time. Santayana says, "The President of Harvard College, seeing me once by chance soon after the beginning of a term, inquired how my classes were getting on; and when I replied that I thought they were getting on well, that my men seemed to be keen and intelligent, he stopped me as if I was about to waste his time. 'I meant,' said he, *'what is the number* of students in your classes.'"

The people have no idea what higher education ought to be because nobody has ever told them. The university is such a conglomerate mass of heterogeneous activities that nobody can tell by looking at it what it is. Any demands can be made upon it because no demand appears to be unsuitable.

Now it looks as though an American will be unable to get a job above the level of manual labor without some kind of certificate, diploma, or degree. Since every American is entitled to a job, it must follow that he is entitled to the certificate, diploma or degree that he needs to get one. Higher education, therefore, must expect to accommodate almost all the young of college age. And, since the popular view is that the best education is that which trains the student in the routines of an occupation, the pressure will be toward a tremendous expansion of the courses purporting to be facsimiles of those routines. All this will take place at the time when technology is opening up the prospect of a workless world and when one of our central problems is what we are to do with ourselves in our free time. The electrical workers in New York who have won a 25-hour week will find this problem of some interest when over-time evaporates.

Of course, the higher learning is expected to help win the Cold War. This aim is perhaps the only one that has been stated clearly to and by the universities of the country and clearly accepted by them and by the public: the universities must help us keep ahead of (or up with) Russia. This has led to enthusiastic emphasis and expenditure on science.

Yet, we might ask ourselves Ortega y Gasset's scornful question: "Do you think that because there are dollars there will be science?" We cannot suppose that, when we have filled the tank with money, science will run out at the faucet. Science is a part, a product, a reflection of a whole culture and a long tradition. It is much more than laboratories, equipment, fellowships, and salaries. Technique and technicians can be developed overnight. A good definition of a technician is that he is a man who lives his life without theory. He does not need to understand anything beyond the mechanical processes that he operates. Science, on the other hand, is a tremendous intellectual enterprise, the resultant of cultural forces streaming from all quarters, from the library as much as the laboratory, from liberal education as much as specialized training, from the long-standing attitudes and appreciations of the people and the standards of their educational system rather than from their sudden determination to meet an emergency by "having science." The notion of producing science on demand is a mournful commentary on the cultural level to which we have sunk.

Since, as Calvin Coolidge said, the business of this country is business, higher education is expected to aid business through research and through the preparation of technicians and what is called "middle management." In the Affluent Society we know the money is to be got. One has the impression that a large part of the time of administrators and professors is now consumed in thinking up the sales gimmicks that will bring the money their way. In this effort they are notably successful. The effects on the quality and direction of higher education in America will be discussed a little later on.

As we enter the closing decades of the 20th century, we find ourselves with a splendid educational plant, with great schools of medicine and engineering, with the largest collections of books in the world, and with a steadily increasing number of distinguished scholars. All that we lack is basic education and true universities.

As to basic education, the remarks of William Riley Parker, professor of English at Indiana University, will suffice: "Without the least exaggeration I can say that, as a teacher of graduate students in English, there is not one single assumption I can make about either knowledge or skill already acquired. I cannot assume a single book read by everyone in my class; I cannot assume knowledge of the simplest Bible story or myth or fairy tale or piece of children's literature. I cannot assume anything except that I have a job that is needlessly difficult."

A true university is a center of independent thought. An American university cannot be a center because its members are not engaged in a common enterprise and because, on account of their lack of basic education and common interests, they cannot be. The importers of the German university forgot to import the *gymnasium* with it. In spite of the deplorable asperity of his language, we must admit that there is a grain of truth in the words of Claude Coleman, director of the Special Honors Program at Southern Illinois University: "Nine-tenths of the faculty at any university are bores, simply because they become complete nincompoops outside their specialties. Most of them take their coffee breaks with their own colleagues in order to avoid the viruses of other disciplines. They are not happy until their undergraduate majors become as narrow as they are themselves."

It is quite natural that the principal opponents of liberal education in the U. S. are the professors of universities distinguished for research and professional training. Liberal education takes time that these professors think should be expended on specialized work. I venture the generalization that liberal education cannot flourish in a university in which liberal education is under departmental control. There can be sudden outbursts of concern, such as the Harvard Report, but they will have no lasting effect on the policies and programs of the faculty.

The commitment of an American professor is not to his university or to education; it is to his subject. In view of the number and miscellaneous quality of subjects, an American university cannot be a center. A phrase often used 40 years ago now has an archaic ring: it was said then that a university was a community of scholars. This community, if it ever existed, has now collapsed.

An American university has a hard time being independent. If public relations, which is nothing but a means to money, is the chief object that those who direct the university must have in view, some shameful things are bound to happen during an era like that of the late Sen. McCarthy. They are likely to continue to happen as long as the Cold War lasts.

The present interest of government and business in the higher learning does not flow from their love of truth. Government and business have their reasons for supporting the universities, but the advancement of knowledge for its own sake is not one of them. In my last year at the University of Chicago, 60% of the money that passed through my hands came by way of one government contract. I could not be indifferent to the demands of the contracting officers, no matter how contrary to the aims of the University they might be.

It is difficult for an American university to concern itself with thought. In the first place, thought implies criticism, and criticism of a social, political, economic system to which one is looking for admiration and support is impossible unless the public, through a long course of education and demonstration, has become convinced that thought, including criticism, is the purpose of the university, that this is what it exists for, and that independent thought and criticism are indispensable to the improvement, and perhaps even the survival, of any society. This long course of education and demonstration has never even gotten started in the U. S.

In the second place, the atmosphere in which students and professors live and the activities in which they engage are hostile to thought. I am not thinking of the popular irrelevancies, such as football, fraternities, and fun. Rather, I would suggest that American professors teach far too much and American students go to class too much. Overteaching inhibits thought. American professors are judged by the amount they write. Therefore, they tend to write material that does not require thought. American students are judged by the amount they remember. They may get better marks if they do not think.

Finally, this is the age of scientism. An American university is unlikely to have two cultures, in the phrase of C. P. Snow. It will have one, the pseudo-scientific. This culture reflects a popular misunderstanding of science, according to which science is the only form of knowledge; everything else is superstition or guesswork. Science consists of the collection of facts. The object of research is the collection of facts and the aim of education is the absorption thereof.

A great mathematician, when he was chairman of the Mathematics Department at the University of Chicago, once told me that a graduate student, who later became a professor of mathematics at Chicago, had promise in his field but was undoubtedly crazy. Since this was said with perfect seriousness, I expressed alarm and asked for evidence of the student's unfortunate condition. The chairman replied, "Mr. Hutchins, he is interested in philosophy!"

Chicago was a great pseudo-scientific institution, with the humanities, the social sciences, and the professional schools all vying with one another to show that they were just as "scientific" as the natural sciences, all eagerly swamping their students with facts and demanding more and more of the students' time so that the sterile stream of their education should not be polluted by infiltrations from other disciplines. I have the impression that a senior in an American medical school knows far more facts than any European professor of the subject.

The American spirit is exemplified by the simultaneous proclamations of Nicholas Murray Butler and William F. Ogburn, not many years ago, that the number of new facts was increasing at such a rate that we should have to prolong adolescence until age 45 in order to have time to pour them all into the students. The collection, transmission, and absorption of facts require very little thought.

Of course, the fact-collecting view of natural science is a caricature of its procedures, which is made no more convincing by the endorsement of some scientists who are misled by the propagandists of science but who would not dream of conforming to the caricature in their laboratories. As I have said, science is an intellectual discipline—this is its claim to be represented in a university—and the scientist who does not think is no scientist at all.

If what we need is basic education and centers of independent thought, how can we get them? Obviously, what we ought to have is a moral and intellectual revolution. Our views of the nature of man and of the good life and the good society are so inadequate and so distorted that we are unlikely to achieve in this century the major reorientation of higher education that the times demand. Perhaps some beginnings can be made. The new colleges associated with Michigan State and Wayne State Universities may be able to shake themselves free from the prevailing academic mores and help to show our people the possibilities of basic education. Eccentric organizations within universities, like the Committee on Social Thought at the University of Chicago, may demonstrate the value of independent thought and suggest ways in which centers, however small, may make their influence felt.

I believe there are great opportunities in the education of adults, largely because nobody has cared enough about it to institutionalize and bureaucratize it. Adult education offers the only sensible answer to the question of what we are going to do with ourselves in a workless world. Since that world is rapidly coming into existence, we may expect our people to take a new attitude toward the continuing education of adults. Perhaps it will turn out that this work can best be conducted far from the red tape, the credits, the departments, and the degrees that strangle education and thought in our universities. If the universities do decide to take adult education seriously, which almost none of them, except possibly the University of California at Los Angeles, has done, then we may hope that this will remain a segregated area into which the miasma of specialization, vocationalism, and pettifogging will not be allowed to penetrate.

The world we are entering is entirely new. The intellectual resources we can bring to bear upon it are meager. To cope with it, we need liberated minds operating in and through intellectual communities. The leading phenomena of our time are technology, bureaucracy, and nationalism. One characteristic they have in common is ambiguity. Technology can smother us all, or it can usher in a world of plenty. Bureaucracy may stifle the political community, or it may be the backbone of democratic government. Nationalism may disrupt the human race, or it may be a necessary step to the world community.

These ambiguities cannot be clarified and the new world cannot be understood or directed by a nation that has no serious higher learning. If we had liberal education and centers of independent thought in the U. S. we might not save ourselves or others, but we might have a better chance of doing so than we have now.

14

International Relations in Higher Education, 1862–1962

WILLIAM W. BRICKMAN

THE FIELD of international education, particularly that part of it dealing with the exchange of professors, teachers, and students, has developed rapidly in the past decade and a half. At the same time, there has been a growing stress, in academic and educational circles, on the furnishing of teachers, instructional materials, and advice to other nations which are in various degrees of development. In general, the accent in these activities has been on the functional and the practical, for understandable reasons. Yet, workers in the area of international education might look back with interest and profit at what has been thought, said, and accomplished before the present.

In another publication, the writer has traced the historical development of international relations among institutions of higher learning from ancient times to our own time.[1] This chapter presents the highlights of international cooperation by universities during the past century. That such co-operation is regarded by governments as of great significance is evident from the fact that both the U.S.S.R. and Czechoslovakia recently have opened international universities for students from Asia, Africa, and Latin America. Further, Atatürk University, Erzurum, Turkey, was opened in 1958 in accordance with the plan of an American land-grant institution, while the Communist Party of Hungary recently has urged that U. S. university courses in business administration and management be introduced in order to improve the level of training in that country.[2]

The period beginning with the second half of the 19th century was marked by the rise of national states and the emergence of groups of nations in an effort to maintain a balance of power. Such international alliances accentuated rivalry and were instrumental in touching off two world wars and several small conflicts. While the struggle in international power politics continued, there were tendencies making for closer and friendlier relations among nations. Among these were the Berne Convention on Copyright (1866), the first modern Olympic Games (1896), the Pan American Union (1900), the Nobel Peace Prize (1897), the Permanent Court of Arbitration (1900), the international expositions in Philadelphia (1876) and Paris (1889), the international conferences and associations of learned men and professionals in every conceivable field, the introduction of such international

---

[1] William W. Brickman, "Introduction to the History of International Relations in Higher Education" (New York: The Author, 1960). This memorandum was prepared for the Ford Foundation.

[2] *New York Times,* April 29, 1962.

languages as Volapük (1880) and Esperanto (1887), the growth of the peace movement, the rise of governmental and private cultural programs in conjunction with other nations, the cultural and educational activities of the League of Nations and other intergovernmental bodies, and so on. While the diminishing distances among nations and the improved methods of communication encouraged warlike activities, they also made possible better and more frequent contacts of a cultural and educational nature among the peoples of the world.

INTERNATIONAL STUDENT EXCHANGE

The tradition of the international migration of students in quest of a higher education can be traced to ancient times in Greece, Egypt, Palestine, Persia, and India. More familiar is the international nature of the medieval university in Western Europe. During the later historical periods, students from various lands ventured forth to pursue higher learning in such institutions as the University of Bologna, the University of Leyden, and the University of Paris. All through the 19th century, the Universities of Berlin and Göttingen in particular and German universities in general attracted students from all over the world. Without doubt, 19th-century Germany was "the Mecca of foreign students, above all of Americans from the United States."[3] In its universities could be found, well into the 20th century, students from all parts of Europe, North and South America, the Middle and the Far East, Africa, and Australia.[4]

---

[3] Reinhold Schairer, "Die Studenten im internationalen Kulturleben" (Münster i.W.: Aschendorffsche Verlagsbuchhandlung, 1927), p. 9.

[4] See the statistical tables covering 1865-66 to 1926 in *ibid.*, pp. 19-22.

American interest in German higher education is traceable to a visit by Benjamin Franklin to the University of Göttingen in 1766. In spite of the claim that Benjamin Smith Barton (1768-1815) of Philadelphia obtained an M.D. in 1788 at the University of Göttingen after apparently less than a year of study, the records of the university do not contain the American's name.[5] In 1815, George Ticknor and Edward Everett enrolled at Göttingen to study modern and ancient languages, respectively. Two years later, at the age of 23, the latter obtained the Ph.D., "the first American and so far as I know, Englishman, on whom it has ever been conferred."[6] These two scholars, who left their impress upon Harvard and upon American higher education in general, were the forerunners of the large contingent of American students who were to study at the German universities during the following century and afterward. Among the American scholars who sat at the feet of the German professors were George Bancroft, Henry Wadsworth Longfellow, and John Lathrop Motley. Other notable students who spread the German idea of higher education were such future university presidents as Henry P. Tappan of Michigan, Charles W. Eliot of Harvard, Daniel C. Gilman of Johns Hopkins, Andrew D. White of Cornell, G. Stan-

[5] Henry A. Pochmann, "German Culture in America: Philosophical and Literary Influences, 1600-1900" (Madison: University of Wisconsin Press, 1957), p. 50. See also B. A. Hinsdale, "Notes on the History of Foreign Influence upon Education in the United States," in "Report of the Commissioner of Education for the Year 1897-98" (Washington: Government Printing Office, 1899), Vol. I, p. 607.

[6] Edward Everett to Stephen Higginson, Sept. 17, 1817, as quoted in Orie W. Long, "Literary Pioneers: Early American Explorers of European Culture" (Cambridge: Harvard University Press, 1935), p. 71.

ley Hall of Clark, and Nicholas Murray Butler of Columbia. Between 1815 and 1914, more than 10,000 young Americans were enrolled in German institutions of higher learning.[7] Americans were attracted to Germany because they could obtain a higher form of higher education without subjection, as at Oxford and Cambridge, to religious tests and because they could avoid the "infidelity" and the "immorality" of France. The "vision of excellence across the seas" resulted in a "transatlantic scholarly migration, one of the most extraordinary examples of cultural interaction in the history of higher education."[8] Hundreds brought back with them the "coveted Ph.D. degree," a distinction which became the "open sesame for virtually any university chair in the United States."[9]

Many an American or other foreign student in Germany must have wondered about the desirability of adopting some or even all the features of German higher education in his own country. In 1874, James Morgan Hart warned that, while "the German method of Higher Education is far above our own, I should be very sorry to see that method adopted at once, and in the lump."[10] However, this is what took place, more or less, two years later when the Johns Hopkins Univer-

---

[7] Charles F. Thwing, "The American and the German University" (New York: Macmillan, 1928), pp. 12-44; John S. Brubacher and Willis Rudy, "Higher Education in Transition: An American History, 1636-1956" (New York: Harper, 1958), pp. 172-173; Friedrich Schneider. "Geltung und Einfluss der deutschen Pädagogik im Ausland" (Munich: Oldenbourg, 1943), p. 313; and Pochmann, op. cit., p. 77.

[8] Brubacher and Rudy, op cit., pp. 173-174.

[9] George P. Schmidt, "The Liberal Arts College: A Chapter in American Cultural History" (New Brunswick, N. J.: Rutgers University Press, 1957), p. 159.

[10] James M. Hart, "German Universities" (New York: Putnam, 1874), pp. vi-vii.

sity was opened as "the first university in America based on the German model" and as "the Göttingen at Baltimore."[11] In this new institution there was a decided stress on advanced instruction and original research through the medium of the seminar. Decades earlier, Tappan's attempt to "Prussianize" higher education in Michigan may have proved a failure, but Daniel Coit Gilman's process of Germanization turned out to be a resounding success at Johns Hopkins.

One of the major imports from Germany was the concept of academic freedom for professors and students: *Akademische Lehr- und Lernfreiheit*. Many of "the leaders and targets in academic-freedom cases" from 1890 to 1914 were former students at German universities, *e.g.*, Richard T. Ely, E. Benjamin Andrews, Edward A. Ross, John M. Mecklin, James McKeen Cattell, Edwin R. A. Seligman, and Arthur O. Lovejoy. Of the 13 individuals who signed the "Report on Academic Freedom" when the American Association of University Professors was founded in 1915, eight had studied in German universities.[12]

The content of the subject matter taught in American colleges and universities also underwent change as the result of the impact of the German university on higher education in the U. S. The field of psychology, for example, was transformed by G. Stanley Hall, a student under Wilhelm Wundt in 1879-80 at the University of Leipzig, and by others who had studied in Germany. It was Hall who arranged to have Sigmund Freud, Carl Gustav Jung, Sandor Ferenczi, and

[11] Richard Hofstadter and Walter P. Metzger, "The Development of Academic Freedom in the United States" (New York: Columbia University Press, 1955), p. 377.

[12] *Ibid.*, p. 396.

other European psychoanalysts lecture at Clark University in 1909, an event which led to the introduction of psychoanalysis into this country. The subject of pedagogy received its impetus in the late 19th century when Charles De Garmo and Charles and Frank McMurry introduced the Herbartianism they had absorbed under Wilhelm Rein at the University of Jena.[13] For decades thereafter, well into the 20th century, college and university departments of education and teachers colleges taught the "Five Formal Steps" and other Herbartian doctrines as the last word in modern education.

The influence of German higher education was apparent in all parts of the world. Students from all continents sought the number-one academic distinction, the German Ph.D. degree. Armed with the ideals and techniques of *Wissenschaft,* they returned to their native lands and sought to promote the German conception of higher education. "The historical seminars in France, the graduate schools in the United States, and the technical schools of Japan as well as similar trends elsewhere all bore the stamp 'made in Germany.' "[14] The German universities deserved their reputation as locales of serious study and careful scientific research, where the acquisition and advancement of knowledge could be accomplished in an atmosphere of full freedom. Many a native German student might have frittered away his time in drinking bouts and in duelling, but the foreign student generally haunted the library and the laboratory.

Although the prevalence of foreign students in their midst was regarded, as a rule, with favor

13 Pochmann, *op. cit.,* p. 281.
14 Koppel S. Pinson, "Modern Germany: Its History and Civilization" (New York: Macmillan, 1954), p. 252.

by the German academicians and students, there was one prominent exception. The growing number of students from Russia, where higher education often was suppressed or restricted during the 19th century, became a matter of concern, suspicion, and finally opposition on the part of the students in some of the German higher institutions. The students of technology, in particular, feared future competition from the foreigners, especially the Russians. The Germans succeeded, in some cases, in exacting special privileges for themselves and disabilities for the foreign students. At least on one occasion, in 1905 in Jena, the outcome of such agitation by the German students was "a serious insult to the foreigners."[15] It is interesting to note that most writings on international student exchange discuss its benefits and glories but very seldom give any hint of friction between the native and foreign students. A study of such conflicts would be a desirable addition to the literature and possibly would yield a better understanding of the complexities of international exchange of students.

During the 20th century, Germany continued to draw foreign students to its universities, but the number varied in accordance with political conditions in the country. During the period of National Socialist power, a foreign observer noted that "Germany is rapidly falling into a quagmire of intellectual provincialism."[16] Contributing to the decline of the German university under Hitler were the dismissals of Jewish and

[15] Friedrich Schulze and Paul Ssymank, "Das deutsche Studententum von den aeltesten Zeiten bis zur Gegenwart," second edition (Leipzig: Voigtländer, 1910), pp. 441-442.
[16] Edward Y. Hartshorne, Jr., "The German Universities and National Socialism" (London: George Allen & Unwin, 1937), p. 172.

other anti-Nazi professors, who then went abroad and enriched higher education in many other countries. Since the recovery of Germany following the defeat in World War II, its universities once more have begun to draw foreigners.[17] Now, however, Germany no longer enjoys the monopoly in the higher education of foreign students as it had during the 19th century. Large numbers of young men and women from all parts of the globe now crowd universities in the U. S., England, France, the U.S.S.R., and other countries.[18]

It would be interesting and instructive to analyze historically the experiences of many countries in having their young citizens taught in foreign universities. However, because of space restrictions, it will be possible to refer only to a few. It is hoped that a fuller account may be given on a later occasion.

A major reason for the exodus of students from one country to other areas is the pressing need for the rapid preparation of personnel to aid an underdeveloped country to transform itself into a modern, scientific-technical society. A typical case is that of Persia (Iran), whose Shah, Nasir-ud-Din, sent out in 1858 a group of 42 students to become competent physicians, engineers, political scientists, and other specialists in European universities. These students subsequently were

[17] See the 376-page *vademecum* to the German universities issued by the German Academic Exchange Service, "The Foreign Student in Germany" (Bonn: Deutscher Akademischer Austauschdienst, 1958).

[18] The French Ministry of Foreign Affairs has found it necessary to publish a 530-page "Guide de l'enseignement supérieure universitaire français" (Paris: Ministère des Affaires Etrangères, 1959) for the guidance of foreign students.

appointed to important positions in the government, and one man was chosen twice to be Minister of Public Instruction.[19] Since Persian higher institutions could not cope with the professional manpower needs of the country during the present century, the government sends many students to study in France, Germany, England, the U. S. A., and other countries.[20]

China became interested in Western higher education in the 1840's. Its first "returned student," Yung Wing, brought with him a B.A. from Yale College (1854) and initiated a drive to recruit young men to study in the U. S. and thereby to ensure the future of the country.[21] Perhaps his greatest success consisted in obtaining approval by the Imperial Court for his plan to experiment with the education of 120 young Chinese in American colleges. The students, aged 12-14 years, were to be sent in "four installments" of 30 and would have 15 years to complete their education. So that these youngsters would not lose contact with their native culture during their formative and impressionable years, "Chinese teachers were to be provided to keep up their

---

[19] Issa K. Sadiq, "Modern Persia and Her Educational System" (New York: Bureau of Publications, Teachers College, Columbia University, 1931), p. 18.

[20] *Ibid.*, pp. 78-79.

[21] Wen-Han Kiang, "The Chinese Student Movement" (New York: King's Crown Press, 1948), p. 14; "A Study of Chinese Students in American Universities and Colleges in the Past One Hundred Years" (New York: China Institute in America, 1954), p. 5. Apparently the first Chinese students in a Western country were the two in France for whom Turgot wrote in the late 18th century his "Reflexions sur la formation et la distribution des richesses." The first Chinese student in Great Britain, Wong Foon, enrolled in 1850 at the University of Edinburgh. *Cf.,* H. F. MacNair, "The Chinese Abroad" (Shanghai: Commercial Press, 1924), pp. 246-249.

knowledge of Chinese while in the United States."[22] In this way, the plan met a potential criticism which had wrecked successfully many a plan for student interchange in previous periods.

The Imperial Government of China authorized Yung Wing in 1871 to organize a Chinese Educational Mission to the U. S.[23] This he did the following year, and until 1875 the four installments of 30 students came annually to study in American educational institutions. Subsequently, because of governmental fears that the students were becoming infected with the ideologies of Christianity, republicanism, and anti-monarchism, the mission was abolished in 1881. The main contributor to this debacle was apparently Yung Wing's co-commissioner, Wu Tze-teng. According to the former, Wu began a clandestine "stream of misrepresentation" that the students "played more than they studied" and that "most of them went to church, attended Sunday schools and had become Christians"; and that, consequently, "the sooner this educational enterprise was broken up and all the students recalled, the better it would be for China."[24]

In spite of the discrediting of the student exchange in official circles, the plan did succeed in

[22] Yung Wing, "My Life in China and America" (New York: Holt, 1909), p. 173.

[23] Thomas E. LaFargue, "China's First Hundred" (Pullman: State College of Washington Press, 1942). See also Arthur G. Robinson, "The Senior Returned Students: A Brief Account of the Chinese Educational Mission under Dr. Yung Wing, 1872-1881" (Tientsin: Tientsin Press, 1932).

[24] Yung Wing, *op. cit.*, pp. 204-205. That there was some basis for these changes is evident from the chapter on "Chinese Schoolmates," by William Lyon Phelps, in "Autobiography with Letters" (New Haven: Yale University Press, 1939), pp. 56-59. Phelps, however, pointed out not merely the social and athletic, but also the academic ability of the Chinese students.

the long run, inasmuch as the "returned students" became the first engineers, railway and telegraph builders, mining specialists, and naval technical officers. One of these, in fact, Tong Shao-yi, several decades later became the Prime Minister of the Chinese Republic.

Interestingly, a century after the student days of Yung Wing, close to 20,000 Chinese had studied in American colleges and universities.[25] To a significant extent, this pedagogical pilgrimage came about as a result of the series of military defeats inflicted upon China—the Sino-Japanese War (1894-95), the Boxer Rebellion (1900), and the Russo-Japanese War (1904-05). Taking a leaf out of the recent experience of Japan in westernization through intimate educational contact with Europe and America, the Chinese government began sending large numbers of students to Japanese universities. The leader of this exchange movement was the viceroy of Hupeh and Hunan provinces, Chang Chih-tung, whose "Ch'uan Hsueh P'ien" ("An Exhortation to Learning") was issued in 1,000,000 copies and was instrumental in bringing about educational reform.[26] The peak of Chinese enrollment in Japanese institutions was in 1907, when 15,000 students were pursuing higher education in the neighboring nation's institutions. This "huge exodus," unprecedented in Chinese history, was attributable to the propaganda of Chang Chih-tung, who favored Japan because of accessibility,

[25] "Chinese Students in the United States, 1948-55" (New York: Committee on Educational Interchange Policy, 1956), p. 2.

[26] Kiang, op. cit., p. 10. The book has been rendered into English as "China's Only Hope" (New York: Revell, 1900) by Samuel I. Woodbridge.

economy, and similiarity of cultural heritage and customs.[27]

The Boxer Rebellion's outcome forced China to pay indemnities to the victors. In 1908, the Congress of the U. S. decided to return $12,000,-000 to the Chinese government in order to pay for the cost of educating "a certain number of Chinese in the United States, hoping thereby to aid in bringing the Chinese to a better understanding of Western civilization."[28] The following year, 47 students, who were selected after a competitive examination, were sent to the U. S. In 1911, the Chinese government organized Tsing Hua College in Peking to prepare the "indemnity students" for the American university. These 'indemnity students," according to a Chinese scholar who wrote a history of this movement, "played a significant part in the modernization of China."[29] The investment of the indemnity funds in higher education was regarded appreciatively by the Chinese as "an event which has done more than anything else to establish the friendly relations between China and the United States. This simple act of goodwill has placed America in a most favorable light in the eyes of the Chinese people and has laid the foundation for closer cooperation and better understanding between the peoples of the two great nations."[30] Unfortunately, these good relations were not potent enough to stand the strain of the Communist assumption of power in continental China from 1949 onward. One major problem was the status of the Chinese students who could

[27] Kiang, *op. cit.*, p. 16.
[28] "A Study of Chinese Students . . . ," *op. cit.*, p. 17.
[29] Kiang, *op. cit.*, p. 19.
[30] "A Study of Chinese Students . . . ," *op. cit.*, p. 16.

not return to mainland China after it had fallen under Communist control.

No doubt, the most famous among the Chinese students in America were Dr. V. K. Wellington Koo, the ambassador, who studied at Columbia University, and Dr. Y. C. James Yen, the initiator of the Mass Education Movement for literacy, who was a graduate of Yale University.[31] An analysis of "Who's Who in China" for 1931 revealed that, of the 960 persons included, 521 had studied in foreign universities, with 286 of them in the U. S.[32]

Japan followed the precedent of China in its policy of educating some of its young people in American higher institutions. Among the earliest Japanese students was Jo Niishima (also known as Joseph Hardy Neesima), who left Japan secretly in 1864 for Amherst College and Andover Theological Seminary. After obtaining a degree from Amherst in 1870, Niishima returned to Japan and in 1874 became the co-founder of Doshisha School (later University), a Christian institution of great influence, in the ancient cultural center of Kyoto.

In the meantime, the Meiji Restoration took place in 1868 and Japan gave notice to the world that a new, modern country was to arise from its medieval status. The Charter Oath of five principles, taken by the Emperor on April 6, 1868, ended with a principle embodying the national educational aim: "Knowledge shall be sought throughout the world, so that the welfare of the Empire may be promoted."[33] This fifth

[31] *Ibid.,* p. 22.
[32] *Ibid.,* p. 21.
[33] Quoted in G. B. Sansom, "The Western World and Japan: A Study in the Interaction of European and Asiatic Cultures" (New York: Knopf, 1950), p. 318.

principle seemed to forecast the policy of student and other forms of interchange with foreign nations in the West. And this is what took place. From 1865 to 1885, American universities had 293 Japanese students, of whom 162 (55%) "occupied positions of responsibility and influence in government, academic, and business life" in Japan.[34] Many of the returnees took teaching positions and were able to influence the modernization of the Japanese school system. Some held high-ranking academic posts, such as Masakazu Toyama (University of Michigan, 1876), Kenjiro Yamakawa (Yale, 1875), and Naokichi Matsui (Columbia and Yale)—all of whom served as presidents of Tokyo Imperial University.[35] Yujiro Matora attended G. Stanley Hall's seminars at Johns Hopkins in the 1880's and then founded the Japan Child Study Society in 1902. Another student of Hall, Toshihide Shinoda was the first professor of child psychology at the Tokyo Higher Normal School for Women. Kanjiro Higuchi introduced Francis Wayland Parker's methods into Japan.[36] American educational theory penetrated into Japan after World War I and II through the intermediacy of Japanese educators who had studied pedagogy in American institutions. It is interesting that the vast majority embraced the Progressivism of John Dewey and William Heard Kilpatrick rather than the nonpragmatic thought of William Chandler Bagley and Herman Harrell Horne.

---

[34] Robert S. Schwantes, "Japanese and Americans: A Century of Cultural Relations" (New York: Harper, 1955), p. 210. See also William E. Griffis, "The Rutgers Graduates in Japan," second edition (New Brunswick, N. J.: Rutgers College, 1916).

[35] *Ibid.*

[36] *Ibid.*, p. 139.

Early in the 20th century, Toyohiko Kagawa, the famous preacher of the social gospel, studied at the Princeton Theological Seminary. His influence, which was profound before the invasion of China in 1937, dwindled during the war period but was revived after World War II.[37] Kagawa made an attempt at one time "to combine instruction in religion and in better methods of agriculture at short-term Farmers' Gospel Schools, patterned after the Grundtvigian folk schools of Denmark."[38]

Japanese educators returned from the lecture rooms and seminars of Wilhelm Rein at the University of Jena with enthusiasm for the doctrines of Herbartian pedagogy. It may seem odd that Japanese educators became enthusiastic over foreign educational theory and practice, because many of the ideas of Herbart, Dewey, and other moderns already had been anticipated by Japanese thinkers of previous centuries. Thus, the "Wazokudojikin" of Ekiken Kaihara (1630-1714), which was published in 1757, five years prior to the appearance of Rousseau's "Emile," recommended a differentiated course of study in accordance with age levels, thereby proposing a Pestalozzian reform decades before the Swiss pedagogue did.[39] But apparently the educational grass was greener in another country and westernization demanded a pedagogy expressed in Western terminology.

As is well known, Japanese schools and col-

[37] *Ibid.*, p. 266.

[38] *Ibid.*, p. 275.

[39] Komao Murakami, "Das japanische Erziehungswesen" (Tokyo: Fuzambo, 1934), p. 42. See also Olaf Graf, "Kaihara Ekiken: Ein Beitrag zur japanischen Geistesgeschichte des 17. Jahrhunderts und zur chinesichen Sung-Philosophie" (Leiden: Brill, 1942), pp. 282-339.

leges, and the general public as well, look upon baseball as their own national pastime. To some extent, the Japanese students might have been influenced to become baseball fans because of their residence in America. In any event, the educational significance of the American national game was recognized officially when the Minister of Education issued in 1932 certain regulations for players.[40]

It is also worthy of note that the transpacific student exchange was not one-sided. Prior to 1941, many American students and teachers, especially those who lived along the West Coast, spent their summers in Japan and thus absorbed much of Japanese culture. During 1930-41, a former student of New York University, Kaju Nakamura, operated in Tokyo the Oriental Culture Summer College in which lectures and exhibits on Japanese culture and life were offered to over 4,000 foreigners.[41] According to Schwantes, furthermore, "Several thousand Japanese-Americans have returned to Japan for intermediate or higher education, but they have contributed more to Japanese knowledge about American life than to our understanding of Japan."[42] Yet, American understanding of Japanese culture and life was enriched as a consequence of the graduate study in the universities of Japan during the 1930's by such scholars as Prof. E. O. Reischauer of Harvard (currently U. S. Ambassador to Japan) and Pres. Hugh Borton of Haverford College. In addition, the translations and monographs of such specialists as Prof. Donald Keene and Prof. Sir George San-

[40] Murakami, *op. cit.*, pp. 215-216.
[41] Schwantes, *op. cit.*, p. 217.
[42] *Ibid.*, p. 214.

som have added considerably to Western knowledge of Japan.

There are many other phases of international interchange of students involving a large number of countries, but only some can be barely mentioned, *e.g.,* the Rhodes Scholarship Fund (1902),[43] the Junior Year Abroad of the University of Delaware (1923) and other institutions, the Norden Association (1918) of Scandinavia, the Institute of International Education (1919), the Deutsche Pädagogische Auslandsstelle (1929), and the like. Attention might also have been paid to the Fulbright Program of the U. S. (Public law 584, 1946) and to other governmental plans for student exchange. Suffice it to say that all through the 20th century, in spite of some reverses owing to international crisis and tensions, the numbers of students involved in exchanges continued to rise.

It is interesting to take note of the statistics of student exchange. The U. S. Bureau of Education reported in 1904 that 2,673 students from 74 countries were attending American colleges, not including the institutions for women. This figure is given significance when one realizes that the total foreign student population in German universities during 1904-05 was 8,786 (3,097 of these in the technical colleges) and that the French universities' foreign attendance was a mere 2,046.[44] Since there was no comparison at that time, from the standpoint of universal re-

---

[43] Frank Aydelotte, "The American Rhodes Scholarships: A Review of the First Forty Years" (Princeton: Princeton University Press, 1946).

[44] Henry H. King, "Outline History of Student Migrations," in W. Reginald Wheeler, *et al.,* editors, "The Foreign Student in America" (New York: Association Press, 1925), p. 11.

pute, between the American and the European institutions, it was clear that the world was paying more and more notice to the potentialities of the American universities. Although 614 students came to the U. S. in 1904 from British North America, 308 came from Mexico, 236 from Cuba, 105 from China, more than 150 from other South and Central American countries, and 46 from the Philippines.[45]

During 1911-12, there were 4,856 regularly enrolled foreign students in the U. S., with a grand total of 5,227 (including summer session attendance). The world appeal of the American university was even more apparent than in 1904 by reference to the breakdown by major countries: Canada (898), West Indies (698), China (549), Japan (415), Mexico (298), United Kingdom (251), India and Ceylon (148), Germany (143), Russia and Finland (120), Brazil (76), Argentina (51), Peru (28), Colombia (28), Chile (19), and other South American nations (72).[46] While one might argue that geographic proximity was a probable factor in this attendance, it also is undeniable that the U. S. was becoming increasingly recognized on the international scene and that many countries wished to develop commercial relations with this rapidly growing industrial power. Nor should the possible factor of the improving reputation of American higher education be overlooked. Significantly, about 13.6% of the total foreign student population in the U. S. during 1911-12 was derived from Great Britain, India, and Russia.

After World War I, during 1920-21, the foreign enrollment rose to 8,357, with 6,901 coming from

[45] *Ibid.*, pp. 11-12.
[46] *Ibid.*, pp. 11-12.

foreign countries and the rest from American overseas possessions: China (1,443), Canada (1,294), South America (563, including 126 from Brazil), Japan (525), West Indies (396), Russia (291), Mexico (282), India (235), Africa (223), France (160), and Great Britain (149). On a continental basis, 2,506 students were from Asia, 1,425 from Latin America, and 1,379 from Europe.[47]

In the course of the following two decades, the foreign figures rose and fell: 9,819 in 1930-31; 5,860 in 1934-35; 7,343 in 1936-37; and 6,004 in 1938-39. During World War II, the foreign attendance was 7,244 (1943-44), but it constantly has been rising in the postwar period. In 1945-46, there were 10,341 foreigners in U. S. colleges and universities, and one year later as many as 18,013.[48] This figure was almost doubled nearly a decade later when it reached 34,232 (1954-55), with 30% of the foreign students coming from the Far East, 25% from Latin America, and 15% from Europe—in all, from 129 countries and geographical units.[49]

The latest available statistics, for the academic year 1961-62, indicate the presence of 58,086 foreign students from 149 countries in the U. S., an increase of about 10% over the figure of the previous year. On the other hand, the most recent data for U. S. students abroad, covering the academic year 1960-61, show 19,836 Ameri-

[47] *Ibid.*
[48] A. J. Brumbaugh, editor, "American Universities and Colleges," fifth edition (Washington: American Council on Education, 1948), p. 134.
[49] Kenneth Holland, "The Foreign Student in the United States," in Mary Irwin, editor, "American Universities and Colleges," seventh edition (Washington: American Council on Education, 1956), p. 91.

cans at 590 higher institutions in 66 countries.[50] The census of the foreign student population in the U. S. has been undertaken annually since 1948 by the Institute of International Education. This is one of the many valuable services performed by this organization, which also administers the Fulbright program for students.

The total number of foreign students in the Soviet universities in 1957 was 14,536, of which 1,966 were graduate students. At the University of Moscow during 1959-60, there were some 1,500 foreigners from 50 countries. Soviet and other foreign students took work at the University of Peking, while from 1950 to 1958 over 14,000 Chinese studied in the U.S.S.R.[51]

On a world-wide scale, Unesco has furnished the figures on students abroad since 1953. Its ninth annual survey for 1961 reveals that "in the academic year 1959/60, the number of such students throughout the world was over 200,000, or about 2% of the whole student body, estimated at 11.5 million in that year."[52] About 25% of all foreign students were in the U. S., although the ratio of foreigners to natives was 1.4% or less than the world average. The countries receiving more than 10,000 foreign students were the Federal Republic of Germany, France, the United

[50] "Open Doors 1962" (New York: Institute of International Education, 1962), pp. 6, 15.

[51] F. Korolev, "Education in the U.S.S.R." (London: Soviet News, 1959), p. 81; "Moskovskii Gosudarstvennii Universitet imeni M. V. Lomonosova (Kratkaya spravka)" (Moscow: Tipografiya MGU, 1960), p. 14; René Goldman, "Peking University Today," *China Quarterly*, July-September, 1961, p. 108; C. T. Hu, "Chinese Higher Education and World Affairs," *Teachers College Record*, Vol. 62, February, 1961, p. 361.

[52] "Study Abroad" (Paris: Unesco, 1961), p. 643.

Kingdom, the U.S.S.R., and probably Argentina.[53]

Clearly, the practice of student interchange is playing an increasing role in higher education all over the world. Universities, governments, and educational organizations are convinced of the significance of international higher education and have prepared surveys and guidance materials of various types to enable the foreign students to get the maximum benefits from foreign study.[54]

INTERNATIONAL UNIVERSITIES

The past century has witnessed the flourishing of international higher educational institutions, an echo no doubt of those of previous eras. It may be difficult at times to define an international university or to distinguish it from a university which has foreign students and foreign professors. However, one might regard as an international university an institution which is estab-

---

[53] *Ibid.*

[54] *E.g.,* James M. Davis, "IIE Survey of the African Student: His Achievements and His Problems" (New York: Institute of International Education, 1961); Edward C. Cieslak, "The Foreign Student in American Colleges" (Detroit: Wayne University Press, 1955); Martena T. Sasnett, editor, "A Guide to the Admission and Placement of Foreign Students" (New York: Institute of International Education, 1962); Cora DuBois, "Foreign Students and Higher Education in the United States" (Washington: American Council on Education, 1956); Richard D. Lambert and Marvin Bressler, "Indian Students on an American Campus" (Minneapolis: University of Minnesota Press, 1961); S. Alvarez Catola, "Universidad Española: Información para extranjeros," second edition (Madrid: Ministerio de Educación Nacional, 1949); R. Giannarelli and F. Leonardi, "L'istruzione universitaria e pre-universitaria in Italia e all'estero" (Florence: Felice Le Monnier, 1949); and Thomas E. Cotner, "International Educational Exchange: A Selected Bibliography," Bulletin 1961, No. 12, U.S. Office of Education (Washington: U.S. Government Printing Office, 1961).

lished specifically to serve students from several nations. Thus, while Columbia University or the University of London may be considered an international university because of its large numbers of foreign students and for other reasons, it is basically a school for persons of the country in which the institution is located. On the other hand, the Collège d'Europe, founded in 1950 in Bruges, Belgium, by the Council of Europe, is a school designed for the training of students from many European countries for international service.

At the beginning of the 1862-1962 period, an international institution, the American University of Beirut, was established modestly (1863) and it ultimately became a center for higher studies in the Mediterranean area. It was also the first of other schools along similar lines which were opened in Turkey, Egypt, and elsewhere in the Middle East.

It is pertinent to call attention to an interesting experimental period in international education during the decade of the 1860's. International secondary schools were organized at Chatou, near Paris, and at Bad Godesberg, near Bonn, but these were probably discontinued when the Franco-Prussian War began. However, the International College at Spring Grove, England, lasted from 1866 to 1889. This school, which, like all European secondary institutions, conducted its higher classes on a level that would be considered higher education in the U. S. and several other countries, was founded under the inspiration of Richard Cobden, chairman of the International Education Society, Thomas H. Huxley, John Tyndall, and other intellectuals. The idea for an international school originally came from a committee set up by the commissioners of the Paris Universal Exposition to conduct an essay contest on the advantages of a school for pupils of various national origins. The curricular emphasis in the International College was on the sciences and the foreign languages, with the pupils learning Latin, Greek, French, German, and Italian. During the early 1870's, the student body comprised a variety of nationalities —French, German, Spanish, Portuguese, Indian, North American, Brazilian, Chilean, Nicaraguan, and Bermudan.[55] In 1879, the College premises were sold to the Borough Road Training College "and all trace of this fascinating international venture is lost."[56]

Only a few of the various types of international higher institutions can be mentioned within the confines of this chapter. The University of Geneva began the first summer courses for foreign students in 1892, a practice which has been adopted in later years by other universities abroad. An international university was planned for Brussels in 1920, but nothing permanent resulted. In 1921, Peter Manniche, a Danish educator, and other internationally-minded persons founded the International People's College at Elsinore, Denmark, where more than 5,000 students attended the regular courses and over 10,000 attended the short courses during the vacation periods. Based on the principles of Bishop Nikolaus F. S. Grundtvig and those of the Danish Folk High School movement fathered by him, this school makes use of Danish and "the main foreign languages" (English, German, French) in its instructional program. The aim of

---

[55] Cyril Bibby, "T. H. Huxley: Scientist, Humanist and Educator" (New York: Horizon Press, 1960), pp. 168-172.
[56] *Ibid.*, p. 72.

this well-known institution is "to promote personal development in the students and to further international understanding and co-operation."[57] Although many of the courses are of a higher educational level, the college is open to young men and women over 18 without any special entrance requirements.

Without going into detail, one might call attention to, among others, the Visva-Bharati ("Universal Culture") University, founded in 1921 at Santiniketan ("Abode of Peace") in India by Rabindranath Tagore; the Italian University for Foreigners in Perugia (1925); the Institut Universitaire de Hautes Etudes (1927); Collège d'Europe, Bruges (1950); and the Collège de l'Europe Libre, Strasbourg (1951).

It also might be of interest to make brief reference to international religious higher institutions. The Jewish tradition of international migration to study theology and other advanced studies goes back to the ancient and the medieval world. The higher academy of Jewish learning (Yeshivah) in East European countries was a center of study for students from many nations. The Yeshivah of Mir, Lithuania, for example, in the present century taught young men from Germany, England, South Africa, the U. S., and other countries.[58] This institution migrated, during World War II, to Japan, China, and eventually New York City. Other Lithuanian Yeshi-

---

[57] "The International People's College, Elsinore, Denmark: Programme" (Elsinore: The College, n.d.), [p.1].

[58] J. D. Epstein, "Yeshivat Mir," in Samuel K. Mirsky, "Mosdot Torah b'Europa B'binyanam uv'churbanam" (New York: Ogen, 1956), p. 107. This Hebrew volume treats the destruction, during World War II, of higher Jewish academies in Europe.

[59] E. Oshry, "Yeshivat Knesset Yisrael d'Slavodka", in Mirsky, op. cit., p. 160; M. Figter, "Yeshivat Telz," in Mirsky, op. cit., pp. 172-173, 177.

vahs with cosmopolitan student bodies were located in Slavodka and Telz (Telshe), with the latter transplanted after the war to Cleveland.[59]

Another important international religious institution is the University of Al-Azhar, whch has served since its founding in 972 as Islam's international center of theological studies. During the present century, Al-Azhar has offered instruction to students from virtually all parts of Africa, the Middle East, the Far East, Southeast Asia, and East Europe.[60]

Of special significance is the new international university, announced by Premier Nikita S. Khrushchev in an address in February, 1960, at Gadjah Mada University, Djojakarta, Indonesia, and actually opened on Oct. 1, 1960, in Moscow as the University of the Friendship of Peoples. Now known as the Patrice Lumumba University of the Friendship of Peoples (Universitet Druzhbi Narodov imeni Patrisa Lumumbi), this institution was designed mainly for students from Asia, Africa, and Latin America. In February, 1961, the university's enrollment consisted of 597 students, of whom 59 were Soviet nationals. The course of study comprises engineering, agriculture, medicine, and the social sciences. Special attention is given to the Russian language, but Soviet students may study English, French, or Spanish. The foreigners are not offered the courses which are required in all Soviet higher institutions—Dialectical and Historical Materialism, Political Economy, and History of the Com-

[60] Bayard Dodge, "Al-Azhar: A Millenium of Muslim Learning" (Washington: Middle East Institute, 1961), p. 165; Roderick D. Matthews and Matta Akrawi, "Education in the Arab Countries of the Middle East" (Washington: American Council on Education, 1949), pp. 103-104.

munist Party of the Soviet Union.[61] It is expected that Lumumba University, which has become the object of bitter criticism by foreign students, will have an enrollment of 3,000-4,000 by 1965.[62] Interestingly, in November, 1961, the Czechoslovak government apparently followed the Soviet example by opening in Prague the University of November 17 for students from Asia, Africa, and Latin America. The name of the new university commemorates the execution, on Nov. 17, 1939, by the Nazi occupational power of nine Czechoslovak student leaders, the closing of all higher institutions, and the deportation of students and professors to concentration camps.[63]

Finally, it is worthy of note that a new project in international higher education was recommended at a conference in April, 1960, held in Bruges under the co-sponsorship of the Collège d'Europe and the Bureau Universitaire du Mouvement Européen. The final report of the conference called for the creation of a University of Europe in which instruction would be Europeanized and all teaching and research would be carried on in complete freedom—"La liberté de la recherche et de l'enseignement en face de tout pouvoir politique, national ou supranational."[64] There also has been some talk of international universities of regional scope, such as a University of the Americas. It remains to be seen to what extent action will follow the words.

[61] Seymour M. Rosen, "The People's Friendship University in the U.S.S.R." (Washington: U. S. Office of Education, 1962), pp. 4, 7, 9.

[62] David Burg, " 'The People's Friendship University,' " *Problems of Communism,* Vol. 10, November-December, 1961, p. 50.

[63] *Youth and Freedom,* Vol. 4, No. 3-4 [1961], pp. 10, 40.

[64] Collège d'Europe, "Université Européene" (Leyden: Sythoff, 1960), p. 37.

OTHER FORMS OF INTERNATIONAL HIGHER EDUCATION

The exchange of professors has been of smaller scope than that of student exchange. Universities and governments have been involved all through the present century in making arrangements for faculty personnel to lecture in each other's universities. Harvard and Paris exchanged professors as far back as 1898, while the Theodore Roosevelt and Kaiser Wilhelm Professorships brought Berlin and Columbia (1904-14) close together.[65] Since World War II, the exchange of professors has become more widespread than ever, with universities often commissioning their personnel not only as lecturers, but also as advisers in technical and educational fields.[66] The U. S. government has promoted professional interchange through the Fulbright (1946) and Smith-Mundt (1948) Acts, the International Cooperation Administration, and currently the Agency for International Development.

Political upheavals and international crises often bring about faculty interchange. The academic refugee has become a familiar fact in the 20th century. Fortunately, displaced scholars have been enabled to relocate themselves in foreign countries and to contribute to the intellectual advancement of their new homelands and the world at large. The educational emigrés from Nazi Germany, for example, continued their work in many countries in Europe, Asia,

---

[65] Guy S. Métraux, "Exchange of Persons: The Evolution of Cross-Cultural Education" (New York: Social Science Research Council, 1952), p. 7 (note).

[66] For the historical background, see Merle Curti and Kendall Birr, "Prelude to Point Four: American Technical Assistance Overseas, 1838-1938" (Madison: University of Wisconsin Press, 1954).

Africa, North and South America, and Australia.[67] The professors from Hungary and other turbulent countries of recent date have found a hearty welcome in the universities of other nations.

Had space been plentiful, one could have discussed at some length the historical development and current status of the study of international relations and culture in universities;[68] such organizations as the International Association of Professors and Lecturers (1948);[69] the international Association of Universities (1950);[70] the work in international higher education accomplished by the Committee on Intellectual Cooperation of the League of Nations, the International Institute of Intellectual Cooperation, and Unesco; the many international learned societies and journals; the miscellaneous inter-university organizations;[71] the international student houses, such as La Cité Universitaire in Paris (1921) and International House in New York City (1923); and student organizations, such as Corda Fratres (1895), the Liga de Estudiantes Americanos (1908), the International Conference

[67] Edward Y. Hartshorne, Jr., "The German Universities and National Socialism" (London: George Allen & Unwin, 1937), pp. 96-97. See also Stephen Duggan and Betty Drury, "The Rescue of Science and Learning" (New York: Macmillan, 1948), and Norman Bentwich, "The Rescue and Achievement of Refugee Scholars: The Story of the Displaced Scholars and Scientists, 1933-1952" (The Hague: Nijhoff, 1953).

[68] Sigmund Skard, "American Studies in Europe," 2 vols. (Philadelphia: University of Pennsylvania Press, 1958).

[69] R. Douglas Laurie, "International Association of University Professors and Lecturers," School and Society, Vol. 69, March 26, 1949, pp. 217-220.

[70] "Report of the International Conference of Universities" (Paris: International Universities Bureau, 1951).

[71] "Organisations Interuniverstaires" (Paris: Association Internationale des Universités, 1954).

of Students (1919), and Pax Romana (1921). New ideas and new forms of international cooperation in higher education—the U. S. Peace Corps, for example—are familiar occurrences. The literature is vastly growing week by week and it is becoming rather difficult to keep up with it. There is a fruitful field for many studies in the historical and contemporary areas of international higher education. Some topics are particularly intriguing, as, for instance, the impact of American professors on scholarly learning and on education in various countries.[72]

CONCLUSION

A recent commentator has expressed the judgment that "in historical perspective the expansion of America's overseas commitments since 1940 has been vast and breathtaking."[73] This has been apparent in many ways through the activities of the universities. However, it is good to be aware of the fact that there have been overseas educational commitments on the part of many other nations and in the centuries gone by. The history of international relations in higher education is 2,000 years old at least. Some of its development has been dramatic, even "breathtaking," but as a rule it went on slowly, methodically, patiently. Much of the history still remains to be written and interpreted.

This chapter has concentrated on the past century of international relations among the universities of the world. During this time,

---

[72] Richard H. Heindel, editor, "American Influences Abroad: An Exploration" (New York: Carnegie Endowment for International Peace, 1950).

[73] Milton J. Esman, "Needed: An Education and Research Base to Support America's Expanded Commitments Overseas" (Pittsburgh: University of Pittsburgh Press, 1961), p. 1.

scholars of one nation began to know the persons, the philosophies, and the publications of the scholars of other nations in different parts of the globe. As time went on, the media of communication and the means of transportation became faster and better, thus expanding the learned man's knowledge and understanding. No longer is the wandering student the rare exception in the world of today; it is possible that the home-bound student will become a rarity in due time.

The shrinking of the intellectual's geographic world brings with it many opportunities—but also responsibilities. For one thing, he must develop a more open mind with regard to learning from foreign persons and to co-operating with them. This means that the scholar and the student must become facile in the reading of several languages and in the speaking of some. It will become increasingly difficult in the decades ahead to maintain a scholarly status on the basis of a monolingual mind.

The study of international higher educational history demonstrates that all types of nations—autocratic or democratic—take part in the dissemination of ideas across national frontiers. One might also learn that it is possible to obtain something of educational value from direct contacts with the newer, developing nations. Furthermore, it becomes clear that international educational relations, however good and effective, do not, by themselves, necessarily bring about peace.

[74] "Formal Programmes of International Co-operation between University Institutions: Report of an International Committee of Experts" (Paris: Unesco, 1960), p. 39.

[75] Report of the Committee on the University and World Affairs, "The University and World Affairs" (New York: Ford Foundation, 1960), p. 46.

Most persons will agree that "international co-operation is of the essence of the university"[74] and that "universities have a major role to play in world affairs."[75] Much has been accomplished; more remains to be done, especially in conjunction with other public and private agencies. It is not seemly for a university to overstress the narrow training of practical functionaries for international service, but it should concentrate rather on the promotion of "economic needs, cultural values, political policies, scientific and scholarly knowledge, and moral wisdom"[76] in an international society. When an over-all evaluation is made of the contribution of the university to world welfare,[77] proper account should be taken of what the university has achieved in the realm of its greatest competence—the creation and advancement of knowledge toward a better understanding of man in his world and toward a more effective co-operation for a world at peace.

[76] Richard McKeon, "Universities in the Modern World," in Charles Frankel, editor, "Issues in University Education" (New York: Harper, 1959), p. 23.
[77] *Cf.*, Edward W. Weidner, "The World Role of Universities" (New York: McGraw-Hill, 1962), p. 10.

Appendix

Chronology of Higher Education in the U.S.A., 1862-1962

*T*HE HISTORICAL EVENTS listed below were compiled from the general and specialized histories of higher education in the U. S., such as those by John S. Brubacher and Willis Rudy, George P. Schmidt, R. Freeman Butts, Richard Hofstadter and Wilson Smith, and Charles F. Thwing; histories of various colleges and universities; miscellaneous works on higher education and educational history; and original documents, such as laws. No claim is made to completeness; there are gaps, particularly in the area of professional education. As far as the dates for the individual institutions are concerned, the writer has tried to give the year when actual instruction or other active work peculiar to a college or university was started. This has not always been easy to determine, and in some instances the charter date or official date of founding had to be used.

BEFORE THE MORRILL ACT OF 1862

The idea of governmental land grants to higher education goes back to the Northwest Ordinance of 1787, under the terms of which the Congress of the Confederation passed on July 23 an act authorizing the sale of 1,500,000 acres along the Ohio River to the Ohio Company of Associates through the agency of the Rev. Manasseh Cutler. This act specified: "Not more than two complete townships to be given perpetually for the purpose of a university. . . ." In 1832, Congress gave land grants to Columbian College (now George Washington University) in Washington, D. C., a Baptist institution, and in the following year it gave such grants to a Catholic institution in the city, Georgetown College (now Georgetown University).

The principle of governmental land grants began to assume the nature of a movement in the 1850's. As early as May 13, 1850, Jonathan Baldwin Turner (1805-1899), former teacher of Latin and Greek ("Professor of Rhetoric and Belles Lettres") at Illinois College, presented in his presidential address to the Illinois Teachers Institute "A Plan for a State University for the Industrial Classes." In this and subsequent statements, Turner proposed the use of income from Federal land sales for a "University for the Industrial Classes in each of the States," where "no species of knowledge should be excluded, practical or theoretical. . . ." Further, "There should be connected with such an institution, in this State, a sufficient quantity of land, of variable soil and aspect, for all its needful annual experiments and processes in the great interests of agriculture and horticulture." The ideas of Turner fell on fertile ground, and eventually, on Feb. 8, 1853, the Illinois General Assembly adopted unanimously a resolution which called upon the U. S. senators and representatives from the state to get Congress to pass a law giving each state "an amount of public lands not less in value than *five hundred thousand dollars,* for the liberal endowment of a system of industrial universities . . . for the more liberal and practical education adapted to the manifold want of a practical and enterprising people. . . . " Significantly, this wording was identical with that of the text of a memorial written in January, 1853, by Turner at the request of the Fourth Industrial Convention of the State of Illinois and signed by Bronson Murray, president of the convention.*

There were two other outstanding pioneers in the land-grant movement. Thomas Green Clemson (1809-88), Superintendent of Agricultural Affairs during President James Buchanan's final year and founder of the Clemson Agricultural College, labored for the land-grant idea in higher education in the South. The best-known of the trio, of course, was U. S. Sen. Justin Smith Morrill (1810-98), the legislator who succeeded in getting Congress to pass two bills to aid higher education in 1862 and 1890. The first Congressional speech for a land-grant law made by Morrill, then a member of the House of Representatives, was on April 20, 1858, after he had introduced a bill on Dec. 14, 1857. The House passed his bill (H. R. 2) on April 22, 1858, and the Senate approved it on Feb. 7, 1859, both by narrow margins, 105-100 and 25-22, respectively. President Buchanan vetoed the bill on

* Based largely on Mary Turner Carriel, "The Life of Jonathan Baldwin Turner" (Urbana: University of Illinois Press, 1961).

Feb. 24, 1859, citing six objections: the government's financial difficulties, the danger to states' rights, potential injury to new states, skepticism as to the advancement of agriculture and the mechanic arts, injurious interference with existing colleges, and unconstitutionality. However, conditions changed with the onset of the Civil War. Morrill introduced a revised bill (H. R. 138) on Dec. 16, 1961, which overcame some opposition and was passed by a vote of 91 to 25 on June 17, 1862. In the Senate, Sen. Benjamin Franklin Wade of Ohio, also a Republican, introduced a land-grant bill (S. 298) on May 2, 1862, which required less time for passage. On June 11, 1862, the Senate adopted Wade's bill with several amendments by a similarly overwhelming vote of 32 to 7.

THE MORRILL ACT AND LATER

1862 (July 2)—President Abraham Lincoln signed "An Act donating public lands to the several states and territories which may provide colleges for the benefit of agriculture and the mechanic arts." The law granted to the states 30,000 acres for each senator and representative, with the income from the sale of these lands to be applied "to the endowment, support, and maintenance of at least one college where the leading object shall be, without excluding other scientific and classical studies, and including military tactics, to teach such branches of learning as are related to agriculture and the mechanic arts, in such manner as the legislatures of the States may respectively prescribe, in order to promote the liberal and practical education of the industrial classes in the several pursuits and professions in life."

1864-88—Frederick A. P. Barnard, president, Columbia College.

1865—Atlanta University. Vassar Female College. Beginning of instruction at Massachusetts Institute of Technology (chartered in 1861).

1867—Howard University.

1868—University of California.

1868-88—James McCosh, president, College of New Jersey, Princeton.

1868-85—Andrew Dickson White, president, Cornell University.

1869—Establishment by Cornell University of the first university press in the U. S.

1869-1909—Charles William Eliot, president, Harvard University. In his inaugural address, Eliot supported "variety, not uniformity, of intellectual product" and "the system of elective studies."

1870—Department of Higher Education, National Teachers' Association (now National Education Association).

1870—University of Cincinnati (formerly Cincinnati College, 1819).

1871-1909—James Burrill Angell, president, University of Michigan.

1872—Establishment of graduate department at Harvard University.

1875—Wellesley College. Hebrew Union College.

1876—Founding of the first real American university, Johns Hopkins University. Daniel Coit Gilman, president, 1876-1901.

1877—Formation of the intercollegiate Young Men's Christian Association.

1878—Ohio State University.

1881—University of Texas.

1882-1910—Elective system, Harvard University.

1885—New England Association of Colleges and Preparatory Schools (secondary schools).

1885—Illinois Industrial University (University of Illinois). Graduate study, Bryn Mawr College.

1886—Etz Chaim Yeshiva, forerunner of Rabbi Isaac Elchanan Theological Seminary (1896) and Yeshiva University (1945)—first Orthodox Jewish theological institution in the U. S.

1887—College Association of Pennsylvania (Middle States Association of Colleges and Secondary Schools).

1887—Hatch Experiment Station Act passed by Congress. Under this law, the Federal government furnished annual appropriations of $15,000 to the states for the establishment of agricultural experiment stations at the land-grant institutions "to aid in acquiring and diffusing among the people of the United States useful and practical information on subjects connected with agriculture and to promote scientific investigation and experiment respecting the principles and applications of agricultural sciences."

1887—Jewish Theological Seminary of America.

1887—Yale College becomes Yale University.

1887—Association of American Agricultural Colleges and Experiment Stations (American Association of Land-Grant Colleges and State Universities, 1920).

1889—Catholic University of America.

1889—Clark University. G. Stanley Hall, president, 1889-1920.

1890—American Society for the Extension of University Teaching.

1890—Association of American Medical Colleges.

1890—The Second Morrill Land-Grant Act, passed by Congress, appropriated funds derived from the sale of public lands to the states and territories "for the more complete endowment and maintenance of colleges for the benefit of agriculture and the mechanic arts" which were established or will be established under the Morrill Act of 1862. The initial annual sum of $15,000 to each state or territory would rise by annual increments for 10 years to $25,000. The Act provided that no money was to be given to "a college where a distinction of race or color is made in the admission of students, but the establishment and maintenance of such colleges separately for white and colored students shall be held to be a compliance with the provisions of this act if the funds received in such State or Territory be equitably divided as hereinafter set forth. . . . "

1891—Stanford University.

1893—Johns Hopkins University School of Medicine.

1893—Founding of the first Newman Club for Catholic students, University of Pennsylvania.

1893—Society for the Promotion of Engineering Education.

1895—North Central Association of Colleges and Secondary Schools. Association of Colleges and Preparatory Schools of the Southern States (Southern Association of Colleges and Secondary Schools).

1896—The College of New Jersey (1746) becomes Princeton University.

1900—Association of American Universities. Association of American Law Schools. College Entrance Examination Board.

1901—Joliet (Ill.) Junior College, the first permanent junior college.

1902-10—Woodrow Wilson, president, Princeton University.

1902-45—Nicholas Murray Butler, president, Columbia University.

1903—General Education Board founded by John D. Rockefeller to support higher education for Negroes.

1903-18—Charles R. Van Hise, president, University of Wisconsin.

1905—Carnegie Foundation for the Advancement of Teaching.

1907—Nelson Amendment to the Morrill Acts of 1862 and 1890 added $5,000 a year for five years beginning in 1908 to the previous funds for the land-grant institutions.

1908—In *Berea College v. Commonwealth of Kentucky* (211 U.S. 45), the U.S. Supreme Court, by upholding the Kentucky school segregation law of 1904, directed Berea College to become segregated.

1910—Abraham Flexner's epoch-making and influential report, "Medical Education in the United States and Canada."

1912—Columbia College (1784), formerly King's College (1754), becomes Columbia University.

1914—The Smith-Lever Act passed by Congress authorized land-grant institutions to offer extension work in communities away from the campus "to aid in diffusing among the people of the United States useful and practical information on subjects relating to agriculture and home economics and to encourage application of the same. . . . "

1914—Association of American Colleges.

1915—American Association of University Professors.

1916—American Association of Collegiate Schools of Business.

1917—Northwest Association of Secondary and Higher Schools.

1918—Thorstein Veblen, "The Higher Learning in America."

1918—American Council on Education.

1919—Institute of International Education. American Council of Learned Societies.

1920—University of Hawaii (formerly College of Agriculture and Mechanic Arts).

1923—Social Science Research Council.

1923—Upton Sinclair, "The Goose-Step."

1923—Hillel Foundations for the counselling of Jewish students.

1924—Southern California Association of Colleges and Universities (Western College Association).

1929—Howard J. Savage's "American College Athletics," a report under the auspices of the Carnegie Foundation, called for the de-emphasis of the "material benefits" of college athletics.

1929-51—Robert Maynard Hutchins, president and chancellor (after 1945) of University of Chicago.

1930—Abraham Flexner's widely discussed critique of American higher education—"Universities: American, English, German."

1932—Engineers' Council for Professional Development.

1933-53—James Bryant Conant, president, Harvard University.

1934—Congress established the National Youth Administration to enable college students to earn money by performing educationally useful tasks and to continue their studies.

1935—University of Alaska (Alaska Agricultural College and School of Mines, 1922).

1935—Congress passed the Bankhead-Jones Act, which added to the annual appropriations for the land-grant colleges and universities and which provided for agricultural research and co-operative agricultural extension work.

1936—Robert Maynard Hutchins, "The Higher Learning in America."

1936—American Association of Theological Schools, a Protestant organization.

1936—The Court of Appeals of Maryland (*Pearson v. Murray*, 169 Md. 478) ordered that a qualified Negro student must be admitted to the University of Maryland Law School, thus breaking the solid front of public educational segregation in the South.

1938—William S. Learned and Ben D. Wood's report for the Carnegie Foundation, "The Student and His Knowledge."

1944—The Servicemen's Readjustment Act (G. I. Bill of Rights), Public Law 346, 78th Congress, provided for the higher education of veterans.

1945—Report of the Harvard Committee, "General Education in a Free Society."

1946—Congress passed the Fulbright Act (Public Law 584, 79th Congress) to enable Americans to study and teach abroad.

1946—Air University, Maxwell Air Force Base, Ala.

1947—Accrediting Association of Bible Institutes and Bible Colleges.

1947-48—Report of the President's Commission on Higher Education, "Higher Education for American Democracy."

1948—State University of New York.

1948—National Association of Foreign Student Advisers. American Association of Colleges for Teacher Education.

1948—The U. S. Information and Educational Exchange Act (Smith-Mundt Act) provided for the international exchange of teachers, students, lecturers, and other specialists.

1949—Mrs. Ada Lois Fisher, a Negro, was admitted to the University of Oklahoma Law School after a successful appeal to the U. S. Supreme Court (*Sipuel v. Board of Regents of University of Oklahoma,* 332 U. S. 631, 1948).

1950—Point Four Program of the U. S. government enacted by Congress (Foreign Economic Assistance Act, Public Law 535, 81st Congress). Subsequently called the International Cooperation Administration. In 1961, it was renamed Agency for International Development.

1950—Congress created the National Science Foundation to improve science and engineering through institutes for college and other teachers.

1952—Veterans' Readjustment Assistance Act (Korean G. I. Bill of Rights), Public Law 550, 82nd Congress.

1952—National Council for Accreditation of Teacher Education.

1956—Council for the Advancement of Small Colleges.

1958—National Defense Education Act provided college student loans, graduate fellowships, and aid for improvement of teaching science, mathematics, and modern foreign languages.

1961—City University of New York.

1961—Report of the U. S. Commission on Civil Rights, "Equal Protection of the Laws in Public Higher Education: 1960." The first recommendation was that Federal funds should be "disbursed only to such publicly controlled institutions of higher education as do not discriminate on grounds of race, color, religion, or national origin."

1962—U. S. Supreme Court dismissed an appeal by two professors of the University of Washington for a review of a Washington State Supreme Court decision which upheld a state law requiring state employees to declare under oath that they were not members of the Communist Party or other subversive group.

Chronology of Higher Education Outside the U.S.A., 1862-1962

WILLIAM W. BRICKMAN

*T*HIS LISTING of events attempts to include the major developments in higher education abroad during the past century. Although not all new institutions were recorded, an effort was made to mention at least one from each country that founded a university during this period. The items were derived from the "International Handbook of Universities," the "Commonwealth Universities Yearbook," "The World of Learning," and the still unsuperseded "Universities of the World outside U.S.A." (1959), edited by M. M. Chambers; monographs such as W. H. G. Armytage's "Civic Universities"; histories of individual universities; histories of education in various countries; and miscellaneous works in several languages on higher education.

1863—University Statute in Russia restored autonomy to the universities, thus bringing about a revival of all institutions and an increase in enrollment. However, women were forbidden to attend, thus forcing many to enroll in foreign universities, particularly at the University of Zürich.

1864—University of Bucharest. University of Odessa.

1866—University of Ottawa, Canada. In 1889, it acquired the status of a Catholic university.

1867—John Stuart Mill defended classical studies in his "Inaugural Address Delivered to the University of St. Andrews, Feb. 1, 1867."

1868—Thomas H. Huxley's inaugural at the University of Aberdeen.

1868—Matthew Arnold, "Higher Schools and Universities in Germany."

1868—Mark Pattison, "Suggestions on Academical Organisation with Especial Reference to Oxford."

1869—Girton College for Women, Oxford.

1870—University of New Zealand, Wellington.

1871—University Tests Act, England, abolishes religious tests for all non-theological degrees at Oxford, Cambridge, and the University of Durham.

1873—Beginnings of extension teaching at Cambridge University.

1873—University of Geneva (founded as Academy in 1559). University of the Cape of Good Hope (now University of South Africa).

1874—New Zealand University Act made an examining body out of the University of New Zealand.

1876—University of Adelaide, Australia.

1877—Imperial University, Tokyo. University of Manitoba, Winnipeg.

1880—Free University of Amsterdam.

1880—Chartering of Victoria University, Manchester, a federation of colleges: Owens College (1851), later University of Manchester (1903); University College (1881), later University of Liverpool (1903); Yorkshire College of Science (1874), later University of Leeds (1904).

1882—University of the Punjab, Lahore (now Pakistan).

1884—University Statute, Russia, deprived faculties of the right to elect the rector and staff.

1887—University of Allahabad, India. University of Göteborg, Sweden.

1889—Creation in England of Committee on Grants to University Colleges (forerunner of University Grants Committee) with an initial fund of £15,000.

1889—University of Fribourg, Switzerland.

1893—University of Wales, comprising University Colleges of Aberystwyth (1872), Bangor (1884), and Swansea (1920).

1895—World's Student Christian Federation.

1896—University of Constantinople (Istanbul).

1896—Re-establishment of 15 universities which had been discontinued during the French Revolution.

1897—Universidad Nacional de La Plata, La Plata, Argentina. Kyoto Imperial University, Japan.

1897—National Peking University, China (see 1952—University of Peking).

1903—Attachment of the Ecole Normale Supérieure to the University of Paris.

1904—Universities Act in India strengthened control by the government over the universities and control by the universities over the colleges.

1906—University of Belgrade.

1907—Imperial College of Science and Technology, London.

1908—University of the Philippines. University of British Columbia.

1909—University of Neuchâtel, Switzerland.

1911—University of Lisbon. The medieval University of Lisbon, which was founded in 1299, was transferred permanently to the University of Coimbra.

1912—Association of Universities of the British Commonwealth.

1914—University of Debrecen, Hungary. University of Frankfurt am Main, Germany.

1915—University of Warsaw, Poland. University of Murcia, Spain.

1917—Chulalongkorn University, Bangkok, Thailand. National University of Indo-China, Hanoi (now North Viet-Nam).

1918—Irkutsk State University, U.S.S.R. University of Cape Town, South Africa.

1919—Abolition of academic degrees at Russian universities. Appointment of "Red Professors," faithful Communists who lacked university degrees.

1919—American University at Cairo, Egypt. Masaryk University, Brno, Czechoslovakia. Azerbaijan State University, Baku, U.S.S.R. University of Hamburg. University of Montreal.

1919—Creation of University Grants Committee to furnish financial aid to universities in England, Wales, and Scotland.

1919—Association of University Teachers of the United Kingdom.

1920—University of Rangoon, Burma. American University of Beirut, Lebanon (originally Syrian Protestant College, 1866). University of Brazil, Rio de Janeiro.

1921—University of the Witwatersrand, Johannesburg, South Africa.

1922—Rabindranath Tagore founded the University of Visva-Bharati, Santiniketan, Bengal, India, as an international institution.

1923—University of Milan, Italy.

1923—Addition of Oxford and Cambridge to the institutions receiving funds from the University Grants Committee.

1925—Hebrew University, Jerusalem (now Israel). University of Cairo, Egypt.

1929—National Autonomous University of Mexico, Mexico City (previous founding dates: 1553, 1910).

1930—José Ortega y Gasset, "Misión de la Universidad: Sobre reforma Universitaria," Madrid.

1933—Uzbek State University, Samarkand, Uzbekistan, U.S.S.R. University of Aarhus, Denmark.

1934—University of Tehran, Iran. University of São Paulo, Brazil.

1942—Mongolian State University, Ulan Bator, Outer Mongolia. University of Ceylon, Colombo.

1943—"Redbrick University," by "Bruce Truscot" (Prof. E. Allison Peers, University of Liverpool), an influential book which stressed the university's functions of research and teaching.

1944—Marie Curie Sklodowska University of Lublin, Poland.

1944—International Association of University Professors and Lecturers.

1945—Reorganization of Taihoku Imperial University (founded by the Japanese in 1928) as National Taiwan University, Taipei.

1946—University of Ankara, Turkey. Seoul National University, Korea. Australian National University, Camberra. University of Kabul, Afghanistan.

1948—University of Bergen, Norway. University of the Saar, Saarbrücken, Germany. Free University of Berlin, West Berlin.

1948—End of the privilege of representation in the House of Commons by Oxford and Cambridge (since 1603) and by other universities.

1949—Sir Walter Moberly, "The Crisis in the University."

1949—Renaming of Friedrich-Wilhelms-Universität (founded in 1809) as Humboldt University, East Berlin.

1949—University of Gadjah Mada, Djojakarta, Indonesia. University of Malaya, Singapore.

1950—University of Indonesia, Djakarta.

1950—Founding of the International Association of Universities with a permanent secretariat, the International Universities Bureau, Paris.

1951—University of Liberia, Monrovia.

1952—Establishment of the University of Peking, comprising the National Peking University (1898), Yenching University (1919), and Tsinghun University (1928).

1953—International Christian University, Tokyo.

1955—University of Exeter, England.

1956—University of Khartoum, Sudan. University of Baghdad, Iraq. University of Viet-Nam, Hanoi, North Viet-Nam.

1956—Lovanium (1947), Leopoldville, Congo, recognized as university by royal Belgian decree.

1957—University of Dakar, Senegal. University of Rabat, Morocco.

1958—Atatürk University, Erzurum, Turkey, opened on the model of the land-grant university in the U.S., with emphasis on agriculture and engineering.

1960—University of Friendship of the Peoples (Patrice Lumumba University), Moscow, for students from Africa, Asia, and South America.

1961—University of Sussex, Brighton, England. University of Addis Ababa, Ethiopia.

1961—University reform program by Korean Ministry of Education abolished 12 private institutions which did not qualify for government charters.

1961—University of November 17th, Prague, for foreign students. The name was derived from the date, Nov. 17, 1939, when the Nazis executed nine Czechoslovakian student leaders, closed all higher educational institutions in Czechoslovakia, and sent thousands of professors and students to concentration camps.

1962—University of Keele (formerly University College of North Staffordshire).

A Bibliographical Introduction to History of U.S. Higher Education

WILLIAM W. BRICKMAN

*I*N RECENT YEARS, there seems to have been a rise of interest in the professional study of higher education. This is evident from the establishment of centers for higher education at Teachers College of Columbia University, the University of Michigan, University of California at Berkeley, and Michigan State University. Courses and departments in higher education had been established previously, too, at such institutions as Stanford University and New York University.

The study and teaching of the history of higher education in the U. S. has been going on for some time. One thinks of the writing and teaching by historians in the liberal arts colleges and graduate schools as well as in schools of education—writing and teaching by such men as Donald G. Tewksbury, Richard Hofstadter, John S. Brubacher, George P. Schmidt, R. Freeman

Butts, W. H. Cowley, Frederick Rudolph, Willis Rudy, Saul Sack, Richard J. Storr, and others. For over a decade, the present writer has conducted at New York University a full-year graduate course on the history of higher education in the U. S. In connection with this course, which was attended by college and university professors and administrators, he has developed a classified, representative listing of published sources and other materials to aid the students in organizing their readings and in getting their specialized research projects under way.

The bibliography is by no means complete. Suggestions and criticisms are welcome for future revisions and expansions. Research workers and students may find this introduction useful as a basis for a more thorough type of study than is possible by reading even the best of textbooks.

A similar bibliography should be prepared on the history of higher education in Europe and other areas of the world. One of the attempts along these lines has been made by the writer in his article, "Colleges and Universities—Development," in the third edition of "Encyclopedia of Educational Research," edited by Chester W. Harris (New York: Macmillan, 1960), pp. 226-243. The references in that article were to volumes in 10 foreign languages.

General Histories of U. S. Higher Education

Brubacher, John S., and Willis Rudy. "Higher Education in Transition: An American History: 1636-1956." New York: Harper, 1958.

Butts, R. Freeman. "The College Charts Its Course: Historical Conceptions and Current Proposals." New York: McGraw-Hill, 1939.

Cowley, W. H. "The University in the United States of America," pp. 37-112, in Edward Bradby, editor, "The University Outside Europe." London: Oxford University Press, 1939.

Duffus, R. L. "Democracy Enters College: A Study of the Rise and Decline of the Academic Lockstep." New York: Scribner, 1936.

Earnest, Ernest. "Academic Procession: An Informal History of the American College, 1636-1953." Indianapolis: Bobbs-Merrill, 1953.

Hofstadter, Richard, and C. DeWitt Hardy. "The Development and Scope of Higher Education in the United States." New York: Columbia University Press, 1952.

Rudolph, Frederick. "The American College and University: A History." New York: Knopf, 1962.

Schmidt, George P. "The Liberal Arts College: A Chapter in American Cultural History." New Brunswick, N. J.: Rutgers University Press, 1957.

Tewksbury, Donald G. "The Founding of American Colleges and Universities Before the Civil War." New York: Bureau of Publications, Teachers College, Columbia University, 1932.

Thwing, Charles F. "A History of Higher Education in America." New York: Appleton, 1906.

Wills, Elbert V. "The Growth of American Higher Education." Philadelphia: Dorrance, 1936.

Histories of Colleges and Universities

Adams, Herbert B. "The College of William and Mary." Circular of Information, No. 1, 1887, U. S. Bureau of Education. Washington: Government Printing Office, 1887.

Ahern, Patrick J. "The Catholic University of America, 1887-1896." Washington, D. C.: Catholic University of America Press, 1949.

Baldwin, Ebenezer. "Annals of Yale College." New Haven: Howe, 1831.

Battle, Kemp P. "History of the University of North Carolina." 2 vols. Raleigh: Edwards and Broughton, 1907.

Bronson, Walter C. "The History of Brown University, 1764-1914." Providence: Brown University, 1914.

Bruce, Philip A. "History of the University of Virginia, 1819-1919." 5 vols. New York: Macmillan, 1920-22.

Cabaniss, James A. "A History of the University of Mississippi." University: University of Mississippi, 1949.

Carmichael, Oliver C., Jr. "New York Establishes a State University." Nashville: Vanderbilt University Press, 1955.

Chaffin, Nora C. "Trinity College, 1839-1892: The Beginnings of Duke University. Durham, N. C.: Duke University Press, 1950.

Chamberlain, J. L., editor. "Universities and Their Sons: Harvard, Yale, Princeton and Columbia." 5 vols. Boston, 1898-1900; "New York University and University of Pennsylvania," 2 vols. Boston: 1901.

Cheyney, Edward P. "History of the University of Pennsylvania, 1740-1940." Philadelphia: University of Pennsylvania Press, 1940.

Chitty, Arthur B., Jr. "Reconstruction of Sewanee." Sewanee, Tenn.: University Press, 1954.

Clap, Thomas. "Annals or History of Yale College (1700-1766)." New Haven: 1766.

Cole, Arthur C. "A Hundred Years of Mount Holyoke College." New Haven: Yale University Press, 1940.

Cordell, E. F. "University of Maryland (1807-1907)." 2 vols. New York: 1907.

Cremin, Lawrence A., David A. Shannon, and Mary E. Townsend. "A History of Teachers College, Columbia University." New York: Columbia University Press, 1954.

Curti, Merle, and Vernon Carstensen. "The University of Wisconsin: A History, 1848-1925." 2 vols. Madison: University of Wisconsin Press, 1949.

Daley, John M. "Georgetown University: Origin and Early Years." Washington: Georgetown University Press, 1957.

Demarest, William H. S. "A History of Rutgers College." New Brunswick, N. J.: Rutgers College, 1924.

Dingeldine, Raymond C., Jr. "Madison College: The First Fifty Years, 1908-1958." Harrisonburg, Va.: Madison College, 1959.

Dunaway, Wayland F. "History of the Pennsylvania State College." State College: Pennsylvania State College, 1946.

Dunigan, David R. "A History of Boston College." Milwaukee: Bruce, 1947.

Easterby, J. H. "A History of the College of Charleston." Charleston, S. C.: 1935.

Edman, Irwin, et al. "A History of Columbia College on Morningside." New York: Columbia University Press, 1954.

Elliott, Orrin L. "Stanford University: The First Twenty-Five Years." Stanford University Press, 1937.

Ellis, John T. "The Formative Years of the Catholic University of America." Washington, D. C.: American Catholic Historical Association, 1946.

Ferrier, W. W. "Origin and Development of the University of California." Berkeley, Calif.: 1930.

Fleming, W. L. "Louisiana State University, 1860-1896." Baton Rouge: Louisiana State University Press, 1936.

Fletcher, Robert S. "A History of Oberlin College From

Its Foundation Through the Civil War." 2 vols. Oberlin, Ohio: Oberlin College, 1943.

French, John C. "A History of the University Founded by Johns Hopkins." Baltimore: Johns Hopkins Press, 1946.

Galpin, W. Freeman. "Syracuse University." 2 vols. Syracuse: Syracuse University Press, 1952-60.

Gates, Charles M. "The First Century at the University of Washington: 1861-1961." Seattle: University of Washington Press, 1961.

Gilbert, Amy M. "ACUNY: The Associated Colleges of Upper New York." Ithaca: Cornell University Press, 1950.

Goodspeed, T. W. "A History of the University of Chicago." Chicago: University of Chicago Press, 1916.

Goebel, Julius, Jr., et al. "A History of the School of Law, Columbia University." New York: Columbia University Press, 1955.

Guild, R. A. "Early History of Brown University, Including the Life, Times, and Correspondence of President Manning, 1756-1791." Providence, R. I.: 1897.

Hawkins, Hugh. "Pioneer: A History of the Johns Hopkins University, 1874-1889." Ithaca: Cornell University Press, 1960.

Hinsdale, B. A. "History of the University of Michigan." Ann Arbor: 1906.

Hollis, Daniel W. "University of South Carolina." 2 vols. Columbia: University of South Carolina Press, 1951-1956.

Hough, Franklin B. "Historical and Statistical Record of the University of the State of New York during the Century from 1784 to 1884." Albany: Weed, Parsons, and Co., 1885.

Jennings, Walter W. "Transylvania: Pioneer University of the West." New York: Pageant, 1955.

Jones, Theodore F., et al. "New York University, 1832-1932." New York: New York University Press, 1933.

Keppel, Frederick P., editor. "History of Columbia University, 1754-1904." New York: Columbia University Press, 1904.

Montgomery, Thomas H. "History of the University of Pennsylvania from Its Foundation to A.D. 1770." Philadelphia: Jacobs, 1900.

Morison, Samuel E. "Harvard College in the Seventeenth Century." 2 vols. Cambridge: Harvard University Press, 1936.

Morison, Samuel E., editor. "The Development of Harvard

University since the Inauguration of President Eliot, 1869-1929." Cambridge: Harvard University Press, 1930.

Morison, Samuel E. "The Founding of Harvard College." Cambridge: Harvard University Press, 1935.

Morison, Samuel E. "Three Centuries of Harvard, 1636-1936." Cambridge: Harvard University Press, 1936.

Oviatt, Edwin. "The Beginnings of Yale (1701-1726)." New Haven: Yale University Press, 1916.

Parks, Joseph H., and Oliver C. Weaver, Jr. "Birmingham-Southern College, 1856-1956." Nashville: Parthenon, 1957.

Peck, Elisabeth S. "Berea's First Century, 1855-1955." Lexington: University of Kentucky Press, 1955.

Pierce, Benjamin. "A History of Harvard University." 2 vols. Cambridge: 1833.

Pierson, George W. "Yale College: An Educational History, 1871-1921." New Haven: Yale University Press, 1952.

Pierson, George W. "Yale: The University College, 1921-1937." New Haven: Yale University Press, 1955.

Plochmann, George K. "The Ordeal of Southern Illinois University." Carbondale: Southern Illinois University Press [1959].

Pollard, James E. "History of the Ohio State University." Columbus: Ohio State University Press, 1952.

Quincy, Josiah. "The History of Harvard University." 2 vols. Cambridge: Owen, 1840.

Richardson, Leon B. "History of Dartmouth College." 2 vols. Hanover, N. H.: Dartmouth College, 1932.

Ross, Earle D. "A History of the Iowa State College of Agriculture and Mechanic Arts." Ames: Iowa State College Press, 1942.

Rudy, S. Willis. "The College of the City of New York: A History, 1847-1947." New York: City College Press, 1949.

Sellers, James B. "History of the University of Alabama: Volume I, 1818-1902." University: University of Alabama Press, 1953.

Stephens, Frank F. "A History of the University of Missouri." Columbia: University of Missouri Press, 1962.

Tyler, W. S. "A History of Amherst College (1821-1891)." New York: 1894.

Viles, Jonas. "The University of Missouri: A Centennial History." Columbia: University of Missouri, 1939.

Waite, Frederick C. "The Story of a Country Medical College." Montpelier: Vermont Historical Society, 1945.

Wertenbaker, Thomas J. "Princeton, 1746-1896." Princeton: Princeton University Press, 1946.

White, Marion C. "History of Barnard College." New York: Columbia University Press, 1954.

Monographs on Specific Aspects of the History of Higher Education

Abbott, Frank C. "Government Policy and Higher Education: A Study of the Regents of the University of the State of New York, 1784-1949." Ithaca: Cornell University Press, 1958.

Adams, Herbert B., editor. "Contributions to American Educational History." U. S. Bureau of Education, Circulars of Information, Nos. 1-36. Washington, D. C.: Government Printing Office, 1887-1903. Monographs on the history of higher education in various states and on the history of individual universities (Alabama, Rhode Island, etc.).

Asgis, Alfred J. "Professional Dentistry in American Society." New York: Clinical Press, 1941.

Bainton, Roland H. "Yale and the Ministry." New York: Harper, 1957.

Becker, Carl L. "Cornell University: Founders and the Founding." Ithaca: Cornell University Press, 1943.

Beesley, Patricia, "The Revival of the Humanities in American Education." New York: Columbia University Press, 1940.

Bevis, Alma D. M. "Diets and Riots." Boston: Marshall, Jones Co., 1936.

Blackmar, Frank W. "History of Federal and State Aid to Higher Education in the United States." U. S. Bureau of Education, Circulation of Information, 1890, No. 1. Washington, D. C.: Government Printing Office, 1890.

Blandin, J. M. E. "History of Higher Education of Women in the South Prior to 1860." New York: 1860.

Boas, Louis S. "Women's Education Begins: The Rise of the Women's Colleges." Norton, Mass.: Wheaton College Press, 1935.

Broome, Edwin C. "A Historical and Critical Discussion of College Admission Requirements." New York: Columbia University, 1902.

Brown, Elmer E. "The Origin of American State Universities." Berkeley: University of California Press, 1903.

Brubacher, John S., et al. "The Development of the Department of Education at Yale University, 1891-1958." New Haven: 1960.

Butler, Vera M. "Education as Revealed by New England

Newspapers Prior to 1850." Ed.D. Thesis, Temple University. Philadelphia: The Author, 1935. (Pp. 3-155.)

Cassidy, Francis P. "Catholic College Foundations in the United States, 1677-1850." Ph.D. Thesis. Washington, D. C.: Catholic University of America, 1924.

Chambers, M. M. "The Colleges and the Courts, 1936-40." New York: Carnegie Foundation for the Advancement of Teaching, 1941.

Chambers, M. M. "The Colleges and the Courts, 1941-1945." New York: Carnegie Foundation for the Advancement of Teaching, 1946.

Chambers, M. M. "The Colleges and the Courts, 1946-50." New York: Columbia University Press, 1952.

Chittenden, R. H. "History of the Sheffield Scientific School of Yale University, 1846-1922." 2 vols. New Haven: Yale University Press, 1928.

Cohen, I. Bernard. "Some Early Tools of American Science." Cambridge: Harvard University Press, 1950.

Cordasco, Francesco. "Daniel Coit Gilman and the Protean Ph.D.: The Shaping of American Graduate Education." Leiden: Brill, 1960.

Coulter, E. Merton. "College Life in the Old South." Second edition. Athens: University of Georgia Press, 1951.

Cowie, Alexander. "Educational Problems at Yale College in the Eighteenth Century." New Haven: Yale University Press, 1936.

Dalton, Van B. "The Genesis of Dental Education in the United States." Cincinnati: The Author, 1946.

Dutcher, George M. "An Historical and Critical Survey of the Curriculum of Wesleyan University and Related Subjects." Middletown, Conn.: Wesleyan University, 1948.

Eckelberry, R. H. "The History of the Municipal University in the United States." U. S. Office of Education, Bulletin 1932, No. 2. Washington, D. C.: U. S. Government Printing Office, 1932.

Eddy, Edward D., Jr. "Colleges for our Land and Time." New York: Harper, 1957.

Eells, Walter C. "Baccalaureate Degrees Conferred by American Colleges in the 17th and 18th Centuries." Circular No. 528, 1958, U. S. Office of Education. Washington, D. C.: U. S. Office of Education, 1958.

Eells, Walter C. "Surveys of American Higher Education." New York: Carnegie Foundation for the Advancement of Teaching, 1937.

Eells, Walter C. "The Junior College." Boston: Houghton Mifflin, 1931.

Elliott, Edward C., and M. M. Chambers. "The Colleges and the Courts." New York: Carnegie Foundation for the Advancement of Teaching, 1936.

Epler, Stephen E. "Honorary Degrees: A Survey of Their Use and Abuse." Washington: American Council on Public Affairs, 1943.

Erbacher, S. A. "Catholic Higher Education for Men in the United States, 1850-1866." Ph.D. Thesis. Washington, D. C.: Catholic University of America, 1931.

Fleming, Donald. "Science and Technology in Providence, 1860-1914." Providence: Brown University, 1952.

Foster, William T. "Administration of the College Curriculum." Boston: Houghton Mifflin, 1911.

Gabriel, Ralph H. "Religion and Learning at Yale: The Church of Christ in the College and University, 1757-1957." New Haven: Yale University Press, 1958.

Godbold, Alben. "The Church College of the Old South." Durham, N. C.: Duke University Press, 1944.

Good, H. G. "The Rise of the College of Education of the Ohio State University." Columbus: College of Education, Ohio State University, 1960.

Goodspeed, T. W. "William Rainey Harper, First President of the University of Chicago." Chicago: University of Chicago Press, 1928.

Gross, John O., editor. "Methodist Beginnings in Higher Education." Nashville: Board of Education, The Methodist Church, 1959.

Haddow, Anna. "Political Science in American Colleges and Universities, 1636-1900." New York: Appleton-Century, 1939.

Hall, G. Stanley. "On the History of American College Textbooks and Teaching in Logic, Ethics, Psychology and Allied Subjects." *Proceedings of the American Antiquarian Society*, New Series IX, April, 1894, pp. 137-174.

Hamlin, Paul M. "Legal Education in Colonial New York." New York: New York University Law Quarterly Review, 1939.

Hardin, Charles M. "Freedom in Agricultural Education." Chicago: University of Chicago Press, 1955.

Harno, Albert J. "Legal Education in the United States." San Francisco: Bancroft-Whitney, 1953.

Herfurth, Theodore. "Sifting and Winnowing: A Chapter in the History of Academic Freedom at the University of Wisconsin." Madison: University of Wisconsin, 1949.

Hill, Davis S. "Control of Tax-Supported Higher Education in the United States." New York: Carnegie Foundation for the Advancement of Teaching, 1934.

Hinsdale, B. A. "President Garfield and Education." Boston: 1895.

Hofstadter, Richard, and Walter P. Metzger. "The Development of Academic Freedom in the United States." Cambridge: Harvard University Press, 1922.

Hollis, Ernest V. "Philanthropic Foundations and Higher Education." New York: Columbia University Press, 1938.

Holmes, D. O. W. "The Evolution of the Negro College." New York: Bureau of Publications, Teachers College, Columbia University, 1934.

Hornberger, Theodore. "Scientific Thought in the American Colleges, 1638-1800." Austin: University of Texas Press, 1945.

Horton, Byrne J. "The Graduate School (Its Origin and Administrative Development)." New York: New York University Bookstore, 1940.

John, Walton C. "Graduate Study in Universities and Colleges in the United States." U. S. Office of Education, Bulletin 1934, No. 20. Washington, D. C.: U. S. Government Printing Office, 1935.

Jones, Edward S. "Comprehensive Examinations in American Colleges." New York: Macmillan, 1933.

Kirkpatrick, J. E. "Academic Organization and Control." Yellow Springs, Ohio: Antioch College Press, 1931.

Knight, G. W. "History of Land Grants for Education in the North-West Territory." New York: Putnam, 1885.

Kolbe, Parke R. "Urban Influences on Higher Education in England and the United States." New York: Macmillan, 1928.

LeDuc, Thomas. "Piety and Intellect at Amherst College, 1865-1912." New York: Columbia University Press, 1946.

Leonard, Eugenia A. "Origins of Personnel Services in American Higher Education." Minneapolis: University of Minnesota Press, 1956.

Lyons, Gene M., and John W. Masland. "Education and Military Leadership: A Study of the R.O.T.C." Princeton: Princeton University Press, 1959.

MacIver, Robert M. "Academic Freedom in Our Time." New York: Columbia University Press, 1955.

Meriwether, Colyer. "Our Colonial Curriculum, 1706-1776." Washington, D. C.: Capital, 1907.

Mollon, Charles. "Les Collèges et le progrès du libéralisme en Nouvelle-Angleterre (période coloniale)." Paris: Vrin, 1929.

Newcomer, Mabel. "A Century of Higher Education for American Women." New York: Harper, 1959.

Norwood, William F. "Medical Education in the United

States before the Civil War." Philadelphia: University of Pennsylvania Press, 1944.

O'Connor, Michael J. L. "Origins of Academic Economics in the United States." New York: Columbia University Press, 1944.

Pangburn, Jessie M. "The Evolution of the American Teachers College." New York: Bureau of Publications, Teachers College, Columbia University, 1932.

Patton, J. S. "Jefferson, Cabell, and the University of Virginia." New York: Neale, 1906.

Pierson, Mary B. "Graduate Work in the South." Chapel Hill: University of North Carolina Press, 1947.

Potter, David. "Debating in the Colonial Chartered Colleges: An Historical Survey, 1642 to 1900." New York: Bureau of Publications, Teachers College, Columbia University, 1944.

Powell, Burt E. "The Movement for Industrial Education and the Establishment of the University, 1849-1870." Urbana: University of Illinois, 1918.

Power, Edward J. "A History of Catholic Higher Education in the United States." Milwaukee: Bruce, 1958.

Range, Willard. "The Rise and Progress of Negro Colleges in Georgia, 1865-1949." Athens: University of Georgia Press, 1951.

Roach, Helen P. "History of Speech Education at Columbia College, 1754-1949." New York: Bureau of Publications, Teachers College, Columbia University, 1950.

Robb, Mary M. "Oral Interpretation of Literature in American Colleges and Universities." New York: Wilson, 1941.

Roelker, William G. "Francis Wayland, A Neglected Pioneer of Higher Education." Worcester: 1944.

Rogers, Walter P. "Andrew D. White and the Modern University." Ithaca: Cornell University Press, 1942.

Ross, Earle D. "Democracy's College." Ames: Iowa State College Press, 1942.

Rudy, Willis. "The Evolving Liberal Arts Curriculum: A Historical Review of Basic Themes." New York: Bureau of Publications, Teachers College, Columbia University, 1960.

Ryan, W. Carson. "Studies in Early Graduate Education." New York: Carnegie Foundation for the Advancement of Teaching, 1939.

Ryan, W. Carson, Jr. "The Literature of American School and College Athletics." New York: Carnegie Foundation for the Advancement of Teaching, 1929.

Sack, Saul. "A History of Higher Education in Pennsylvania." Harrisburg: Pennsylvania Historical Museum Commission, 1962 (in press).

Schmidt, George P. "Intellectual Crosscurrents in American Colleges, 1825-1855," *American Historical Review,* vol. 42, October, 1936, pp. 46-67.

Sears, Jesse B. "Philanthropy in the History of American Higher Education." U. S. Bureau of Education, Bulletin 1932, No. 26, Washington, D. C.: U. S. Government Printing Office, 1932.

Selden, William K. "Accreditation: A Struggle over Standards in Higher Education." New York: Harper, 1960.

Sheldon, Henry D. "History and Pedagogy of American Student Societies." New York: Appleton, 1901.

Shirley, J. M. "The Dartmouth College Cases and the Supreme Court of the United States." Chicago: Jones, 1895.

Shores, Louis. "Origins of the American College Library, 1638-1800." Nashville: George Peabody College for Teachers, 1934.

Smallwood, Mary L. "An Historical Study of Examinations and Grading Systems in Early American Universities." Cambridge: Harvard University Press, 1935.

Snavely, Guy E. "The Church and the Four-Year College." New York: Harper, 1955.

Snow, Louis F. "The College Curriculum in the United States." New York: Teachers College, Columbia University, 1907.

Storr, Richard J. "The Beginnings of Graduate Education in America." Chicago: University of Chicago Press, 1953.

Sutton, Albert A. "Education for Journalism in the United States from Its Beginning to 1940." Evanston, Ill.: Northwestern University, 1945.

Sugg, Redding S., Jr., and George H. Jones. "The Southern Regional Education Board: Ten Years of Regional Cooperation in Higher Education." Baton Rouge: Louisiana State University Press, 1960.

Swift, Fletcher H. "The Athenian Oath of Allegiance in American Schools and Colleges." Berkeley: University of California Press, 1947.

Ten Brook, Andrew. "American State Universities, Their Origin and Progress." Cincinnati: Clarke, 1875.

Thomas, Russell. "The Search for a Common Learning: General Education, 1800-1960." New York: McGraw-Hill, 1962.

Trytten, M. H., editor. "Baccalaureate Origins of the Science Doctorates Awarded in the United States from 1936 to 1950 Inclusive." Washington: National Academy of Sciences—National Research Council, 1955.

Walsh, James J. "Education of the Founding Fathers of the Republic: Scholasticism in the Colonial Colleges." New York: Fordham University Press, 1935.

Walters, Raymond. "Four Decades of U.S. Collegiate Enrollments." New York: Society for the Advancement of Education, 1960.

Wesley, Edgar B. "Proposed: The University of the United States." Minneapolis: University of Minnesota Press, 1936.

Woody, Thomas. "A History of Women's Education in the United States." 2 vols. Lancaster, Pa.: Science Press, 1929.

Young, Edward J. "Subjects for Master's Degree in Harvard College from 1655-1791." *Proceedings of the Massachusetts Historical Society*, XVIII, pp. 119-151.

Zimmer, Agatho. "Changing Concepts of Higher Education in America since 1700." Washington: Catholic University of America, 1938.

Theory of Higher Education

Barzun, Jacques. "Teacher in America." Boston: Little, Brown, 1945.

Barzun, Jacques. "The House of Intellect." New York: Harper, 1959.

Benjamin, Harold. "Democracy in the Administration of Higher Education." New York: Harper, 1950.

Boewe, Charles E., and Roy F. Nichols, editors. "Both Human and Humane: The Humanities and Social Sciences in General Education." Philadelphia: University of Pennsylvania Press, 1960.

Butler, Nicholas M. "Scholarship and Service: The Policies of a National University in a Modern Democracy." New York: Scribner, 1921.

Butler, Nicholas M. "The Meaning of Education." New York: Scribner, 1915.

Carmichael, Oliver C. "Graduate Education: A Critique and a Program." New York: Harper, 1961.

Clap, Thomas. "Religious Constitution of Colleges, Especially Yale College in New Haven, in the Colony of Connecticut." New London, Conn.: Green, 1754.

Conant, James B. "The Citadel of Learning." New Haven: Yale University Press, 1956.

Eliot, Charles W. "Educational Reform." Boston: Houghton Mifflin, 1898.

Eliot, Charles W. "University Administration." Boston: Houghton Mifflin, 1908.

Fletcher, C. Scott, editor. "Education: The Challenge Ahead." New York: Norton, 1962.

Flexner, Abraham. "A Modern College and a Modern School." Garden City, N.Y.: Doubleday, Doran, 1923.

Flexner, Abraham. "The American College." New York: Appleton-Century, 1908.

Flexner, Abraham. "Universities: American, English, German." New York: Oxford University Press, 1930.

Foerster, Norman. "The American State University." Chapel Hill: University of North Carolina Press, 1937.

Frankel, Charles, editor. "Issues in University Education." New York: Harper, 1959.

Fraser, Mowat G. "The College of the Future." New York: Columbia University Press, 1937.

Gideonse, Harry D. "The Higher Learning in a Democracy." New York: Farrar and Rinehart, 1937.

Gilman, Daniel C. "The Launching of a University and Other Papers." New York: Dodd, Mead, 1906.

Gilman, Daniel C. "University Problems in the United States." New York: Appleton-Century, 1898.

Gould, Samuel B. "Knowledge Is Not Enough: Views on Higher Education." Yellow Springs, Ohio: Antioch Press, 1959.

Griswold, A. Whitney. "In the University Tradition." New Haven: Yale University Press, 1959.

Griswold, A. Whitney. "Liberal Education and the Democratic Ideal." New Haven: Yale University Press, 1959.

Harper, William R. "The Trend in Higher Education." Chicago: University of Chicago Press, 1905.

Highet, Gilbert. "The Art of Teaching." New York: Knopf, 1950.

Hutchins, Robert M. "Freedom, Education, and the Fund: Essays and Addresses, 1946-1956." New York: Meridian, 1956.

Hutchins, Robert M. "No Friendly Voice." Chicago: University of Chicago Press, 1936.

Hutchins, Robert M. "Some Observations on American Education." Cambridge: University Press, 1956.

Hutchins, Robert M. "The Conflict in Education in a Democratic Society." New York: Harper, 1953.

Hutchins, Robert M. "The Higher Learning in America." New Haven: Yale University Press, 1936.

Hutchins, Robert M. "The University of Utopia." Chicago: University of Chicago Press, 1953.

Jones, Howard M. "One Great Society: Humane Learning in the United States." New York: Harcourt, Brace, 1959.

Jones, Howard M. "Reflections on Learning." New Brunswick: Rutgers University Press, 1958.

Jordan, David S. "The Care and Culture of Men." San Francisco: Whitaker and Ray, 1896.

Jordan, David S. "The Voice of the Scholar." San Francisco: Elder, 1903.

Lawler, Justus G. "The Catholic Dimension in Higher Education." Westminster, Md.: Newman, 1959.

Lowell, A. Lawrence. "At War with Academic Traditions in America." Cambridge: Harvard University Press, 1934.

McConnell, T. R. "A General Pattern for American Public Higher Education." New York: McGraw-Hill, 1962.

McCosh, James. "The New Departure in College Education." New York: 1885.

Meiklejohn, Alexander. "The Experimental College." New York: Harper, 1932.

Meiklejohn, Alexander. "The Liberal College." Boston: Jones, 1920.

Nock, Albert J. "The Theory of Education in the United States." New York: Harcourt, Brace, 1932.

Patton, Leslie K. "The Purposes of Church-Related Colleges: A Critical Study, A Proposed Program." New York: Bureau of Publications, Teachers College, Columbia University, 1940.

Porter, Noah. "American College and the American Public." New Haven: Chatfield, 1870.

Quincy, Josiah. "Remarks on the Nature and Probable Effects of Introducing the Voluntary System in the Studies of Greek and Latin." Cambridge: 1841.

Shuster, George N. "Education and Moral Wisdom." New York: Harper, 1960.

Sinclair, Upton. "The Goose-Step: A Study of American Education." Pasadena, Calif.: The Author, 1923.

Smith, Huston. "The Purposes of Higher Education." New York: Harper, 1955.

Tappan, Henry P. "University Education." New York: 1851.

Taylor, Harold, editor. "Essays in Teaching." New York: Harper, 1950.

Taylor, Harold. "On Education and Freedom." New York: Abelard-Schuman, 1954.

Ticknor, George. "Remarks on Changes Lately Proposed or Adopted in Harvard College." Boston: 1825.

Trueblood, Elton. "The Idea of a College." New York: Harper, 1959.

Veblen, Thorstein. "The Higher Learning In America." New York: Huebsch, 1918.

Wayland, Francis. "Report to the Corporation of Brown University on Changes in the System of Collegiate Education." Providence: 1850.

Wayland, Francis. "Thoughts on the Present Collegiate System in the United States." Boston: 1842.

Weatherford, Willis D., Jr., editor. "The Goals of Higher Education." Cambridge: Harvard University Press, 1960.

Wechsler, James. "Revolt on the Campus." New York: Covici Friede, 1935.

Williams, George. "Some of My Best Friends Are Professors." New York: Abelard-Schuman, 1958.

Wriston, Henry M. "Academic Procession: Reflections of a College President." New York: Columbia University Press, 1959.

Wriston, Henry M. "The Nature of a Liberal College." Appleton, Wis.: Lawrence College Press, 1937.

Biographies

Carriel, Mary T. "The Life of Jonathan Baldwin Turner." Urbana: University of Illinois Press, 1961 (original edition, 1911).

Corner, Betsy C. "William Shippen, Jr.: Pioneer in American Medical Education." Philadelphia: American Philosophical Society, 1951.

Craig, Hardin. "Woodrow Wilson at Princeton." Norman: University of Oklahoma Press, 1960.

Dexter, Benjamin F. "Biographical Sketches of the Graduates of Yale College, with Annals of the College History." 6 vols. New Haven: Yale University Press, 1912.

Dorfman, Joseph, and R. G. Tugwell. "Early American Policy: Six Columbia Contributors." New York: Columbia University Press, 1960.

Fisher, George P. "Life of Benjamin Silliman." 2 vols. New York: Scribner, 1866.

Fisher, Samuel H. "Litchfield Law School, 1774-1833: Biographical Catalogue of Students." New Haven: Yale University Press, 1946.

Franklin, Fabian. "The Life of Daniel Coit Gilman." New York: Dodd, Mead, 1910.

Freidel, Frank. "Francis Lieber, Nineteenth-Century Liberal." Baton Rouge: Louisiana State University Press, 1937.

James, Henry. "Charles W. Eliot, President of Harvard University, 1896-1909." Boston: Houghton Mifflin, 1930.

Kuehl, Warren F. "Hamilton Holt: Journalist, Internationalist, Educator." Gainesville: University of Florida Press, 1960.

Parker, W. B. "The Life and Public Services of Justin Smith Morrill." Boston: Houghton Mifflin, 1924.

Perry, Charles M. "Henry Philip Tappan—Philosopher and University President." Ann Arbor: University of Michigan Press, 1933.

Rudolph, Frederick. "Mark Hopkins and the Log: Williams College, 1836-1872." New Haven: Yale University Press, 1956.

Sears, Jesse B., and Adin D. Henderson. "Cubberley of Stanford and His Contribution to American Education." Stanford: Stanford University Press, 1957.

Schneider, Herbert, and Carol Schneider, editors. "Samuel Johnson, President of King's College: His Career and Writings." 4 vols. New York: Columbia University Press, 1929.

Sibley, J. L., and Clifford K. Shipton. "Biographical Sketches of Graduates of Harvard University." 8 vols. Cambridge: Harvard University Press, 1873-1952.

Weld, William E., and Kathryn W. Sewny. "Herbert E. Hawkes: Dean of Columbia College, 1918-1943." New York: Columbia University Press, 1958.

Wilkins, Burleigh T. "Carl Becker: A Biographical Study in American Intellectual History." Cambridge: M.I.T. Press, 1961.

Yeomans, Henry A. "Abbott Lawrence Lowell: 1856-1943." Cambridge: Harvard University Press, 1948.

Autobiographies, Memoirs, and Reminiscences

Atkinson, Brooks, editor. "College in a Yard: Minutes by Thirty-nine Harvard Men." Cambridge: Harvard University Press, 1957.

Bowen, Robert O., editor. "The New Professors." New York: Holt, Rinehart and Winston, 1960.

Burgess, John W. "Reminiscences of an American Scholar: The Beginnings of Columbia University." New York: 1934.

Butler, Nicholas M. "Across the Busy Years." Vol. I. New York: Scribner, 1939.

Cohen, Morris R. "A Dreamer's Journey." Boston: Beacon, 1949.

Corner, George W., editor. "The Autobiography of Benjamin Rush." Philadelphia: American Philosophical Society, 1948.

Flexner, Abraham. "An Autobiography." New York: Simon and Schuster, 1960.

Fulton, John. "Memoirs of Frederick A. P. Barnard." New York: Macmillan, 1896.

Hammond, William G. "Remembrance of Amherst: An Undergraduate's Diary, 1846-1848." New York: Columbia University Press, 1946.

Hitchcock, Edward. "Reminiscences of Amherst College." Northampton, Mass.: 1863.

Lewis, William D., editor. "The Diary of a Student at Delaware College: August, 1853, to November, 1954." Baltimore: Furst, 1951.

McClure, David. "Memoirs of the Reverend Eleazar Wheelock." Newburyport, Mass.: Little, 1811.

Mecklin, John M. "My Quest for Freedom." New York: Scribner, 1945.

Robinson, G. Canby. "Adventures in Medical Education." Cambridge: Harvard University Press, 1957.

Shuster, George N. "The Ground I Walked on: Reflections of a College President." New York: Farrar, Straus and Cudahy, 1961.

Smith, Homer W. "Life and Correspondence of the Rev. William Smith, D.D." Philadelphia: Ferguson, 1880.

Spectorsky, A. C., editor. "The College Years." New York: Hawthorne, 1958.

[Ticknor, George.] "Life, Letters, and Journals of George Ticknor." 2 vols. Boston: Osgood, 1876.

Wayland, Francis, and Herman L. Wayland. "A Memoir of the Life and Labors of Francis Wayland, D.D." 2 vols. New York: Sheldon, 1867.

White, Andrew D. "Autobiography of Andrew Dickson White." 2 vols. New York: Century, 1905.

Notable Reports

"A Master Plan for Higher Education in California, 1960-1975." Sacramento: California State Department of Education, 1960.

Cooperative Study in General Education. "Cooperation in General Education." Washington, D. C.: American Council on Education, 1947.

Educational Policies Commission. "Higher Education in a Decade of Decision." Washington: National Education Association, 1957.

Flexner, Abraham. "Medical Education in the United States and Canada." New York: Carnegie Foundation for the Advancement of Teaching, 1910.

"Higher Education in the Forty-Eight States: A Report to the Governors' Conference." Chicago: Council of State Governments, 1952.

Learned, William S., and Ben D. Wood. "The Student and His Knowledge." New York: Carnegie Foundation for the Advancement of Teaching, 1938.

President's Committee on Education beyond the High School. "Second Report to the President." Washington: U. S. Government Printing Office, 1957.

Report of the Harvard Committee. "General Education in a Free Society." Cambridge: Harvard University Press, 1945.

Report of the President's Commission on Higher Education. "Higher Education for American Democracy." New York: Harper [1947].

Savage, Howard J., et al. "American College Athletics." New York: Carnegie Foundation for the Advancement of Teaching, 1929.

"The Substance of Two Reports of the Faculty of Amherst College to the Trustees." Amherst, Mass.: Amherst College, 1948. (Facsimile of Report of 1827.)

United States Commission on Civil Rights. "Equal Protection of the Laws in Public Higher Education: 1960." Washington: U. S. Government Printing Office, 1961.

Yale Faculty, "Original Papers in Relation to a Course of Liberal Education." *American Journal of Science and Arts*, vol. 15, January 1829, pp. 297-351. (Text of the Yale Report of 1828.)

Documentary Collections

Butterfield, L. H. "John Witherspoon Comes to America." Princeton: Princeton University Press, 1953.

Cole, Arthur H., editor. "Charleston Goes to Harvard." Cambridge: Harvard University Press, 1940.

Dexter, Franklin B., editor. "Documentary History of Yale University." New Haven: Yale University Press, 1916.

Dexter, Franklin B., editor. "The Literary Diary of Ezra Stiles." 3 vols. New York: Scribner, 1901.

Elliott, Edward C., editor. "The Rise of a University: Volume II, The University in Action." New York: Columbia University Press, 1937. (Writings of Nicholas M. Butler.)

Elliott, Edward C., and M. M. Chambers, editors. "Charters and Basic Laws of Selected American Universities and Colleges." New York: Carnegie Foundation for the Advancement of Teaching, 1934.

"Federal Laws and Rulings Relating to Morrill and Supplementary Morrill Funds for Land-Grant Colleges and Universities." U.S. Office of Education, Pamphlet No. 91. Washington, D. C.: Government Printing Office, 1940.

"Harvard College Records." Publications of the Colonial Society of Massachusetts, vols. XV, XVI, XXXI, 1925-1935, 3 vols.

Hofstadter, Richard, and Wilson Smith, editors. "American Higher Education: A Documentary History." 2 vols. Chicago: University of Chicago Press, 1961.

Irwin, Ray W., and Edna L. Jacobsen, editors. "A Columbia Student in the Eighteenth Century: Essays by Daniel D. Tompkins." New York: Columbia University Press, 1940.

Knight, Edgar W. "What College Presidents Say." Chapel Hill: University of North Carolina Press, 1940.

Knight, Edgar W., editor. "A Documentary History of Education in the South Before 1860: Volume III, The Rise of the State University." Chapel Hill: University of North Carolina Press, 1952.

Russell, William F., editor. "The Rise of a University: Volume I, The Later Days of Old Columbia College." New York: Columbia University Press, 1937. (Writings of F. A. P. Barnard.)

Weaver, David A., editor. "Builders of American Universities." Vol. I. Alton, Ill.: Shurtleff College Press, 1950.

Weaver, David A., editor. "Butler's Commencement Addresses." Alton, Ill.: Shurtleff College Press, 1951.

Miscellaneous Monographs and Other Publications

Axt, Richard G. "The Federal Government and Financing Higher Education." New York: Columbia University Press, 1952.

Babbidge, Homer D., Jr., and Robert M. Rosenzweig. "The Federal Interest in Higher Education." New York: McGraw-Hill, 1962.

Barish, Norman N., editor. "Engineering Enrollment in the United States." New York: New York University Press, 1957.

Bartlett, Lester W. "State Control of Private Incorporated Institutions of Higher Education." New York: Bureau of Publications, Teachers College, Columbia University, 1926.

Bauer, Ronald C. "Cases in College Administration." New York: Bureau of Publications, Teachers College, Columbia University, 1955.

Beck, Hubert P. "Men Who Control Our Universities." New York: King's Crown Press, 1947.

Berelson, Bernard. "Graduate Education in the United States." New York: McGraw-Hill, 1960.

Blauch, Lloyd E., editor. "Accreditation in Higher Education." U. S. Office of Education. Washington, D. C.: U. S. Government Printing Office, 1959.

Blauch, Lloyd E., editor. "Education for the Professions." U. S. Office of Education. Washington: U. S. Government Printing Office, 1955.

Blegen, Theodore C., and Russell M. Cooper, editors. "The Preparation of College Teachers." Washington: American Council on Education, 1950.

Bonthius, Robert H., et al. "The Independent Study Program in the United States." New York: Columbia University Press, 1957.

Bowles, Frank H. "Admission to College: A Perspective for the 1960's." Princeton: College Entrance Examination Board, 1960.

Brody, Alexander. "The American State and Higher Education: The Legal, Political, and Constitutional Relationships." Washington: American Council on Education, 1935.

Brown, Nicholas C., editor. "Higher Education: Incentives and Obstacles." Washington: American Council on Education, 1960.

Buckley, William F., Jr. "God and Man at Yale." Chicago: Regnery, 1951.

Burns, Gerald P., editor. "Administrators in Higher Education: Their Functions and Coordination." New York: Harper, 1962.

Byse, Clark, and Louis Joughin. "Tenure in American Higher Education: Plans, Practices, and the Law." Ithaca: Cornell University Press, 1959.

Caplow, Theodore, and Reece J. McGee. "The Academic Marketplace." New York: Basic Books, 1958.

Carmichael, Oliver C. "Universities: Commonwealth and American." New York: Harper, 1959.

Caullery, Maurice. "Universities and Scientific Life in the United States." Cambridge: Harvard University Press, 1922.

Chambers, M. M. "The Campus and the People." Danville, Ill.: Interstate Printers and Publishers, 1960.

Cole, Charles C., Jr. "Encouraging Scientific Talent." New York: College Entrance Examination Board, 1956.

Cooper, Russell M., editor. "The Two Ends of the Log: Learning and Teaching in Today's College." Minneapolis: University of Minnesota Press, 1958.

Corson, John J. "Governance of Colleges and Universities." New York: McGraw-Hill, 1960.

Dodds, Harold W. "The Academic President—Educator or Caretaker?" New York: McGraw-Hill, 1962.

Dressel, Paul L., *et al*. "Evaluation in Higher Education." Boston: Houghton Mifflin, 1961.

Du Bois, Cora. "Foreign Students and Higher Education in the United States." Washington: American Council on Education, 1956.

Eddy, Edward D., Jr. "The College Influence on Student Character." Washington: American Council on Education, 1959.

Edwards, Marcia. "Studies in American Graduate Education." New York: Carnegie Foundation for the Advancement of Teaching, 1944.

Eells, Walter C., and Harold A. Haswell. "Academic Degrees." Bulletin 1960, No. 28, U. S. Office of Education. Washington: U. S. Office of Education, 1960.

Fisher, James A., editor. "The Humanities in General Education." Dubuque, Iowa: Wm. C. Brown Co., 1960.

Gallagher, Buell G. "American Caste and the Negro College." New York: Columbia University Press, 1938.

Glenny, Lyman A. "Autonomy of Public Colleges: The Challenge of Coordination." New York: McGraw-Hill, 1959.

Goldsen, Rose K., *et al*. "What College Students Think." Princeton: Van Nostrand, 1960.

Good, Carter V. "Teaching in College and University: A Survey of the Problems and Literature of Higher Education." Baltimore: Warwick and York, 1929.

Gordon, Robert A., and James E. Howell. "Higher Education for Business." New York: Columbia University Press, 1959.

Harris, Seymour E., editor. "Higher Education in the United States: The Economic Problems." Cambridge: Harvard University Press, 1960.

Havemann, Ernest, and Patricia S. West. "They Went to College: The College Graduate in America Today." New York: Harcourt, Brace, 1952.

Havighurst, Robert J. "American Higher Education in the 1960's." Columbus: Ohio State University Press, 1960.

Henderson, Algo D. "Policies and Practices in Higher Education." New York: Harper, 1960.

Hill, Alfred T. "The Small College Meets the Challenge: The Story of CASC." New York: McGraw-Hill, 1959.

Hillway, Tyrus. "The American Two-Year College." New York: Harper, 1958.

Hollinshead, Byron S. "Who Should Go to College." New York: Columbia University Press, 1952.

Holstein, Edwin J., and Earl J. McGrath. "Liberal Education and Engineering." New York: Bureau of Publications, Teachers College, Columbia University, 1960.

Hook, Sidney. "Heresy, Yes—Conspiracy, No." New York: Day, 1953.

Jacob, Philip E. "Changing Values in College: An Exploratory Study of the Impact of College Teaching." New York: Harper, 1957.

Justman, Joseph, and Walter H. Mais. "College Teaching: Its Practice and Its Potential." New York: Harper, 1956.

Keezer, Dexter M. "Financing Higher Education: 1960-70." New York: McGraw-Hill, 1959.

Kelly, Robert L. "The American Colleges and the Social Order." New York: Macmillan, 1940.

Kent, Raymond A., editor. "Higher Education in America." Boston: Ginn, 1930.

Kidd, Charles V. "American Universities and Federal Research." Cambridge: Harvard University Press, 1959.

Kirk, Russell. "Academic Freedom: An Essay in Definition." Chicago: Regnery, 1955.

Kirkpatrick, John E. "Academic Organization and Control." Yellow Springs: Antioch Press, 1931.

Klapper, Paul. "College Teaching." Yonkers: World Book Co., 1920.

Knapp, Robert H., and Hubert B. Goodrich. "Origins of American Scientists." Chicago: University of Chicago Press, 1952.

Knapp, Robert H., and Joseph J. Greenbaum. "The Younger American Scholar: His Collegiate Origins." Chicago: University of Chicago Press, 1953.

Knight, Douglas M., editor. "The Federal Government and Higher Education." Englewood Cliffs, N. J.: Prentice-Hall, 1960.

Lazarsfeld, Paul F., and Wagner Thielens, Jr. "The Academic Mind: Social Scientists in an Age of Crisis." Glencoe, Ill.: Free Press, 1956.

McGlothlin, William J. "Patterns of Professional Education." New York: Putnam, 1960.

McGrath, Earl J. "Liberal Education in the Professions." New York: Bureau of Publications, Teachers College, Columbia University, 1959.

Medsker, Leland L. "The Junior College: Progress and Prospect." New York: McGraw-Hill, 1960.

Millett, John D. "Financing Higher Education in the

United States." New York: Columbia University Press, 1952.

Moos, Malcolm, and Francis E. Rourke. "The Campus and the State." Baltimore: Johns Hopkins Press, 1959.

Noble, Jeanne L. "The Negro Woman's College Education." New York: Bureau of Publications, Teachers College, Columbia University, 1956.

Perkins, Dexter, John L. Snell, et al. "The Education of Historians in the United States." New York: McGraw-Hill, 1962.

Pierson, Frank C., et al. "The Education of American Businessmen: A Study of University-College Programs in Business Administration." New York: McGraw-Hill, 1959.

Reid, Robert H. "American Degree Mills." Washington: American Council on Education, 1959.

Rogers, Francis M. "Higher Education in the United States: A Summary View." Third edition. Cambridge: Harvard University Press, 1960.

Ruml, Beardsley, and Donald H. Morrison. "Memo to a College Trustee." New York: McGraw-Hill, 1959.

Sanford, Nevitt, editor. "The American College: A Psychological and Social Interpretation of the Higher Learning." New York: Wiley, 1962.

Shryock, Richard H. "The University of Pennsylvania Faculty: A Study in American Higher Education." Philadelphia: University of Pennsylvania Press, 1959.

Stewart, George R. "The Year of the Oath." New York: Doubleday, 1950.

Stoke, Harold W. "The American College President." New York: Harper, 1959.

Swift, Richard N. "World Affairs and the College Curriculum." Washington: American Council on Education, 1959.

Thompson, Ronald B. "Estimating College Age Population Trends: 1940-1970." Columbus: The Author, Ohio State University, 1953.

Tyler, Ralph W., chairman, et al. "Graduate Study in Education." Part I, Fiftieth Yearbook, National Society for the Study of Education. Chicago: University of Chicago Press, 1951.

Valentine, P. F., editor. "The American College." New York: Philosophical Library, 1949.

Walter, Erich A., editor. "Religion and the State University." Ann Arbor: University of Michigan Press, 1958.

Weidner, Edward W. "The World Role of Universities." New York: McGraw-Hill, 1962.

Wilson, Logan. "The Academic Man." New York: Oxford University Press, 1942.

Wise, W. Max. "They Come for the Best of Reasons—College Students Today." Washington: American Council on Education, 1958.

Wolfle, Dael. "America's Resources of Specialized Talent." New York: Harper, 1954.

Woodburne, Lloyd S. "Principles of College and University Administration." Stanford: Stanford University Press, 1958.

Reference Works

American Association of Colleges for Teacher Education. *Yearbook.*

Association of Graduate Schools in the Association of American Universities. *Journal of Proceedings and Addresses.* Annual since 1949.

Blackwell, Thomas E. "College Law: A Guide for Administrators." Washington: American Council on Education, 1961.

Bogue, Jesse P. "American Junior Colleges." Fifth edition. Washington: American Council on Education, 1960.

"Current Issues in Higher Education." Annual. Association for Higher Education, National Education Association.

Hollis, Ernest V., *et al.* "Survey of State Legislation Relating to Higher Education." U.S. Office of Education. Annual.

Institute of International Education. "Handbook on International Study." A guide for foreign students in the United States and for American students abroad. Third edition, 1961.

Institute of International Education. "Open Doors." Annual statistics of foreign students in the universities in the United States and of American students in foreign universities.

Irwin, Mary, editor. "American Colleges and Universities." Eighth edition. Washington: American Council on Education, 1960.

Keiser, Albert. "College Names: Their Origin and Significance." New York: Bookman Associates, 1952.

Ness, Frederic W., editor. "A Guide to Graduate Study: Programs Leading to the Ph.D. Degree." Second edition. Washington: American Council on Education, 1960.

United States Office of Education. "Education Directory: Part 3, Higher Education." Annual.

United States Office of Education. "Biennial Survey of Education in the United States": chapter 4, section I,

"Statistics of Higher Education—Faculty, Students, and Degrees"; Section II, "Statistics of Higher Education—Receipts, Expenditure, and Property."

Wilkins, Theresa B. "Accredited Higher Institutions: 1960." Bulletin 1960, No. 24, U. S. Office of Education. Washington: U. S. Government Printing Office, 1960.

Periodicals

American Association of University Professors Bulletin.

American Journal of Pharmaceutical Education.

American Quarterly Register and Journal of the American Education Association (1829-43).

American Scholar.

College and Research Libraries.

College and University.

College and University Bulletin.

College and University Business.

College and University Journal (formerly *Pride* and previously *College Public Relations Quarterly*).

College Board Review.

College Art Journal.

College English.

Graduate Comment (Wayne State University).

Graduate Journal (University of Texas).

Graduate School Record (Ohio State University).

Harvard Educational Review.

Higher Education.

Higher Education in the West.

Improving College and University Teaching.

Journal of Chemical Education.

Journal of Dental Education.

Journal of Engineering Education.

Journal of General Education.

Journal of Higher Education.

Journal of Legal Education.

Journal of Medical Education.

Journal of the American Association of University Women.

Journal of the Association of American Medical Colleges.

Journal of the National Association of Women's Deans and Counselors.

Journal of Negro Education.

Journal of Teacher Education.

Junior College Journal.

Liberal Education (formerly *Association of American Colleges Bulletin*).

North Central Association Quarterly.

NUEA Spectator (National University Extension Association).

Overseas (formerly *News Bulletin, Institute of International Education*).

Quarterly Review of Higher Education for Negroes.

School and Society.

Teacher Education (Illinois State Normal University).

Teacher Education Quarterly.

Women's Education.

Bibliographies

American Council on Education. "Publications Catalog." Washington, D. C.

Bigelow, Karl W. "Selected Books for the College and University Administrator." New York: Bureau of Publications, Teachers College, Columbia University, 1958.

Blessing, James H., compiler. "Graduate Education: An Annotated Bibliography." Bulletin 1961, No. 26, U. S. Office of Education. Washington: U. S. Government Printing Office, 1961.

Bloomfield, Maurice. "Bibliographia Hopkinsiensis, 1876-1893." Baltimore: Johns Hopkins University, 1892-94.

Brickman, William W. "College and University History." *School and Society,* Vol. 64, Dec. 28, 1946, pp. 465-471.

Brickman, William W. "Colleges and Universities—Development," in Chester W. Harris, editor, "Encyclopedia of Educational Research," third edition. New York: Macmillan, 1960, pp. 226-243.

Brickman, William W. "Education for the Professions," *School and Society,* Vol. 75, April 26, 1952, pp. 262-267.

Brickman, William W. "Education in the College and University," *School and Society,* Vol. 72, Sept. 2, 1950, pp. 148-154.

Brickman, William W. "Higher Educational History," *School and Society,* Vol. 69, May 28, 1949, pp. 385-391.

Brickman, William W. "History of Colleges and Universities," *School and Society,* Vol. 76, Dec. 27, 1952, pp. 415-421.

Brickman, William W. "The M.A. and the Ph.D.," *School and Society,* Vol. 66, Aug. 30, 1947, pp. 169-174.

Dibden, Arthur J. "A Bibliography of College and University Life." Fourth edition. Galesburg, Ill.: Knox College, 1959.

Dissertation Abstracts (formerly *Microfilm Abstracts*). "Doctoral Dissertations Accepted by American Universities." Annual.

Eells, Walter C. "American Dissertations on Foreign Education." Washington: National Education Association, 1959.

Eells, Walter C., and Ernest V. Hollis. "Administration of Higher Education: An Annotated Bibliography." Bulletin 1960, No. 7, U.S. Office of Education. Washington: U.S. Government Printing Office, 1960.

Eells, Walter C., and Ernest V. Hollis. "The College Presidency, 1900-1960: An Annotated Bibliography." Bulletin 1961, No. 9, U.S. Office of Education. Washington: U.S. Government Printing Office, 1961.

Eells, Walter C. "College Teachers and College Teaching." Atlanta: Southern Regional Education Board, 1957.

Engleman, Lois E., and Walter C. Eells. "The Literature of Junior College Terminal Education." Washington: American Association of Junior Colleges, 1941.

Good, H. G. "Colleges and Universities—I. Historical Development in the United States," in Walter S. Monroe, editor, "Encyclopedia of Educational Research," second edition. New York: Macmillan, 1950.

"Index to American Doctoral Dissertations." Ann Arbor, Mich.: University Microfilms. Appears every year.

Layton, Elizabeth N. "General Education: Bibliography." Bulletin 1954, No. 3, U.S. Office of Education. Washington: U.S. Government Printing Office, 1954.

Layton, Elizabeth N. "Higher Educational Administration and Organization: Annotated Bibliography, 1940-1950." U.S. Office of Education. Washington: U.S. Government Printing Office, 1951.

Layton, Elizabeth N. "Innovations in Curriculum Organization and Instructional Methods in Colleges and Universities: Bibliography." Circular No. 240. Washington: U.S. Office of Education, 1948.

Layton, Elizabeth N. "Surveys of Higher Education in the United States: 1937-1949." Circular No. 257. Washington: U.S. Office of Education, 1949.

MacMinn, Paul, *et al.* "Research in School and College Personnel Services: Summaries of Unpublished Studies, September 1956-September 1958." Bulletin 1960, No. 10, U.S. Office of Education. Washington: U.S. Office of Education, 1960.

Mattingly, Richard C. "Scholarships and Fellowships: A Selected Bibliography." Bulletin 1957, No. 7, U.S. Office of Education. Washington: U. S. Government Printing Office, 1957.

Morrison, D. G., and S. V. Martorana. "The 2-Year Community College: An Annotated List of Studies and Surveys." Bulletin 1958, No. 14, U. S. Office of Education. Washington: U. S. Government Printing Office, 1958.

Muller, Leo C., editor. "Selected Bibliography on College Public Relations and Development." Washington: American College Public Relations Association, 1960.

Muller, Leo C. "Selected Bibliography on the Advancement and Support of Higher Education." Washington: American College Public Relations Association, 1962.

Parsons, Algene, et al. "Student Housing in Colleges and Universities." Pasadena, Calif.: Western Personnel Institute, 1961.

Paulsen, F. Robert. "Selected Bibliographies for Administration in Higher Education." Ann Arbor: Center for the Study of Higher Education, University of Michigan, 1960.

Peterson, Dora W. "Reading List on Student Personnel Work: A Selected Bibliography." Pasadena, Calif.: Western Personnel Institute, 1955.

Reporter. Clearinghouse of Studies on Higher Education. U. S. Office of Education. Appears at periodic intervals.

"Selected Bibliography of Publications on American Higher Education." Washington: American Council on Education, 1959.

SPECIAL NOTE: See the excellent bibliography in R. Freeman Butts, "The College Charts Its Course" (1939) and the comprehensive footnote references in John S. Brubacher and Willis Rudy's "Higher Education in Transition" (1958). See also the *Review of Educational Research*, Vol. 30, No. 4, October, 1960, issue on "Higher Education," which is a review of the research literature for 1954-60. For previous surveys, see the October, 1954, and earlier issues.

Related Writings

The American College
and University
A History
by **FREDERICK RUDOLPH,** *Williams College*

This outstanding newly published text draws parallels
between the development on the college campus and the
concurrent forces shaping American life. Professor Rudolph
describes and explains how the history of American higher
education is also social and intellectual history.

1962; 540 pp.; $5.00 *text*

The Transformation
of the School
by **LAWRENCE A. CREMIN,** *Teachers College,*
Columbia University

A masterly work of intellectual history. It will be the
definitive study of the history of progressive education in
America, and moreover, a joy to read.

—Lewis Feuer, *University of California*
1961; 352 pp.; $4.00 *text*

An Introduction to Education
in American Society
by **RAYMOND E. CALLAHAN,** *Washington University*

An excellent comprehensive treatment of education in
America. It begins with the trumpet sound of great issues
that are relevant to the education of mankind as a race,
and it ferrets into every nook and cranny of professional
education of the present day. The illustrative readings from
the professional literature, which illuminate the text, are
highly apropos and well chosen. Quality is a hallmark of
this book.—Paul D. Leedy, *The American University*

1960; 483 pp.; $5.75 *text*

ALFRED A. KNOPF, Publisher
College Department ● 501 Madison Avenue ● New York 22